中再集团
CHINA RE

专业 让保险更保险

中国再保险行业发展报告

（2023）

中国再保险（集团）股份有限公司等 ◎ 编著

中国金融出版社

责任编辑：王雪珂
责任校对：李俊英
责任印制：陈晓川

图书在版编目(CIP)数据

中国再保险行业发展报告. 2023 / 中国再保险（集团）股份有限公司
等编著. — 北京: 中国金融出版社，2023.9
ISBN 978-7-5220-2173-7

Ⅰ.①中…　Ⅱ.①中…　Ⅲ.①再保险 — 保险业 — 经济发展 — 研究报告 —
中国 — 2023　Ⅳ.① F842.69

中国国家版本馆CIP数据核字 (2023) 第177062号

中国再保险行业发展报告（2023）
ZHONGGUO ZAIBAOXIAN HANGYE FAZHAN BAOGAO (2023)

出版
发行　**中国金融出版社**

社址　北京市丰台区益泽路2号
市场开发部　(010) 66024766，63805472，63439533 (传真)
网 上 书 店　www.cfph.cn
　　　　　　(010) 66024766，63372837 (传真)
读者服务部　(010) 66070833，62568380
邮编　100071
经销　新华书店
印刷　北京侨友印刷有限公司
尺寸　169毫米×239毫米
印张　24.75
字数　315千
版次　2023年9月第1版
印次　2023年9月第1次印刷
定价　168.00元
ISBN 978-7-5220-2173-7

如出现印装错误本社负责调换　联系电话 (010) 63263947

编委会名单

主　　　编：和春雷

执行副主编：庄乾志

副　主　编：朱海林　　朱晓云　　雷建明

　　　　　　田美攀　　曹顺明

编委会成员：张仁江　　张　健　　张　青

　　　　　　庞　卫　　孔奕丰（Ivan Gonzalez）

　　　　　　李文明　　冯　键　　朱日峰

　　　　　　卞江生　　钭旭杰　　刘　扬

序　言

　　2022年，党的二十大胜利召开，明确了以中国式现代化全面推进中华民族伟大复兴的历史使命，擘画了全面建成社会主义现代化强国的宏伟蓝图，凝聚起全国人民团结奋斗、加快发展的强大力量。

　　当前，百年未有之大变局加速演进，世界进入新的动荡变革期，地缘政治形势持续紧张，气候变化等全球性问题凸显。中国经济发展的外部环境更趋复杂严峻，风险和不确定性进一步增加。保险，作为降低风险、减少不确定性的主要手段，在提供风险保障、服务实体经济、护航人民美好生活中将发挥更加重要的作用。

　　在国家金融监督管理总局的正确领导下，随着中国经济的持续增长和行业的共同努力，中国已成为全球第二大保险市场和最重要的新兴保险市场，并有望伴随中国经济的发展于2035年成为世界第一大保险市场。站在"两个一百年"的历史关口，中国保险业始终坚守服务中国式现代化的责任使命，积极践行ESG可持续发展理念，围绕国家治理体系和治理能力现代化、绿色能源转型、高水平科技自立自强、乡村振兴与农业现代化、养老保障体系与"三医"联动改革等关键领域，加快产业融合，强化创新驱动，逐步实现从被动的损失分摊向主动的风险减量全过程治理转型，从单一风险保障的提供者向综合风险解决方案的提供者转型，全面融入社会风险管理大生态系统，充分发挥保险保障功能，有力服务国家战略、参与社会治理、保障人民群众的生命财产安全，将行业的涓涓细流汇入国家和人民事业的大江大河，与民族复兴的时代脉搏同频，与人民对美好生活的追求向往共振。

数字化成为保险业转型升级、迈向高质量发展的关键驱动力量。人工智能、区块链、云计算、大数据、物联网、生物识别、5G、增强现实、量子通讯等数字化技术加速创新，正在全面融入产品设计、营销创新、核保核赔、运营管理、再保安排等保险全流程，推动保险机构深度融入大健康、新能源汽车、农业现代化等多个产业，实现内部运营效能提升与外部产业生态建设双向发展。数字化正在改变保险业务链与价值链，重塑经营逻辑，推动保险机构从点和面的技术应用向体系化的生态构建转变，从改良型的科技赋能向改革型的商业模式变革转变，从硬实力的科技应用向软实力的企业组织文化变革转变。

放眼世界，厄尔尼诺现象正在加剧全球气候危机。2022年，伊恩飓风等自然灾害造成的经济损失预计高达2 750亿美元，其中保险损失高达1 250亿美元，远高于此前五年和十年平均水平。加之俄乌冲突、能源危机、疫情形势延宕反复、主要发达经济体货币政策大幅收紧等多重因素影响，全球保险市场传统资本和新兴资本均明显减少，保险价格走硬趋势较为明显。中国保险业紧紧把握金融业双向开放机遇，加快国际化发展步伐，以响应"一带一路"倡议为着力点，积极参与国际保险市场竞争，主动融入全球保险价值链，有力提升了中国保险业的国际影响力。

从国际保险业发展历程中可以看到，任何一个发达保险市场背后，都有一个强大和完善的再保险体系的支持。再保险，作为"保险的保险"，在中国金融业中率先全面开放，现已形成500多家中外资、在岸离岸机构争相竞争的市场格局，充分发挥了风险分散、技术引导和资金融通作用，成为中国保险市场的"稳定器"和"调控器"。作为中国再保险行业的奠基人和主力军，中国再保险（集团）股份有限公司（以下简称中再集团或中再）始终以习近平新时代中国特色社会主义思想为指导，坚决贯彻落实党的二十大精神，落实党中央、国务院各项决策部署，坚守再保险主责主业，打造再保险生态圈，加快数字化转型，助力完善行业基础设施，推进产品和服务创新，携手合作伙伴打造一站式、定制化的风险管理综合解决方案，全力服务国家重大战略、分散经济运行风险、护航人民美好生活、参与全球风险治理。

2022年，中再集团组织编写行业首部年度发展报告——《中国再保险行业发展报告（2022）》，得到了原中国银行保险监督管理委员会和中国保险行业协会的悉心指导，以及国内保险、再保险同业的大力支持。今年，中再集团进一步聚合行业力量，共同编写了新一版《中国再保险行业发展报告（2023）》，总结和展示了行业发展的新面貌、新特点、新趋势，希望能为广大读者全面了解和深入研究中国再保险行业发展状况提供有益参考，对扩大国内外行业交流、提升再保险行业社会影响力起到积极的促进作用。

展望未来，在中国式现代化新征程上，中国再保险行业仍处于重要的战略机遇期，但也存在不少困难与挑战，需要汇聚多方智慧认真研究解决。中再集团将主动作为、加强研究，与行业一同，为中国保险再保险行业高质量发展献计献策，为服务党和国家事业全局、实现中华民族伟大复兴的"中国梦"作出更大贡献！

中再集团董事长　和春雷

2023年9月

前 言 ①

2022年，是党和国家历史上极为重要的一年。党的二十大胜利召开，描绘了全面建设社会主义现代化国家的宏伟蓝图。2022年，也是风险挑战复杂艰巨的一年，百年变局和世纪疫情交织叠加，世界经济下行风险加大，外部发展环境的复杂性、严峻性和不确定性显著上升。以习近平同志为核心的党中央团结带领全国各族人民迎难而上，统筹国内国际两个大局，统筹疫情防控和经济社会发展，统筹发展与安全，加大宏观调控力度，实现经济平稳运行、发展质量稳步提升、社会大局保持稳定。2022年，中国国内生产总值超过121万亿元，同比增长3.0%，稳居世界第2位，物价总水平保持稳定，进出口总额同比增长7.7%，数字经济规模占GDP比重提升至41.5%，国民经济发展总体呈现持续恢复的良好态势，为保险再保险业稳健发展营造稳固的宏观环境。

2022年，中国再保险行业坚持以习近平新时代中国特色社会主义思想为指导，积极落实党的二十大精神，围绕党中央、国务院决策部署和监管机构工作部署，深刻把握金融工作的政治性、人民性，持续提升创新能力，深入推进数字化转型，不断强化风险防范，着力服

---

① 本报告中的"中国再保险行业"或"中国保险业"是指中国大陆保险再保险行业及市场，不含港澳台地区。本报告中主要数据来自历年《中国保险年鉴》、国家金融监督管理总局、原中国银行保险监督管理委员会、再保险公司年报等公开披露数据信息，以及撰写期间再保险行业调研数据信息。

务保险业供给侧结构性改革大局，发挥好保险市场安全阀和稳定器的作用，行业综合实力不断增强，服务实体经济能力不断提升。2022年，中国保险市场分出保费2 782.8亿元，同比增长13.3%；再保险行业分保费收入2 250.2亿元，同比增长7.7%；再保险行业总资产规模6 719.5亿元，较年初增长10.9%；中国再保险市场规模占全球份额约9.0%。再保险行业呈现直再合作持续深化（Collaboration）、创新迭代不断提速（Creation）、境内外市场深化融合（Convergence）的"3C"特点。

2022年，再保险行业将自身发展与服务党和国家战略全局紧密结合，以更高站位、更大力度，扛起服务国家战略和经济社会发展的政治责任、经济责任和社会责任。落地国内首创、行业首创的新能源汽车芯片质量安全责任保险，为科技自立自强和制造强国战略作出积极贡献。以乡村振兴和共同富裕为己任，为农业生产提供风险保障超过2万亿元，服务保障农户超过3亿户次。助力地方政府提升公共安全管理水平，工程质量潜在缺陷保险（IDI保险）累计保障面积超过1.78亿平方米。积极支持健康中国和应对人口老龄化战略，累计为116个城市提供惠民保产品设计和服务方案，惠及人群超过1.2亿人次。"一带一路"再保险共保体成员公司为中国"走出去"企业和海外利益（财产类）提供近3.3万亿元的保险保障，同比增长19.0%。

针对中国再保险行业呈现的新面貌、新特点和新趋势，《中国再保险行业发展报告（2023）》（以下简称《报告》）拓展研究视角、丰富研究素材，以"主报告+专题报告"形式，点面结合、立体展现了中国再保险市场发展全貌。《报告》基于对国际国内宏观经济、政策环境、市场变化、灾害风险等影响行业发展关键因素的分析，重点介绍了再保险行业发展最新情况，包括市场规模、市场格局、业务结构、创新实践等，在梳理总结再保险行业新时代十年来发展成效与实践经验的基础上，深入研究行业发展面临的新机遇、新风险，并展望未来发展趋势。行业数字化转型正在加速推进，《报告》也邀请了推动保险科技协同创新平台——分子实验室共同参与撰写。

在《报告》编写过程中，始终得到原中国银行保险监督管理委员会财产保险监管部（再保险监管部）李有祥主任的悉心指导，在此致以诚挚的谢意！

《报告》的出版发行，离不开中国保险和再保险行业相关单位领导和专家同仁的大力支持。感谢原中国银行保险监督管理委员会财产保险监管部（再保险监管部）再保险公司监管处王君、金学群、郑琬冬，在《报告》体例框架、监管内容把关等方面的指导！感谢中国保险行业协会在行业调研安排和意见征求等方面的组织协调！

《报告》由中再集团牵头，以下单位参与了编写工作：

中国再保险（集团）股份有限公司

中国财产再保险有限责任公司

中国人寿再保险有限责任公司

中国农业再保险股份有限公司

人保再保险股份有限公司

太平再保险（中国）有限公司

瑞士再保险股份有限公司北京分公司

分子实验室

《报告》由中再集团张健、钭旭杰负责统稿。各章撰写分工如下：

主报告部分由中再负责，第一章官兵，第二章孙涛，第三章金笑权、李非，第四章薛源、刘爽，第五章郑利娜、范令箭、张坤。专题报告部分，第一章金笑权、于洋（中再），第二章王克、陈蔡春子（中国农再），第三章娄鹏、袁新芳、王广智、张冰玉、邹逸菲［太平再（中国）、中国亚太再保险研究中心］，第四章戴鑫、陈亚新、王晓阳（瑞再），第五章刘扬（分子实验室），第六章马晓静（中再），第七章岳溪柳、冯键、杜越、王明昌（中再），第八章刁宁、李忠益（人保再）。英文版由中再集团王少康审校。

《报告》的出版发行是再保险行业共同努力的成果，是行业智慧的结晶。向所有参与编写工作的机构与同仁表达诚挚的谢意。向慕再、汉再、法再、通用再等所有为《报告》提供资料、素材、数据并提出专业意见建议的再保险同业，表示衷心感谢。

最后，衷心希望《中国再保险行业发展报告（2023）》在理论与实践方面的探索，能够启迪智慧、促进交流，为中国再保险行业高质量发展贡献绵薄之力！

中国再保险（集团）股份有限公司

2023年9月

目　录

第一章

2022年中国再保险市场整体情况及发展展望

一、再保险市场发展环境

二、再保险市场发展情况

三、再保险行业服务经济社会发展情况

四、再保险市场发展展望

2022年，面对新冠疫情反复延宕与复杂的内外部环境，中国再保险行业保持稳健运行，市场规模稳步增长，创新动能持续提升，风险防控有力有效，国际影响力不断增强，高质量发展实现新突破，整体呈现"3C"特点：一是直再合作（Collaboration），再保险对直保市场支持作用持续提升，直再合作更为紧密，为直保客户持续创造价值的能力进一步增强；二是创新提速（Creation），再保险行业更为注重产品、技术、服务与模式创新，各领域创新成果不断涌现；三是内外融合（Convergence），通过设立境内机构或境外离岸参与、增强资本实力等方式，全球再保险机构持续看好中国再保险市场的广阔发展前景。

一、再保险市场发展环境

（一）全球

2022年，世界经济处于动荡变革期，受俄乌冲突、能源危机、贸易保护、疫情形势延宕反复、发达经济体货币政策大幅紧缩等因素影响，世界经济增速从上一年的6.1%下滑至3.4%，经济发展和贸易增长动能减弱，而通胀水平从2021年的4.6%上升至近40年来最高水平的9.0%[①]，欧美发达经济体衰退风险加大，全球债务水平处于高位，金融市场剧烈波动，大宗商品价格巨幅涨落。

2022年，全球保险市场受经济放缓、高通胀和利率快速上升影响，经通胀调整后的全球保费收入约6.8万亿美元，实际增速放缓至−1.1%左右，未能延续2021年3.4%的增长态势。其中，非寿险市场保费收入约4.0万亿美元，实际增速约0.5%；寿险市场保费收入约2.8万

---

① 数据来源：世界银行*World Economic Outlook*，2023年4月。

亿美元，实际增速约−3.1%[①]。

2022年，全球再保险市场机遇与挑战并存。新冠疫情的冲击有所减弱，但伊恩飓风等自然灾害导致的保险损失超过近年来平均水平，主要发达经济体短时间内大幅加息引发金融市场动荡和债券投资浮亏，造成传统再保险资本和第三方资本供给均大幅减少。在多种因素综合影响下，2022年全球财产再保险市场走硬特征较为明显。全球人身再保险市场因新冠疫情死亡率风险可控及较为健康的风险调整后资本收益水平，整体运行较为平稳。

（二）中国

2022年，中国有效应对多重超预期因素对经济运行的冲击，针对有效需求不足的突出矛盾，加大宏观调控力度，稳住了经济大盘，国内生产总值超过121万亿元，全年经济增速约3.0%，稳居世界第2位。国内供求总体平衡；物价总水平保持平稳；高技术行业、新能源产业和数字经济发展新动能持续增强；高水平开放不断拓展，发展质量稳步提升[②]。

2022年，中国保险市场保费收入约46 958.0亿元，同比增长4.6%，全球第二位置更为稳固；保险密度约3 369元人民币/人，保险深度约3.9%[③]，虽与全球发达保险市场还有一定差距，但也预示着中国保险市场仍具有较大发展潜力。

2022年，中国财产保险公司保费收入14 867.0亿元，同比增长约

---

① 数据来源：2023年第3期Sigma报告"世界保险业：经受扰动，温和增长"，瑞再研究院。

② 信息来源：《2022年国民经济和社会发展统计公报》，国家统计局，2023年2月28日。

③ 根据瑞再研究院2023年第3期Sigma报告"世界保险业：经受扰动，温和增长"的全球统计数据为基础，按2022年12月31日银行间外汇市场人民币汇率：1美元=6.89元人民币测算。

8.7%；非车险业务规模同比增长12.5%，占比约44.6%，成为财产险直保市场和再保险市场的增长引擎。人身保险公司保费收入32 091.0亿元，同比增长约2.8%[①]，行业仍处于转型调整期，新单保费收入和新业务价值增速继续负增长，人身保险分出需求整体稳定。截至2022年末，中国保险资金运用余额约25.1万亿元，同比增长7.9%，行业财务收益率中位数位于3.25%~3.5%，保险资金收益水平相对平稳[②]。

二、再保险市场发展情况

（一）市场规模

1. 原保险市场分出

（1）原保险市场分出规模

2022年，国内保险市场分出保费2 782.8亿元，同比增长13.3%。同期，国内原保险保费收入46 958.0亿元，同比增长4.6%（见图1、表1）。2022年，分出保费增长率高于原保险保费收入约8.7个百分点，主要源于保险市场受经济周期影响，部分直保公司偿付能力充足率有所下滑。同时，原中国银行保险监督管理委员会（以下简称原中国银保监会）于2022年1月1日正式实施的《保险公司偿付能力监管规则（Ⅱ）》（以下简称"偿二代"二期工程），更为强调风险导向，资本认定和资本监管更为严格，从而提升了直保公司分出需求。

---

① 数据来源：原中国银保监会。2022年数据不包含处于风险处置阶段的保险公司保费收入数据。

② 数据来源：原中国银保监会、中国保险资产管理协会发布的《2022—2023年中国保险资产管理行业运行调研报告》。

图1　2012—2022年原保险保费、分出保费及增长率情况

（数据来源：《中国保险年鉴》、原中国银保监会）

表1　2012—2022年分出保费、原保险保费及再保险分出率情况

单位：亿元，%

年份	分出保费	增长率	原保险保费	增长率	再保险分出率
2012	879.4		15 487.8		5.7
2013	1 164.0	32.4	17 222.1	11.2	6.8
2014	2 867.2	146.3	20 234.7	17.5	14.2
2015	1 501.6	−47.6	24 282.4	20.0	6.2
2016	1 323.8	−11.8	30 959.0	27.5	4.3
2017	1 661.2	25.5	36 580.9	18.2	4.5
2018	1 808.5	8.9	38 016.6	3.9	4.8
2019	1 881.6	4.0	42 644.8	12.2	4.4
2020	2 427.1	29.0	45 257.3	6.1	5.4
2021[1]	2 456.8	1.2	44 900.2	−0.8	5.5
2022[2]	2 782.8	13.3	46 958.0	4.6	5.9

注1、2：2021年、2022年的原保险保费收入数据不含处于风险处置阶段的保险公司数据。

数据来源：《中国保险年鉴》、原中国银保监会。

2022年，国内保险市场分出保费中，财产保险公司分出保费1 629.5亿元，同比增长11.6%，占总分出保费的58.6%；人身保险公司分出保费1 153.3亿元，同比增长15.8%，占总分出保费的41.4%（见图2）。

从历年分出保费结构看，财产保险公司与人身保险公司分出保费占比约为6∶4。

图2　2012—2022年财产险与人身险公司分出保费占比情况

（数据来源：《中国保险年鉴》、原中国银保监会）

2012—2022年，伴随中国保险市场的不断发展，再保险需求持续提升，分出保费规模从879.4亿元增长至2 782.8亿元，年均增长率约12.2%。同期，中国原保险保费收入由15 487.8亿元增长至46 958.0亿元，年均增长率约11.7%（见图1、表1）。

近十年来，分出保费与原保险保费平均增速基本一致，但各年增速差异较大。2014—2016年出现较大波动，主要源于"偿二代"影响。"偿二代"建设于2012年启动，2015年2月正式发布并进入实施过渡期，2016年第一季度起正式实施。相较于以规模为导向的"偿一代"，"偿二代"强调以风险为导向，显著影响保险公司对再保险的分出需求及分保策略。2016—2017年以及2019—2020年分出保费大幅增加，主要源于人身保险公司的分出规模增加。

（2）原保险市场分出率

2022年，国内保险市场分出率约5.9%（见图3）。其中，财产保险公司分出率约11.0%，人身保险公司分出率约3.6%。由于财产保险的风险更为多元且巨灾风险突出，相较人身保险，财产保险对再保险需求更大，分出率也更高。

2012—2022年，国内保险市场分出率平均约6.1%，其中2014—2016年"偿二代"监管政策过渡期间，分出率大幅波动，2014年分出需求猛增，分出率高达14.1%，随后逐步回落。不考虑2014—2016年波动影响，分出率平均约5.4%。2016年至今，分出率总体呈稳步上升趋势，体现出保险市场对再保险的风险分散需求正在逐步增强。

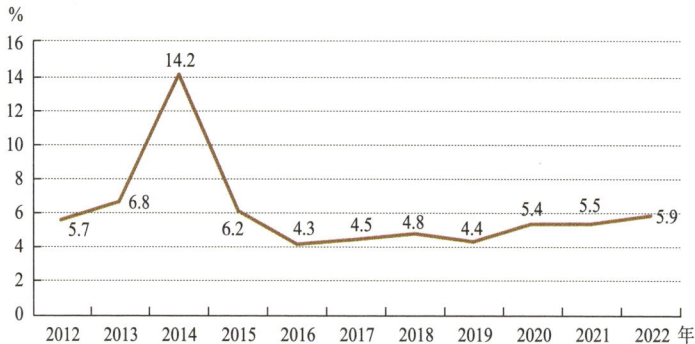

图3　2012—2022年原保险市场分出率情况

（数据来源：《中国保险年鉴》、原中国银保监会）

与全球市场相比，中国保险市场分出率相对较低，保费自留率较高。据国际保险监督官协会（IAIS）测算，2021年，全球保险市场分出率约为8.0%，北美市场分出率近12.0%，欧洲市场分出率约为8.5%[①]。

---

① 数据来源：国际保险监督官协会（International Association of Insurance Supervisors，IAIS），Global Insurance Market Report，2022。

2．再保险市场分保费收入

2022年，国内再保险市场分保费收入2 250.2亿元，同比增长7.7%，高于原保险保费增速，行业整体呈现良好发展态势。其中，6家中资公司分保费收入1 625.5亿元，同比增长14.2%，占比约72.2%；8家外资公司分保费收入624.7亿元，同比下降6.4%，占比约27.8%。

2012—2022年，国内再保险市场分保费收入从691.2亿元增长至2 250.2亿元，年均增长率约12.5%（见图4）。总体来看，再保险分保费收入与原保险保费收入、原保险市场分出保费平均增速基本一致，但再保险分保费收入各年增速差异较大、波动性较高。特别是2014—2016年间，受"偿二代"监管政策过渡期影响，再保险公司分保费收入显著波动。自2016年"偿二代"正式实施后，分保费收入呈逐年增长趋势。

图4　2012—2022年再保险公司分保费收入及增长率情况

（数据来源：《中国保险年鉴》、原中国银保监会）

2012—2022年，中资再保险公司分保费收入保持正增长；外资再保险公司分保费收入波动性较大，2014年分保费收入增长率超过100%，2015年下降近47%，2022年降低约6.4%（见表2、图5），体现了中资公司与外资公司经营策略的差异性。

表2　　　　　　　2012—2022年中资再保险公司与外资再保险公司
分保费收入及增长率情况

单位：亿元，%

年份	分保费收入	中资公司分保费收入	增长率	占比	外资公司分保费收入	增长率	占比
2012	691.2	400.3		57.9	290.9		42.1
2013	948.6	466.8	16.6	49.2	481.8	65.6	50.8
2014	1 486.0	502.5	7.6	33.8	983.5	104.1	66.2
2015	1 066.3	543.4	8.1	51.0	522.9	−46.8	49.0
2016	958.6	552.0	1.6	57.6	406.6	−22.2	42.4
2017	1 099.6	778.7	41.1	70.8	320.9	−21.1	29.2
2018	1 370.1	949.8	22.0	69.3	420.2	31.0	30.7
2019	1 576.1	1 044.9	10.0	66.2	533.0	26.8	33.8
2020	1 809.2	1 180.1	13.1	65.2	629.1	18.0	34.8
2021	2 090.2	1 422.9	20.6	68.1	667.3	6.1	31.9
2022	2 250.2	1 625.5	14.2	72.2	624.6	−6.4	27.8

数据来源：《中国保险年鉴》、原中国银保监会。

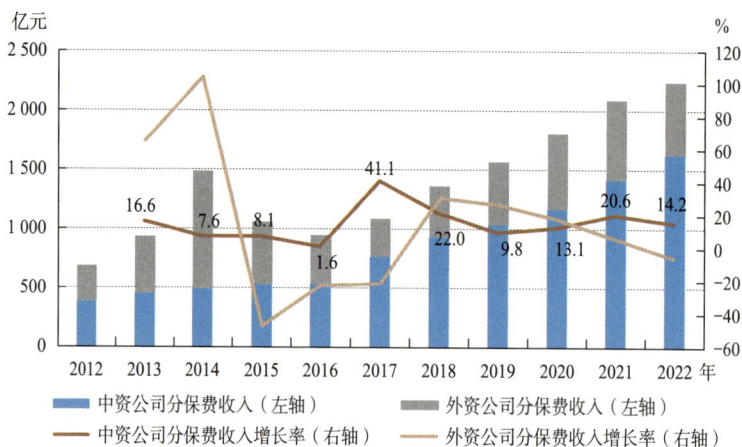

图5　2012—2022年中资再保险公司与外资再保险公司分保费收入及增长率情况

（数据来源：《中国保险年鉴》、原中国银保监会）

3．再保险赔付支出

2022年，国内再保险行业赔付支出为1 154.6亿元，同比增长35.4%，占当年分保费收入约51.3%（见图6）。其中，6家中资公司赔付支出为831.9亿元，同比增长69.4%，主要原因是部分公司的赔付支出大幅增加；8家外资公司赔付支出为322.7亿元，同比降低10.8%（见表3、图7）。

图6　2012—2022年再保险业赔付支出情况

（数据来源：《中国保险年鉴》、原中国银保监会）

表3　　　　　　　2012—2022年再保险业赔付支出情况

单位：亿元，%

年份	赔付支出	中资再保险公司赔付支出	中资再保险公司赔付支出增长率	占比	外资再保险公司赔付支出	外资再保险公司赔付支出增长率	占比
2012	303.8	151.8		50.0	151.9		50.0
2013	383.7	180.6	18.9	47.1	203.1	33.7	52.9
2014	433.2	210.5	16.6	48.6	222.6	9.6	51.4
2015	668.5	263.3	25.1	39.4	405.2	82.0	60.6
2016	1 119.4	301.2	14.4	26.9	818.1	101.9	73.1
2017	489.0	254.4	−15.6	52.0	234.6	−71.3	48.0
2018	541.2	278.3	9.4	51.4	262.9	12.1	48.6

11

续表

年份	赔付支出	中资再保险公司赔付支出	中资再保险公司赔付支出增长率	占比	外资再保险公司赔付支出	外资再保险公司赔付支出增长率	占比
2019	670.3	350.4	25.9	52.3	320.0	21.7	47.7
2020	746.5	432.7	23.5	58.0	313.8	−1.9	42.0
2021	852.6	491.0	13.5	57.6	361.6	15.2	42.4
2022	1 154.6	831.9	69.4	72.1	322.7	−10.8	27.9

数据来源：《中国保险年鉴》、原中国银保监会。

图7　2012—2022年中资再保险公司与外资再保险公司赔付支出和增长率情况

（数据来源：《中国保险年鉴》、原中国银保监会）

2012—2022年，国内再保险行业赔付支出从303.8亿元增长至1 154.6亿元，年均增长率约14.3%（见图6）。总体来看，再保险赔付支出在2016年"偿二代"实施初期大幅增长，其中人身再保险赔付支出大幅增加，2017年明显回落，政策变化期的波动性较大。

4．再保险总资产

2022年末，国内再保险行业总资产规模6 719.5亿元，较年初增长10.9%，低于分保费收入增速3.3个百分点。2012—2022年，国内再保险行业总资产规模从1 437.2亿元增长至6 719.5亿元，年均增长率约16.7%，高于再保险分保费收入年均增长率（见图8）。总资产规模同样受到"偿二代"影响，在2014—2016年呈较大波动性。自2016年开始，再保险行业总资产规模呈增长趋势，与分保费收入变化趋势保持一致。

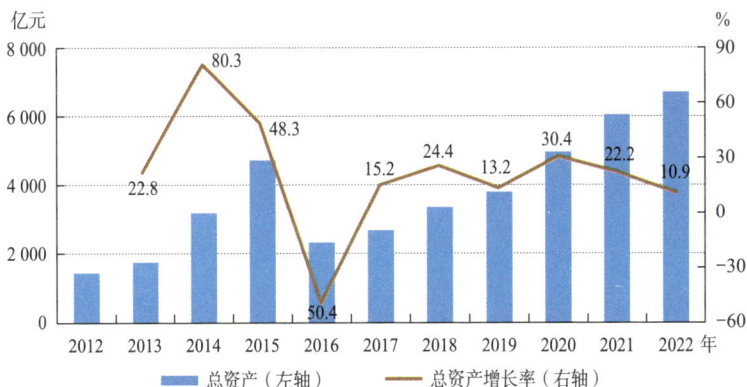

图8　2012—2022年再保险业总资产及增长率情况

（数据来源：《中国保险年鉴》、原中国银保监会）

2012—2022年，再保险行业总资产占保险业总资产规模比重相对稳定，2022年底占保险业总资产规模约2.5%，体现了再保险行业伴随保险市场发展而逐步发展壮大，在监管政策与市场环境变化下保持整体稳步增长。同时，保险业总资产占金融业总资产规模比重稳步上升，从2018年的5.6%上升至2022年的6.5%，保险业在金融行业中的作用和地位不断增强（见表4）。

表4　2012—2022年再保险业、保险业、金融业总资产规模及占比情况

单位：亿元，%

年份	再保险业总资产	保险业总资产	再保险业总资产占保险业比重	金融业总资产	保险业总资产占金融业比重
2012	1 437.2	68 425.6	2.1		
2013	1 765.4	77 576.7	2.3		
2014	3 183.2	96 177.8	3.3		

续表

年份	再保险业总资产	保险业总资产	再保险业总资产占保险业比重	金融业总资产	保险业总资产占金融业比重
2015	4 722.0	119 295.7	4.0		
2016	2 343.9	142 659.0	1.6		
2017	2 699.3	146 816.7	1.8		
2018	3 358.3	163 641.0	2.1	2 940 000	5.6
2019	4 261.3	187 495.6	2.3	3.186 900	5.9
2020	4 956.3	216 156.5	2.3	3 531 900	6.1
2021	6 057.5	248 874.0	2.4	3 819 500	6.5
2022	6 719.5	271 500.0	2.5	4 196 400	6.5

数据来源：《中国保险年鉴》、原中国银保监会、中国人民银行网站。

（二）市场格局

1．市场主体不断丰富

经过多年发展，中国再保险市场逐渐形成境内专业再保险人为主体、境外离岸再保险人和直保公司共同参与的多元发展格局。

在专业市场主体方面，截至2022年底，国内再保险市场专业再保险公司共15家，其中7家中资再保险公司（含1家集团公司，即中再集团），8家外资再保险公司（见表5）。2022年8月，西班牙曼福再保险公司（MAPFRE）获批筹建北京分公司，注册地为北京，营运资金为5亿元人民币。

在离岸市场主体方面，近年来，未在国内设立分支机构，但通过离岸交易接受国内分出业务的境外离岸再保险人的参与力度不断加大。2022年，与超过500家离岸再保险人开展业务往来，向境外分出保费约471.3亿元，分出规模基本稳定。

此外，境内百余家财产险和人身险直保公司不同程度地参与再保险市场竞争，部分直保公司通过业务互换等方式与境外市场开展再保险业务往来。

公司名称	成立时间	注册地	注册性质	企业性质
中国再保险（集团）股份有限公司	1996年	北京	集团公司	中资
中国财产再保险有限责任公司	2003年	北京	公司	中资
中国人寿再保险有限责任公司	2003年	北京	公司	中资
慕尼黑再保险公司北京分公司	2003年	北京	分公司	外资
瑞士再保险股份有限公司北京分公司	2003年	北京	分公司	外资
德国通用再保险股份公司上海分公司	2004年	上海	分公司	外资
法国再保险公司北京分公司	2008年	北京	分公司	外资
汉诺威再保险股份公司上海分公司	2008年	上海	分公司	外资
信利再保险（中国）有限公司[2]	2011年	上海	公司	外资
RGA美国再保险公司上海分公司	2014年	上海	分公司	外资
太平再保险（中国）有限公司	2015年	北京	公司	中资
前海再保险股份有限公司	2016年	深圳	公司	中资
人保再保险股份有限公司	2017年	北京	公司	中资
大韩再保险公司上海分公司	2020年	上海	分公司	外资
中国农业再保险股份有限公司	2020年	北京	公司	中资

表5　　　　　　　　　国内专业再保险公司情况概览[1]

注：1. 各再保险主体名称在下文中使用以下简称：中再集团或中再、中再产险或中再、中再寿险或中再、慕再或慕再北分、瑞再或瑞再北分、通用再或通用再上分、法再或法再北分、汉再或汉再上分、信利再、RGA美再或RGA美再上分、太平再（中国）、前海再、人保再、大韩再或大韩再上分、中国农再。

2. 信利保险（中国）有限公司于2011年成立，2020年变更为信利再保险（中国）有限公司。

资料来源：《中国保险年鉴》、各再保险公司年报。

2012—2022年，国内再保险市场主体数量不断增加，从9家增至15家，其中中资公司新增4家，外资公司新增2家。2014—2017年，每年均新设一家再保险公司，2020年增加2家再保险公司，2022年批准筹建1家再保险公司。

2．双向开放格局初步形成

在"引进来"方面，自中国2001年加入世界贸易组织（WTO）以来，中国再保险市场成为中国金融业开放最早、开放力度最大的领域之一，全球主要再保险公司均在国内设立分支机构、开展业务，为国内再保险市场发展带来人才、技术和资本支持。近年来，中国再保险行业积极落实党中央要求，进一步深化高水平对外开放，不断完善与国际接轨的制度与标准体系，持续激活行业发展内生动力，增强服务创新能力。

党的十八大以来，中国不断加快上海国际再保险中心建设，取得积极成效。截至2022年底，上海已汇聚了40多家保险法人机构、8家再保险机构（见表6）、10家保险资产管理公司、232家保险专业中介法人机构。上海国际再保险中心建设将聚焦打造再保险"国际板"，开设面向全球的再保险分入业务交易市场，吸引全球要素在上海集聚，增强配置全球资源的能力，打造具有全球影响力的、在岸与离岸相结合的全球再保险交易中心，形成再保险国内大循环的中心节点、国内国际双循环的战略链接。

表6　　　　　　　　　专业再保险公司国内机构布局情况

公司名称	机构布局情况
中国再保险（集团）股份有限公司	总部位于北京
中国财产再保险有限责任公司	总部位于北京，在上海、深圳设有分公司
中国人寿再保险有限责任公司	总部位于北京，在上海、深圳设有分公司
慕尼黑再保险公司北京分公司	分公司位于北京
瑞士再保险股份有限公司北京分公司	分公司位于北京
德国通用再保险股份公司上海分公司	分公司位于上海
法国再保险公司北京分公司	分公司位于北京
汉诺威再保险股份公司上海分公司	分公司位于上海
信利再保险（中国）有限公司	公司位于上海
RGA美国再保险公司上海分公司	分公司位于上海
太平再保险（中国）有限公司	总部位于北京，在上海设有分公司
前海再保险股份有限公司	公司位于深圳
人保再保险股份有限公司	公司位于北京
大韩再保险公司上海分公司	分公司位于上海
中国农业再保险股份有限公司	公司位于北京

在"走出去"方面，中国保险市场通过离岸交易形式接受境外业务分入。2022年，境外分入保费规模约283亿元。与此同时，中资再保险企业加快走出国门，积极布局境外市场，经营视野明显拓宽，国际竞争能力不断提升。中再集团已成为全球第八大再保险集团，是国际化程度最高的中资金融保险企业之一，海外经营机构已扩展到11个国家和地区，境外拥有500余人的再保险专业团队，境外（再）保险业务占比超过17.8%[①]，财产险板块境外业务占比达32.0%。

（三）业务结构

1．分业务类型分保费收入

2022年，国内再保险市场分保费收入2 250.2亿元，其中合约业务分保费收入2 240.6亿元，同比增长8.2%，占比约97.9%；临分业务分保费收入48.0亿元，同比减少3.1%，占比约2.1%[②]（见图9）。合约业务保持稳健增长，临分业务增长速度有所放缓。

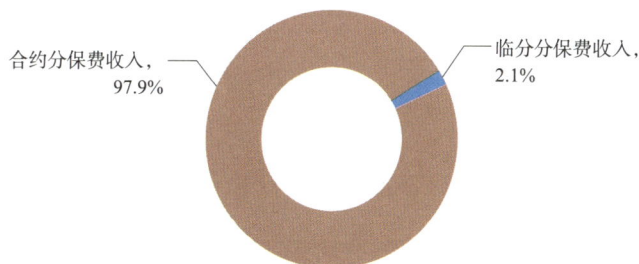

合约分保费收入，97.9%　　临分分保费收入，2.1%

图9　2022年再保险合约与临分业务分保费收入占比情况

（数据来源：原中国银保监会）

2012—2022年，合约业务分保费收入由681.9亿元增长至2 240.6亿元，年均增长率约12.6%；临分业务分保费收入由9.3亿元增加至48.0亿

---

① 为中再集团境外所有保险业务收入与集团总保费收入的比值。

② 分保费收入已考虑公司间关联交易影响，分合约类型分保费收入未考虑关联交易影响。

元，年均增长率约17.8%（见表7、图10）。总体来看，合约业务为再保险主要业务类型，占比保持在95%以上，发展速度较为平稳；临分业务占比较小，发展速度较快，但历年增长速度有较大波动，与业务性质密切相关。

表7　2012—2022年再保险合约与临分分保费收入、增长率及占比情况

单位：亿元，%

年份	合约业务分保费收入	增长率	占比	临分业务分保费收入	增长率	占比
2012	681.9		98.7	9.3		1.3
2013	940.3	37.9	99.1	8.3	−10.7	0.9
2014	1 476.7	57.1	99.4	9.3	11.6	0.6
2015	1 055.2	−28.5	99.0	11.0	19.2	1.0
2016	917.9	−13.0	95.8	37.9	243.7	4.0
2017	1 080.2	17.7	98.2	19.4	−48.9	1.8
2018	1 339.4	24.0	97.8	30.7	58.5	2.2
2019	1 539.8	15.0	97.7	36.3	18.1	2.3
2020	1 774.3	15.2	97.5	45.8	26.2	2.5
2021	2 070.7	16.7	97.7	49.5	8.1	2.3
2022	2 240.6	8.2	97.9	48.0	−3.1	2.1

数据来源：《中国保险年鉴》、原中国银保监会。

图10　2012—2022年合约、临分分保费收入及增长率情况

（数据来源：《中国保险年鉴》、原中国银保监会）

2．分险种分保费收入

2022年，国内再保险市场财产险分保费收入1 220.5亿元，同比增长13.5%，占比约54.2%；寿险分保费收入433.4亿元，同比减少2.6%，占比约19.3%；健康险分保费收入532.2亿元，同比增长7.2%，占比约23.7%；意外险分保费收入64.1亿元，同比减少12.3%，占比约2.8%（见图11）。

总体来看，一是各险种分保费收入增长率有所分化，财产险增长较快，其次为健康险，寿险和意外险规模与上年基本持平；二是健康险分保费收入增速较往年明显放缓，与保险市场健康险发展态势一致，健康险分保需求在2022年减速明显；三是与2021年相比，财产险分保费收入占比小幅上升，寿险、健康险和意外险的分保费收入占比小幅下降，体现了保险市场业务结构调整对再保险的影响。

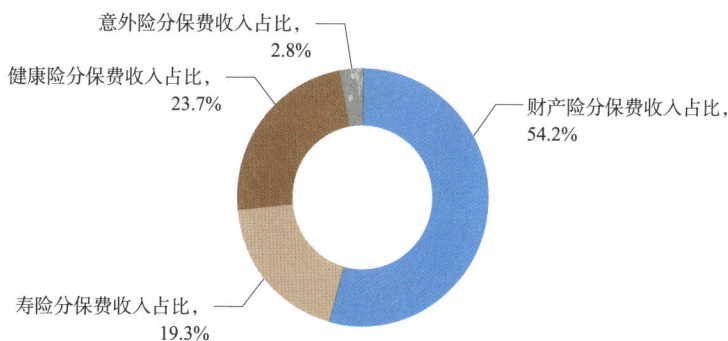

意外险分保费收入占比，2.8%
健康险分保费收入占比，23.7%
财产险分保费收入占比，54.2%
寿险分保费收入占比，19.3%

图11　2022年各险种分保费收入占比

（数据来源：原中国银保监会）

2012—2022年，国内再保险市场财产险分保费收入由462.6亿元增长至1 220.5亿元，年均增长率约10.2%；寿险业务由153.0亿元增长至433.4亿元，年均增长率约11.0%；健康险业务由50.6亿元增长至532.2亿元，年均增长率约26.5%；意外险业务由25.0亿元增长至64.1亿元，年均增长率约9.9%（见表8、图12）。其中，健康险是增长最快的险种，保费占比逐年上升，2019年首次超过20%，2020年分保费规模超过400亿元（见图13），是发展潜力最大的险种，但近年来健康险增长速度正在放缓。随着财产险公司健康险业务比重的不断上升，对健康险的再保险分出需求也在持续增加，特别是对短期健康险需求的增加带来了较高的分保费收入。

表8　　　　　　　　2012—2022年各险种分保费收入及增长率

单位：亿元，%

年份	财产险	增长率	寿险	增长率	健康险	增长率	意外险	增长率
2012	462.6		153.0		50.6		25.0	
2013	562.8	21.7	297.3	94.3	63.5	25.6	24.8	-0.6
2014	588.0	4.5	799.6	168.9	65.7	3.4	32.7	31.7
2015	598.1	1.7	320.9	-59.9	112.1	70.7	35.1	7.4
2016	480.7	-19.6	285.9	-10.9	100.1	-10.8	43.5	23.9
2017	484.9	0.9	430.2	50.5	136.1	36.0	48.4	11.3
2018	600.4	23.8	484.4	12.6	218.2	60.4	67.1	38.5
2019	729.9	21.6	421.3	-13.0	353.1	61.8	73.6	9.7
2020	840.1	15.1	441.6	4.8	454.5	28.7	73.1	-0.7
2021	1 075.6	28.0	445.0	0.79	496.5	9.2	73.1	0.0
2022	1 220.5	13.5	433.4	-2.6	532.2	7.2	64.1	12.3

数据来源：《中国保险年鉴》、原中国银保监会。

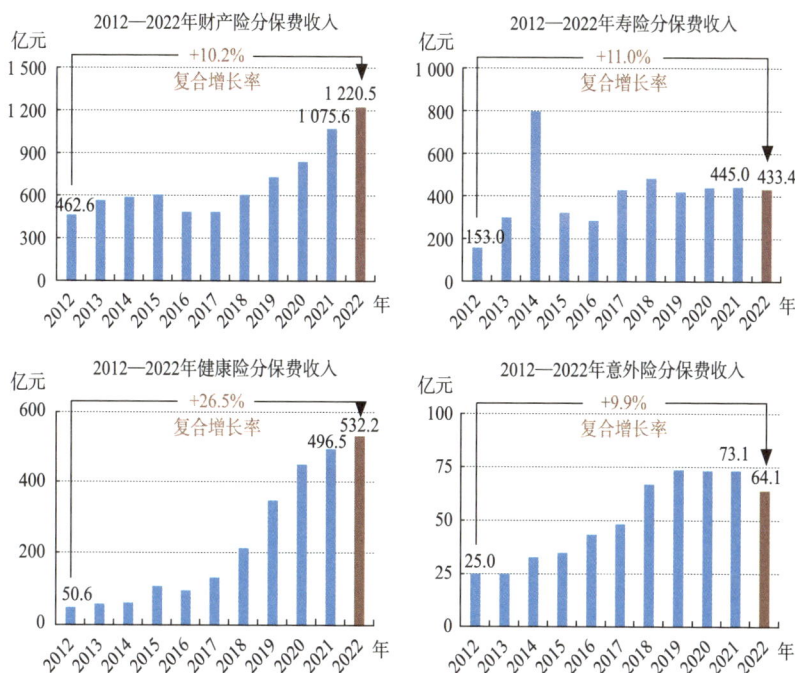

图12　2012—2022年各险种分保费收入

（数据来源：《中国保险年鉴》、原中国银保监会）

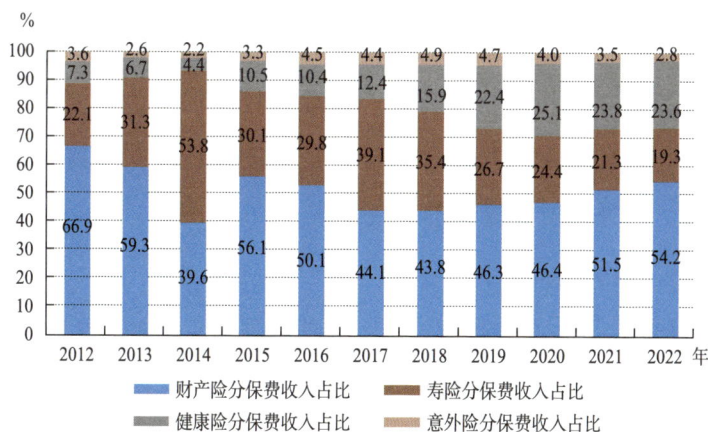

图13　2012—2022年分险种分保费收入占比情况

（数据来源：《中国保险年鉴》、原中国银保监会）

3．再保险产品服务创新

以比例合约为基础的传统再保险服务始终是再保险企业提供稳定承保能力支持、改善直保公司偿付能力、维护直再长期合作关系、实现互利共赢的基本方式和手段。部分再保险企业探索加强传统再保险业务的周期管理和组合管理，协助保险行业优化资本投放，稳定风险回报水平。

近年来，中国保险行业加快布局新风险、新领域、新市场。再保险行业也发挥数据优势、产品开发与定价优势，逐步从幕后走向前台，与直保公司前置合作更为密切，提供产品开发、方案设计、数据分析、自动核保、智能理赔与风控等综合型服务，积极融入产业生态服务，提供"一站式"、定制化解决方案，满足直保公司个性化需求，助力客户价值增值。

（四）风险管理

近年来，再保险行业不断增强风险管理意识，强化风险管理主体责任，搭建较为完整的风险管理架构，制定较为全面的风险管理制度，风险管理工作机制更为合理，风险管控手段更为丰富。2022年，再保险公司偿付能力与风险综合评价整体表现较好，为其业务拓展、风险管理、声誉形象等提供了有效支撑。

1．偿付能力情况[①]

核心偿付能力充足率是保险公司核心资本与最低资本的比值，衡量公司高质量资本的充足状况，监管达标值为50%；综合偿付能力充足率是实际资本与最低资本的比值，衡量公司资本的总体充足状况，

---

① 下文中偿付能力相关数据均为"偿二代"二期规则下的统计数据。

监管达标值为100%。

2022年四个季度，再保险公司的平均核心偿付能力充足率分别为267.5%、281.2%、278.5%和268.5%，均高于监管达标值和当季财产险公司、人身险公司的充足率水平。

2022年四个季度，再保险公司的平均综合偿付能力充足率分别为298.5%、310.4%、309.1%和300.1%（见图14），均高于监管达标值和当季财产险公司、人身险公司的充足率水平。

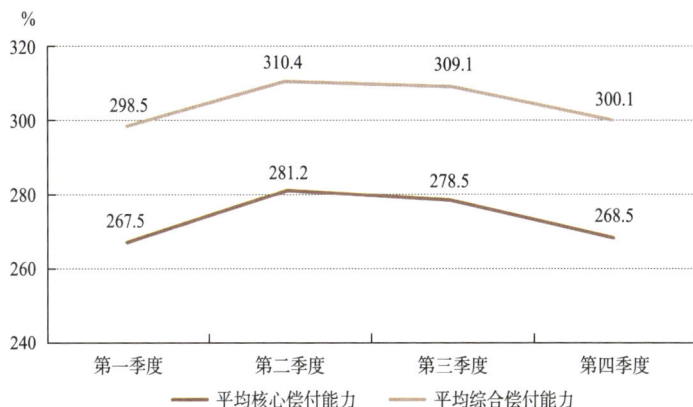

图14　2022年再保险公司偿付能力

（数据来源：原中国银保监会）

与2021年相比，随着新偿付能力准则的切换与再保险业务规模的扩大，2022年再保险行业保险风险最低资本上升幅度较大，最低资本较上年末有所增加，因此，2022年综合偿付能力充足率和核心偿付能力充足率有所下降。

2．风险综合评级（IRR）情况

风险综合评级是对保险公司偿付能力综合风险的评价，衡量保险公司总体偿付能力风险的大小，分为A、B、C、D四类，监管达标值为B类。

2022年，共有14家再保险公司披露了季度风险综合评级情况，评级结果均在B类及以上。

3．风险管理能力（SARMRA）情况

偿付能力风险管理要求与评估（SARMRA）是保险业功能监管的重要内容，是通过制度健全性和遵循有效性的评估反映保险公司的风险管理水平，对于提升保险公司风险管理水平、增强行业防范化解风险能力具有重要意义。SARMRA评估分值高于80分可提高偿付能力充足率。

2022年，监管部门对8家再保险公司开展了SARMRA现场评估，再保险公司得分为79.73分，比2021年增加1.11分，并有6家再保险公司得分在80分以上[①]。

（五）再保险经纪市场发展情况

再保险经纪人是国内再保险与直保公司、国内公司与境外公司之间建立分保关系的重要桥梁和纽带，也是中国保险、再保险公司获得国际专业服务的重要渠道。再保险经纪人凭借其对市场信息全面及时掌握，丰富的专业知识和实务经验，为再保险交易双方提供高质量的服务，设计再保险方案、落实再保险安排、提供专业培训。

中国再保险经纪市场是最为开放的金融领域之一。与境内经纪公司类似，境外经纪公司在中国再保险登记系统注册并通过审核，即可在境外发起再保险业务。中国再保险登记系统信息显示，截至2023年7月，再保险经纪人共244家，其中境外机构122家，境内机构122家。

中国再保险经纪市场主体主要由国际再保险经纪人、国内再保

[①] 数据来源：原中国银保监会发布2022年度保险公司偿付能力风险管理评估结果，原中国银保监会网站。

经纪人、国内直保经纪人兼营再保险业务等组成。国内再保险经纪人市场主要由佳达、怡安、韦莱三家全球排名前列的外资专业再保经纪人组成，其服务全面、团队专业，资源充足，能在全球范围内进行复杂的再保安排；国内再保险经纪人及直保经纪人的市场份额较外资低，中天、五洲、江泰等国内专业再保险经纪人具有市场化程度高、了解客户需求等特点，有细分险种的专业团队，服务较为全面。

合约再保险是国内再保险经纪市场的主要业务，国际再保险经纪人占据主导地位。中资再保险经纪人较多参与临分业务，结合自身资源或技术优势，参与特定行业或企业的再保险临分业务。

（六）监管政策

2022年，监管部门聚焦服务国家大局，出台多项具有重大行业影响的规则、指引及指导意见，引导市场主体积极发挥保险职能，促进行业规范化运营。"偿二代"二期自2022年起正式落地实行，在制度层面引领行业整体风控能力提升。完善保险资金运用、关联交易管理、公司治理机制、保险机构监管评估体系、保险公司资本补充和计量、数据出境监管等方面的规章制度，提升行业高质量发展能力。出台疫情防控、乡村振兴、交通强国、中小微企业、新市民群体、绿色发展、普惠保险、数字化转型等政策文件，指导行业更好地服务国家战略、服务实体经济。

三、再保险行业服务经济社会发展情况

再保险是保险的保险，是支持保险业分散风险、财务稳定和创新发展的重要手段，也是宏观经济增长和保险市场稳定发展的重要保

障。2022年，中国再保险行业坚持创新引领、深化改革开放，加快高质量发展，在服务经济发展、民生保障、社会治理、对外开放等方面持续贡献专业价值。

（一）做风险减量的践行者，服务实体经济提质增效

服务制造强国领域，中再瞄准"卡脖子"技术领域，为国产大飞机C919试验和首飞提供风险保障，为航空航天产业提供坚实保障；研发首台（套）重大技术装备保险，全面覆盖海洋工程、轨道交通、环保装备等高端制造领域。

服务数字中国领域，中再大力支持培育数字经济，与工业和信息化部启动产融合作，共促信息技术等新兴产业发展。与中关村科技园区朝阳园、360集团等多方共建网络安全保障体系，提升产业信息化深度。

服务科技自立自强领域，中再全面保障国家重点科技专项"国和一号"首堆核保险投保工作，重点支持中国具有完全自主知识产权的第三代核电技术"华龙一号"等示范工程。落地首单商业化新能源汽车国产芯片质量安全责任保险，是国内首创、行业首创，有效解决了新能源汽车企业使用国产芯片的后顾之忧，增强了中国汽车产业链韧性和自主研发的信心。

服务绿色发展领域，再保险行业持续为海上风电、新能源汽车等可再生能源企业提供风险保障。中再发布国内首个新能源汽车保险定价风控模型"再·途"，促进保险业与新能源汽车行业融合创新与协同发展。人保再承接海上风电等清洁项目数十个，建立海上风电自动承保机制，累积提供承保能力支持突破200亿元。瑞再协助直保企业开发全国首个湿地碳汇生态价值保险方案并落地宁波，为杭州湾国家湿地公园碳汇等生态价值提供风险保障。

专栏：中再服务中国汽车产业"强芯稳链"积极助力制造强国

近年来，中国加快推进新能源汽车领域国产替代、实现"强芯稳链"，迫切需要保险业更好地发挥防灾防损、风险转移、经济补偿功能，实现"科技+产业+保险"良性循环。中再牢记国之大者，充分发挥科技保险、供应链保险领域产品创新和风险管理技术优势，发布国内新能源汽车全产业链综合风险解决方案，包括国产芯片产品质量安全责任保险产品、新能源汽车定价风控模型等，有效助力中国新能源汽车全产业链高质量发展。

一是推出国内首款新能源汽车国产芯片质量安全责任保险产品。中再联合保险公司成功推出并独家再保支持的国内首单商业化新能源汽车国产芯片质量安全责任保险业务，在著名芯片设计研发和芯片加工企业——紫光微电子有限公司落地，首单产品提供综合风险保障500万元。该产品有效解决了新能源汽车企业使用国产芯片的后顾之忧，增强了汽车产业链韧性和自主研发的信心，为加快国产芯片替代之路提供坚实的风险保障。

在此基础上，在工业和信息化部相关司局指导下，中再纵向延伸国产芯片替代保障范围，创新开发出国内首款国产芯片应用于整车、供应商和芯片设计企业的全产业链保险保障产品，包括产品质量、产品责任、科研费用、召回等汽车电子元器件系列风险保障方案，为完善汽车芯片国产替代风险保障体系、破解国家汽车产业链芯片"卡脖子"难题、支持芯片国产替代科技自主自强提供重要支持。

二是开发国内首款新能源汽车定价风控模型——"再·途"模型。模型分为保险定价模型和风控报警模型，采用国际前沿精算技术和人工智能神经网络方法，具有可解释、高精度、可迭代等特点，有效满足车辆电池热失控、车辆损失和危险驾驶行为所引发的相关风险的定价及风控需要。在产业端，模型充分利用保险行业的数据分析和风控能力，协助新能源汽车行业优化各项技术的安全性，提升火灾管控能力。在消费端，模型通过合理的风险定价，为新能源汽车消费者提供优质保险保障和风险管理服务，促进新能源汽车消费需求提升。

（二）做新发展格局的建设者，服务乡村振兴与共同富裕

在服务乡村振兴和农业强国建设方面，再保险行业从后端承保能力支持和产品创新开发，到前端运用科技手段助力客户风险减量，均取得了较好的成效。中国农再在分散农业大灾风险、推动农业保险高质量发展方面发挥了重要作用，过去两年，通过约定分保为农业生产提供风险保障近2万亿元，服务保障农户约3亿户次。中再积极扩大承保能力，助力中国政策性农业保险市场稳健发展，同时，创新商业农险发展模式，引领行业完成高标准农田建设创新保障方案并在12个省落地，提升农田建设与管护水平，上线农业气象指数保险产品研发平台，落地十余款地方特色产品，各类新型农险风险保障近900亿元。人保再近三年累计提供农业保险相关风险保障近200亿元，其中农房项目风险保障覆盖20余个省份，提供风险保障近亿元。瑞再发布"信瑞智农"智能农业风险管理平台2.0版，为保险公司提供多灾因多尺度、实时且即时的风险量化评估，帮助农业保险行业提升风险管理能力。

在支持共同富裕方面，中再服务小微企业，探索中小企业营业中断保险，精准保障75.7万家中小企业；创新服务外卖小哥等新市民群体2.3亿人次；"防返贫保险"为甘肃、内蒙古、黑龙江等20个省份脱贫地区180.58万户脱贫群众提供风险保障237.08亿元。

（三）做社会管理的共治者，服务国家治理体系现代化

在巨灾风险管理方面，中再深度参与了全国地震巨灾保险制度设计和各地综合性巨灾保险试点工作，在80%的地方巨灾保险试点项目中担任首席再保人，提供灾害风险评估、风险分担机制研究、保险方案设计、费率测算等技术服务，全年新增保障覆盖4 000万人，累计覆

盖1.3亿人，为抗灾救灾和灾后重建提供有力保障。人保再主动加入城乡居民地震共保体，积极参与广东、广西、湖北、河南、厦门、宁波、深圳等省市的政府巨灾保障，全面保障超过3亿名城乡居民的生命财产安全。

在公共安全管理方面，中再引领环境污染责任险、建设工程安全生产责任险、建筑质量潜在缺陷保险等保险产品创新，其中建筑质量潜在缺陷保险（IDI保险）累计保障面积1.78亿平方米，有效减少社会矛盾纠纷，助力社会管理创新，建设和谐社会。人保再积极参与疫苗接种、服务类企业纾困及复工复产类业务，保障超过7亿剂次新冠疫苗接种，并提供近700万元摊赔支持，助力全民免疫屏障构筑，充分发挥央企责任担当。

（四）做百姓全生命周期的守护者，服务健康中国和应对人口老龄化战略

在保障民生健康方面，中再作为境内首席再保人，积极参与城市定制型商业医疗保险（以下简称惠民保）发展，提供包括产品开发、数据精算、风险承保、系统运营等全方位的支持，"一城一策"推动创新型的普惠型保险解决方案落地，累计为116个城市提供保障方案，惠及人群累计覆盖1.2亿人次。中再还联合国家心血管中心高血压专病医联体，在青海省循化县建立全省首个"三高共管综合防控示范区"，为首批1 500名高血压患者免费提供"慢病管理+保险保障"系统解决方案，防止因病致贫返贫，该项目作为首批典型案例，被国家乡村振兴局在全国推介。

在应对老龄化战略方面，中再发挥保险产品设计能力与保险资金投资专业优势，从承保和投资两端支撑初创期的养老保险机构，协同

构建国家养老金第三支柱；配合监管完善长护险相关制度，聚焦老年险、失能险、护理险三大新型需求，引领行业落地新产品20款，为老年人提供"一站式"照护服务。

（五）做国际合作的参与者，服务"双循环"新格局

中再担任中国"一带一路"再保险共同体主席单位和管理机构。2022年，在中国"一带一路"再保险共同体积极推动下，成员公司共为中国海外利益（财产类）提供近3.3万亿元人民币的保险保障，同比增长19%。人保再持续增强服务"一带一路"沿线区客户能力，创建国际中收业务模式，近两年先后完成阿根廷、智利监管注册，已累计为华为、金风科技、中铁建等重点客户和科兴疫苗支援拉美国家抗疫斗争提供风险保额106亿元，保费收入1 750万元，获得良好的社会效益。太平再（中国）积极参与粤港澳大湾区建设，参与超过40个项目，如粤港澳大湾区深圳都市圈城际铁路深惠城际、穗莞深城际前海至皇岗口岸等重大项目，提供超过78亿元的承保保障。

（六）做保险市场稳定器和行业发展助推器，赋能保险行业高质量发展

中再成立中国保险业首家专注巨灾风险管理的保险科技公司——中再巨灾风险管理股份有限公司，2022年，开发上线国内首个具有自主知识产权的中国洪涝巨灾模型，迭代开发中国台风、地震巨灾模型，形成中再品牌的中国地震、台风、洪涝三大巨灾模型谱系，实现巨灾模型国产化自主可控，让巨灾风险"看得清、算得明、管得好"，有力提升防灾减灾能力。目前，中国地震和台风巨灾模型已在30多家保险和政府机构应用。中再牵头开展人身险行业基础建设，积极参与

第四套生命表编制工作，完成全行业9.04亿件保单和1 001万件理赔的数据收集、清洗及测算工作，科学反映人身险死亡及长寿风险，夯实行业数据基础。人保再开发的交易信息数据交换系统获得"全球保险科技案例奖"，中再巨灾风险管理有限公司获得"全球保险科技企业奖"。瑞再与百度联合落地业界首个为百度Apollo自动驾驶定制的保险解决方案，即自动泊车产品险，荣获《亚洲保险》（*Insurance Asia*）杂志公布的"2022年度汽车保险创新大奖"。慕再在非寿险领域，2022年4月成立了保险解决方案部，以技术型数据分析为依托，以产品开发和咨询服务为导向，致力于帮助保险公司高效改善承保质量，严格加强承保管理；在寿险健康险领域，面向中国市场推出了量身定制的数字化核保风控解决方案——iRISK，帮助保险公司实现简化核保流程、提高承保效率、减少逆选择风险的目的。

四、再保险市场发展展望

2023年，中国再保险行业将持续深化改革、守正创新，回归风险保障本源，加快经营模式转型，实现质的有效提升和量的合理增长，走好特色发展之路。

（一）机遇与挑战

1．机遇

从经济增长看，2023年，主要发达经济体货币政策收紧步伐放慢，中国股市、债市、汇市面临的外部压力将有所减轻。中国走出疫情阴霾，消费环境、消费秩序逐步改善，市场预期和信心平稳，稳增长政策效果持续显现，经济运行有望企稳恢复，预计全年经济增速约5.0%，全球经济增量中有1个百分点来自中国，占全球经济增量的1/3。中国经济具有巨大的发展韧性和潜力，长期向好的基本面没有改变，将为保险市场高质量发展奠定重要基础。

从发展动能看，投资仍是当前推动经济稳定恢复的重要手段，预计传统基建与新基建投资持续发力，拉动工程险、货运险、新能源领域保险发展。国家将更加注重发挥消费的拉动作用，车险、家财险预计继续保持增长态势。稳外贸、发挥出口的重要作用是中国长期发展战略，"一带一路"建设、中国企业海外投资布局及海外利益保障尚有巨大保险缺口。随着国家总体安全观战略实施，粮食、能源、产业链安全等领域带来农险、安责险、企财险等险种的保险需求前景广阔。国家将更加重视运用保险手段助力社会治理转型，保险行业将在食品药品、安全生产、环境保护、劳动保障等更多领域发挥补齐公共服务不足和社会管理不足的"短板"。个人养老金制度、医保商保信息共享、税优健康险扩面、人寿保险与长期护理保险责任转换等利好政策的出台，有望推动养老年金保险、健康保险走向"快车道"。在加快弥合风险保障缺口、深化高质量发展中，再保险需求也将不断释放。

2．挑战

一是宏观环境复杂多变。2023年，中国发展的外部环境不确定性加大，全球通胀仍处于高位，世界经济和贸易增长动能减弱，国际主要央行政策紧缩效应显现，外部压力不断上升。国际货币基金组织预计2023年全球经济前景黯淡，经济增速将放缓至2.8%的历史低位，金融稳定风险上升。

中国经济企稳向上的基础仍需巩固，总需求不足仍然是当前经济运行面临的突出矛盾，经济转型升级面临新的阻力。中美宏观周期错位，制约中国宏观政策作用空间。气候变化导致巨灾事件频发，经济社会风险复杂性提高，导致风险管理难度加大，再保险公司经营面临的外部风险因素不断增加。

二是政策影响持续深化。国际会计准则IFRS17在境内外上市企业率先落地，预计2026年在全行业实施。国内新一轮车险综改政策已实施，2023年6月1日前将在全国范围内扩大车险自主系数浮动范围，将进一步加剧车险费率波动。"偿二代"二期工程实施满一年，对保险公司经营行为影响深远。政策变化对再保险公司的产品形态、服务模式、服务领域和技术水平提出新的挑战，改革发展面临的约束条件和规则要求显著增多。

三是市场竞争越发激烈。财产险领域，车险竞争更趋激烈，综合成本率抬升；非车非农领域增收不增利现象较为普遍；工程、水险、特殊险等险种定价回升乏力，部分商业险种风险敞口累积严重，考验再保险企业的业务选择和风险管控能力。人身险领域，行业仍将处于转型调整阶段，低利率环境对传统寿险及年金产品冲击较大，对业务交易、精算假设产生长期持续影响；健康险发展进入平台期，重疾险经验恶化、医疗险赔付率持续提升，均对人身再保险市场发展带来影响。再保险领域，传统业务承保能力充足，同质化竞争加剧。直保客户需求更为丰富多元，对再保险公司产品创新速度、客户服务效率和平台运营能力提出更高要求。

（二）趋势展望

一是再保险行业持续向好的发展态势不会改变。未来一段时期内，宏观经济将保持稳定上行，利率水平稳中有降，投资和消费动能逐步恢复，保险需求回升，再保险市场发展的外部环境持续向好。再保险行业将继续推动以客户为中心的战略转型，深入推进云计算、大数据和人工智能等科技手段运用，加快数字化、智能化和平台生态化发展步伐，提升专业化、精细化、集约化管理水平，打造再保险特色生态圈，推动产业链与合作网络建设，稳中向好的发展态势进一步显现。

二是再保险行业发展将更加注重与国家战略相结合。再保险行业围绕经济建设、科技创新、数字经济、绿色发展、民生保障、社会治理、"一带一路"倡议等国家发展重点领域，将着力发挥数据积累、风险识别、风险定价和产品创新等方面的技术优势，加强负债端和资产端的双轮驱动和协同配合，前移服务端口，着力"保险增量、风险减量"，为财产损失和人身健康，特别是一系列新兴风险提供风险预防、风险管理和损失融资等更加全面的保险保障与服务，不断拓宽保险保障领域和内容，持续提升服务效率和质量。

三是再保险市场双向开放、融合发展的层次和水平不断提升。2023年6月，国家金融监督管理总局联合上海市人民政府出台了推进上海国际再保险中心建设的实施细则，正式在上海开设面向全球的国际再保险交易市场，对再保险中心建设路径和配套支持进行明确，预计上海再保险交易中心建设进一步提速。与此同时，中国再保险行业将积极把握新一轮金融业对外开放机遇，以服务"双循环"新发展格局为契机，推动国际化战略落地，加快全球化发展步伐，提升跨境服务能力和国际化经营水平，增强国际竞争力，提升国际市场话语权。

四是再保险行业政策体系不断优化完善。中国再保险行业政策体系将朝着不断提升行业竞争力、市场吸引力和国家安全力的方向持续完善。再保险营商环境不断优化，提升中国再保险市场的全球吸引力；加快贸易信用、海事、航空、战争等特殊风险的再保险风险管理能力建设，补齐重大风险、新兴风险等领域再保险供给不足的"短板"，提升再保险服务国民经济的深度和广度；优化再保险组织体系，强化再保险的"最后风险承担者"功能，提升服务国内大循环和国际国内"双循环"的能力。

第二章

2022年中国财产再保险市场回顾及展望

一、财产再保险市场规模

（一）分出保费规模

2022年，国内财产保险公司分出保费1 629.5亿元，同比增长11.6%；同期，财产保险公司原保险保费收入14 867.0亿元，同比增长8.7%；分出保费增速高于同期原保险保费收入增速约2.9个百分点（见图1、表1）。

2012—2022年，国内财产保险公司分出保费由739.0亿元增长至1 629.5亿元，年均增长率约8.2%；同期，财产保险公司原保险保费收入由5 529.9亿元增长至14 867.0亿元，年均增长率约10.4%，再保险分出保费年均增速低于同期原保险保费收入约2.2个百分点（见图1、表1）。

图1　2012—2022年财产保险公司分出保费、原保险保费及增长率情况

（数据来源：《中国保险年鉴》、原中国银保监会）

表1　　2012—2022年财产保险公司分出保费、原保险保费及分出率情况

单位：亿元，%

年份	分出保费	增长率	原保险保费	增长率	分出率
2012	739.0		5 529.9		13.4
2013	865.2	17.1	6 481.2	17.2	13.3
2014	929.8	7.5	7 544.4	16.4	12.3
2015	946.0	1.7	8 423.3	11.6	11.2
2016	887.9	−6.1	9 266.2	10.0	9.6
2017	938.8	5.7	10 541.4	13.8	8.9
2018	1 072.3	14.2	11 755.7	11.5	9.1
2019	1 207.7	12.6	13 016.3	10.7	9.3
2020	1 383.4	14.5	13 583.7	4.4	10.2
2021	1 460.5	5.6	13 676.5	0.7	10.7
2022	1 629.5	11.6	14 867.0	8.7	11.0

数据来源：《中国保险年鉴》、原中国银保监会。

（二）分出率

2022年，国内财产保险公司的分出率约11.0%，较上年提升0.3个百分点（见图2），连续第三年超过10%。

2012—2015年，财产保险分出率逐年下降，但均高于10%；2016—2022年，分出率呈现先降后升的变化趋势。2016年主要受"偿二代"实施的影响，分出率大幅下降至不足10%；2017年"偿二代"影响延续，分出率降至不足9%；2018年以来，受非车险业务增长的拉动，分出率逐年提升；2020年，分出率提升至10%以上；2021—2022年，分出率进一步上升，2022年分出率较2016年高出约1.4个百分点。

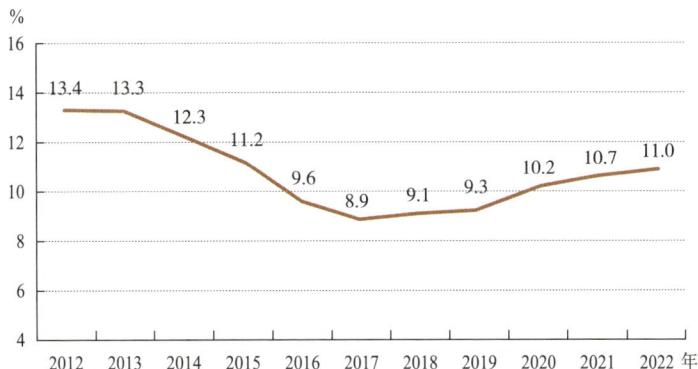

图2 2012—2022年财产保险公司再保险分出率情况

（数据来源：《中国保险年鉴》、原中国银保监会）

二、财产再保险需求侧分析

（一）财产保险公司分出保费分布情况

2022年，分出保费规模超过100亿元的财产保险公司共4家，合计分出保费1 034.3亿元，占行业分出保费规模的63.5%；分出保费规模在10亿~100亿元的财产保险公司共15家，合计分出保费391.8亿元，占行业分出保费规模的24.0%；分出保费规模在1亿~10亿元的财产保险公司共50家，合计分出保费196.4亿元，占行业分出保费规模的12.1%；分出保费规模不足1亿元的财产保险公司共18家，合计分出保费7.1亿元，占行业分出保费规模的0.4%（见表2）。

表2　　　　　　　　2022年财产保险公司分出保费的规模分布情况

单位：家，亿元，%

规模	数量	合计分出保费	占全行业分出保费的比例
分出保费规模超过100亿元	4	1 034.3	63.5
分出保费规模在10亿~100亿元	15	391.8	24.0

规模	数量	合计分出保费	占全行业分出保费的比例
分出保费规模在1亿~10亿元	50	196.4	12.1
分出保费规模不足1亿元	18	7.1	0.4

数据来源：原中国银保监会。

（二）财产保险公司分出保费变化情况

2022年，分出保费较上年增长的财产保险公司数量65家，占比74.7%。其中，较上年增长10%以内的公司数量16家，占比18.4%；较上年增长10%~20%的公司数量18家，占比20.7%；较上年增长超过20%的公司数量31家，占比35.6%（见表3）。

表3　　　　　　　　2022年财产保险公司分出保费的增速分布情况

单位：家，%

	数量	占比
分出保费较上年增长的财产保险公司	65	74.7
其中：较上年增长10%以内的公司	16	18.4
较上年增长10%~20%的公司	18	20.7
较上年增长超过20%的公司	31	35.6

数据来源：原中国银保监会，不包含劳合社中国的业务。

（三）财产保险公司分出率分布情况

2022年，分出率超过20%的财产保险公司数量41家，较上年增加2家、占比47.1%；分出率15%~20%的公司数量6家，较上年增加1家，占比6.9%；分出率10%~15%的公司数量10家，较上年增加2家，占比11.5%；分出率5%~10%的公司数量16家，较上年减少2家，占比18.4%；分出率低于5%的公司数量14家，较上年减少4家，占比16.1%（见表4）。

表4　　　　　2016—2022年各财产保险公司再保险分出率分布情况

单位：家

年份 分出率区间	2016	2017	2018	2019	2020	2021	2022
>20%	26	26	28	34	32	39	41
15%~20%	4	5	8	2	10	5	6
10%~15%	12	12	11	15	7	8	10
5%~10%	14	17	15	11	12	18	16
<5%	24	24	25	25	27	18	14
合计	80	84	87	87	88	88	87

数据来源：原中国银保监会。

三、财产再保险供给侧分析

2022年，在境内注册、经营财产再保险业务的专业再保险公司共12家。其中，市场份额超过20%的专业再保险公司1家，中再产险充分发挥国内再保险市场主渠道作用，市场份额排名第一位；市场份额10%~15%的专业再保险公司1家，市场份额5%~10%的专业再保险公司3家，市场份额低于5%的专业再保险公司7家。

（一）车险业务

2021年，在财产再保险市场中，专业再保险公司的车险分保费收入204.5亿元，同比下降10.3%；2012—2021年，年均增长率约-3.4%，业务规模整体呈下降态势。从车险业务逐年分保费收入来看，2013年增幅较大，增速达27.7%；2016年降幅最大，降低约42.6%；从2016年开始，业务规模由超过300亿元降低为200亿元左右（见表5）。

表5　　　　2012—2021年专业再保险公司车险业务分保费收入情况

单位：亿元

	2012	2013	2014	2015	2016	2017	2018	2019	2020	2021
中再产险	147.0	170.0	174.9	181.5	94.3	91.2	88.4	83.5	98.1	81.0
慕再北分	39.3	65.6	46.6	45.5	43.3	30.3	41.6	28.3	28.7	25.7
瑞再北分	78.2	103.1	106.3	83.1	38.3	38.5	33.8	42.9	44.7	42.9
法再北分	3.7	9.1	14.1	16.4	14.6	12.5	12.1	10.6	4.5	4.3
通用再上分		0.1	0.1	0.2	0.2	0.2	0.2	0.2	0.2	0.2
汉再上分	10.3	3.7	3.4	20.7	6.2	4.6	8.2	12.0	14.4	14.6
太平再（中国）		4.0	4.6	6.4	6.3	7.6	11.5	11.8	11.9	11.6
前海再						1.4	2.5	5.2	3.9	3.8
人保再						15.6	10.1	10.6	21.6	20.4
大韩再										0.1
合计	278.4	355.5	350.0	353.8	203.2	201.8	208.4	205.1	228.1	204.5

数据来源：《中国保险年鉴》、原中国银保监会。

从各市场主体车险分保费收入情况来看，中再产险位于行业第1位，2021年分保费收入81.0亿元，其他公司的车险分保费收入均在50亿元以下。

（二）非车险业务

2021年，在财产再保险市场中，专业再保险公司的非车险分保费收入823.1亿元，同比增长48.6%；2012—2021年，年均增长率约18.1%，业务规模整体呈较快增长态势。从非车险业务逐年分保费收入来看，除2015年和2017年出现下降外，其余年度均实现增长；非车险业务的增长性较好，分保费收入在2018年和2019年先后突破400亿元和500亿元，2021年突破800亿元（见表6）。

表6　　2012—2021年专业再保险公司非车险业务分保费收入情况

单位：亿元

	2012	2013	2014	2015	2016	2017	2018	2019	2020	2021
中再产险	93.5	114.2	118.1	114.8	123.6	128.9	162.9	203.7	235.4	269.3
慕再北分	25.4	23.1	26.3	27.6	41.2	16.5	41.5	46.6	38.9	50.3
瑞再北分	46.2	53.2	52.6	60.3	59.3	37.0	58.8	76.7	81.0	95.9
法再北分	12.6	15.2	18.3	19.2	23.1	22.8	21.3	22.1	23.0	29.7
通用再上分	0.2	0.3	0.5	0.4	0.3	0.7	1.5	1.9	3.2	2.2
汉再上分	6.3	5.5	30.7	10.5	16.2	20.7	33.4	54.5	81.4	68.4
信利再										4.8
太平再（中国）		9.4	11.0	12.0	14.2	22.8	32.4	38.9	39.0	39.8
前海再						4.7	19.1	18.2	21.3	25.5
人保再						19.1	38.8	47.0	29.9	40.6
大韩再									0.7	5.0
中国农再										191.7
合计	184.2	220.8	257.4	244.8	278.1	273.2	409.8	509.6	553.8	823.1

数据来源：《中国保险年鉴》、原中国银保监会。

从各市场主体非车险分保费收入情况来看，中再产险位于行业第1位，2021年分保费收入269.3亿元，其余公司的非车险分保费收入均在200亿元以下。

四、财产再保险市场机遇与挑战

（一）财产险市场发展机遇

受宏观经济景气度回升、政策利好不断释放的积极推动，财产险市场主要在以下四个领域面临发展机遇。

1. 保险助力绿色转型

第一，"碳达峰、碳中和"的"1+N"政策体系逐步完善，各部门、各地区先后颁布行动方案，也为保险业勾画了展业地图，保险公司能够对接相应保障需求、开展产品创新、实现增量发展。第二，监管部门新近发布了《银行业保险业绿色金融指引》，提出从战略高度推进绿色金融，要求金融机构加大对绿色、低碳、循环经济的支持，要求确定绿色金融发展战略、制定绿色金融目标、报送和披露绿色金融情况，将进一步促进绿色保险业务的发展。

保险助力绿色转型主要包括以下细分领域。一是新能源汽车保险。2022年上半年新能源汽车保有量突破1 000万辆，产销再创历史新高，新车销售拉动保费增量，承保业绩也有望改善。二是绿色电力保险。2021年风电、光伏发电装机容量双双突破3亿千瓦后，对照国家规划目标仍有近一倍的增长空间，同时抽水蓄能项目规模化建设、核电项目积极安全有序发展，迎来历史性的发展机遇期。三是绿色建筑保险。中国建筑全过程能耗占全国能源消费总量的45%，碳排放量占全国排放总量的50.6%[①]，建筑行业的绿色转型对于实现"双碳"目标至关重要。目前，北京、宁波、湖州等多地市已实现业务试点落地。四是林草碳汇保险。巩固生态系统固碳作用，提升碳汇能力，推动林草碳汇保险发展成为创新热点，各类"首单"不断。下一步产品创新方向将围绕碳资产保险、碳超额排放费用损失保险等与碳交易相关的细分领域展开。

2．保险支持科技创新

在关键核心技术攻关的新型举国体制下，保险发挥风险保障作用、支持科技创新打开了新的空间。与此同时，"服务战略性新兴产业情况"也已纳入财政部《商业保险公司绩效评价办法》的评价指标体系，推动保险支持科技创新加速落地。

---

① 数据来源：《2022中国建筑能耗与碳排放研究报告》，中国建筑节能协会。

保险支持科技创新主要包括以下细分领域。一是集成电路全产业链保险。组建集成电路共保体，共同解决集成电路产业"卡脖子"问题。二是知识产权保险。目前已覆盖5 000家企业、提供200余亿元的风险保障。三是首台套/新材料保险。与绿色发展领域有交集的电力装备绿色低碳创新行动值得期待。下一步产品创新方向将围绕国产汽车芯片保险、智能机器人保险等细分领域。

3．保险参与风险共治

第一，国家治理体系和治理能力现代化建设不断深化，将从制度层面推动大量潜在风险保障需求转化为实际投保需求。第二，保险行业通过与第三方机构合作，以"保险+"的方式推进风险减量管理，有利于实现经营闭环，提升风险管控水平。

保险参与风险共治主要包括以下细分领域。一是参与建筑质量管控的IDI业务累计保障面积1.78亿平方米，保费规模已超过80亿元。二是已形成"保前体检+保中监测"风控理念和管控模式的网络安全保险，行业主体参与围绕网络安全保险及服务标准的编制工作。三是要求保险提供事故预防服务的安全生产责任保险，正式成为法定保险刚过一年，预计未来市场规模有望达到千亿元。四是参与建设及管护环节风险管理的高标准农田保险，较多地市先后开展试点。除以上领域外，保险参与法律风险服务也将成为新的探索领域。

4．保险服务民生保障

服务民生保障直接体现"保险姓保"的本质属性，有效对接粮食与能源安全、健康中国等重大战略。"服务社会民生情况"也已纳入财政部《商业保险公司绩效评价办法》的评价指标体系。监管部门也先后出台指导意见，要求银行业保险业加强新市民金融服务、支持小微企业发展，为推动保险业加强民生服务保障指明了目标方向。

保险服务民生保障主要包括以下细分领域。一是惠民保。目前已覆盖过亿参保人群、实现超百亿元的保费体量。随着医保和商保实现信息共享，医疗体制改革深化发展，惠民保仍将面临扩大保障范围和提升保障程度的机遇。二是突发公共卫生事件相关保险。疫苗责任险持续发挥积极作用，部分地市由政府部门投保疫情防控保险以保障市场服务型主体的复工复产。三是针对三亿可保群体的新市民保险。相关数据显示，该类群体社会保障参与度低，保险意识尚不足，39%的新市民未购买商业保险[①]，有待深挖业务机遇。四是巨灾保险。巨灾试点项目仍持续增加，越来越兼顾灾害管理和民生保障双重因素。此外，粮食安全和能源安全与民生保障密切相关，保险保障也不可或缺。

（二）财产再保险市场发展机遇

一是高质量发展成为行业普遍共识，再保险作用进一步凸显。财产保险公司普遍提高对业务承保质量的管控要求，确保实现承保效益已成为多数行业主体的核心经营指标。安全有效的再保险安排在稳定承保业绩、支持优质业务发展方面的作用和价值进一步凸显。

二是车险进入新一轮发展阶段，再保险助力行业精细化经营管理。车险综改压力释放，市场竞争秩序好转；市场主体的经营应变能力增强，风险定价精准度显著提升，费用管控效果明显。新能源汽车保险业务规模快速增长，已成为车险业务的战略性增长点，也是车险市场新一轮发展的重要增长引擎，但"高增长、高赔付"的特点加剧经营挑战，专业再保险公司将积极协同直保公司及第三方专业机构开展数据分析挖掘，优化定价模型、改善承保业绩。

---

① 数据来源：中国平安联合第三方调研机构发布的《2022年新市民金融服务白皮书》，2022年7月8日。

三是非车险领域的产品创新和服务创新加速，再保险参与协同创新。聚焦于助力绿色转型、支持科技创新、参与风险共治、服务社会民生，财产再保险公司在服务国家战略、融入经济大盘中将发挥更专业的风险管理职能，并同步实现自身业务的增长。产品创新试点加快落地，在新兴险种及创新产品领域的再保需求保持强劲。

（三）财产险与再保险市场面临的风险挑战

一是中国是全球气候变化敏感区，所受影响趋强。气候变化是全球性话题，世界气象组织最新报告显示：未来5年，全球气温上升有近50%的可能性将突破1.5摄氏度[①]，即突破《巴黎协定》所确定的全球气温上升控制的努力目标。2022年《中国气候变化蓝皮书》再次确认，中国升温速率高于同期全球平均水平，是气候变化的敏感区，高温、强降水等极端天气气候事件趋多、趋强[②]。同时，多部委联合发布《国家适应气候变化战略2035》认为，气候变化向经济社会系统蔓延渗透，可能引发系统性经济与金融风险，涉及农业生产、身体健康、基础设施和居住环境等方面，均与保险业务场景密切相关。

二是中国的自然灾害仍较重，损失呈上升趋势。自然灾害是影响财产保险行业承保业绩的主要因素。2022年上半年，极端天气灾害再现，广东遭遇历史性"龙舟水"和特大洪水，"超百年一遇""六十年以来最强"。其中，广东省17个地市触发巨灾指数保险的理赔条件，部分地市甚至触发了两次赔付。2022年，台风灾害带来新的损失，3号台风"暹芭"重创海上风电。海上风电施工船"福景001轮"在阳江海域防御台风时，走锚遇险沉没，同时因碰撞及拖拽导致邻近海域的海上

---

① 世界气象组织：《全球年际至十年际气候最近通报（2023—2027）》，2023年5月。

② 中国气象局气候变化中心：《中国气候变化蓝皮书（2022）》，2022年8月。

风电机组及海缆损失，经济损失及保险赔付巨大。

三是绿色产业、绿色标的风险暴露增长较快。海上风电项目大规模建设并投产运营，台风的影响已经由风险隐忧演变为实际损失案例，但尚缺乏模型工具等量化风险分析手段。屋顶光伏等分布式光伏项目的新增装机超过集中式项目，更多资产暴露在自然环境下，与农业、农房等标的形成风险叠加，灾害情景下的累计损失风险加重。为稳定电网运行的电化学储能项目即将大规模配建，其火灾风险引起广泛关注。

四是房地产行业风险及对上下游产业链影响值得关注。近年来，受多重因素影响，中国房地产领域停工、逾期交房问题突出。据奥维云网（AVC）地产罗盘大数据平台监测数据显示，2022年精装修楼盘计划交付3 162个项目，但延期交付项目占比高达30%以上，意味着有将近1/3的项目延期到2023年后交房。将对工程履约保证保险、农民工工资支付保证险业务产生较大的负面影响。

五是更多保险险种与产品受境外风险影响。如新兴的亚马逊平台卖家商业综合责任保险、知识产权海外纠纷法律费用保险等，都受境外风险影响。随着产品不断创新，承保业务组合中涉及的境外风险，开始从以中国海外利益为代表的资产类风险向法律责任类风险延伸，给保险行业的风险管控带来更大挑战。

六是公共安全事件、安全生产事故风险。2022年以来，东航坠机、网络攻击等危及公共安全的事件，以及石化厂火灾爆炸等安全生产领域事故等，均提升了社会公众的风险意识，也为保险产品创新带来发展机遇。

七是法律环境的变化。中国版证券市场集体诉讼司法实践已落地。多家上市公司因涉嫌信息披露违法违规，被证监会立案调查；众多投资者因上市公司存在虚假陈述行为遭受经济损失，提出证券索赔请求。

八是疫情影响。疫情对中小微企业经营的冲击更为显著，以小微企业经营者为主要客群之一的融资性保证险业务赔付显著上升。同时，中国台湾地区的防疫保险遭遇理赔高峰，上海疫情推高隔离险的赔付，应加强管控此类可能显著影响经营稳定性的重大风险因素。

五、财产再保险市场发展展望

（一）对再保险分出需求变化的展望

传统险种领域，财产保险公司的再保险需求保持整体平稳。稳定经营业绩、分散巨灾风险、减轻资本压力成为再保险安排的主要诉求。一是传统险种的再保分出率整体保持在合理区间，进一步拓展优质业务对再保险支持的需求更为刚性。二是在再保险硬市场环境下，多数财产保险公司能够接受市场对再保险合约条件一定程度的调整。三是在超赔合约保障的再保险安排中，多数财产保险公司能够提高成本预算，以保证其在再保险市场硬周期下能够获得足额的风险保障。

新兴险种及创新产品领域，财产保险公司的再保需求保持强劲。一是绿色保险领域的产品创新和再保险保障需求强劲。监管部门要求金融企业从战略高度推进绿色金融，加大对绿色、低碳、循环经济的支持，将进一步促进绿色保险业务的发展。绿色电力保险、绿色建筑保险、林草碳汇保险、碳资产保险等领域，产品创新活跃，再保合作需求旺盛。二是科技保险的再保险服务需求强劲。监管出台多部指导意见，要求银行保险业支持高水平科技自立自强、服务制造业高质量发展。围绕集成电路全产业链保险、知识产权保险、首台套及新材料保险、国产汽车芯片保险、智能机器人保险等领域，组建保险共同体、保险生态圈成为保险服务高科技产业的创新模式，再保险支持是其中必不可少的重要环节。三是"再保险+数据""再保险+服务"等综合风险服务更加契合财产保险公司的业务发展需求。专业再保险公司更积极地输出数据能力和经验、整合服务资源和网络，与直保公司合作开发创新型保险产品和风险解决方案。在巨灾保险、网络安全保险等新兴领域，再保险公司持续增加资源投入并强化价值输出，从供给端助推业务发展需求向再保险合作的转化。

（二）对专业再保险公司业务承保策略变化的展望

国内再保险市场的承保能力供给紧张，市场排分难度将显著增加。财产再保险市场将延续"硬市场"周期，离岸再保人继续将承保能力向价格涨幅大的国家和地区转移，对国内市场的再保险承保能力供给整体下降。财产保险公司的再保险排分难度将显著增加，部分领域已出现的再保险排分缺口将延续甚至进一步扩大。

国际再保险市场的价格上涨将向国内市场传导。首先，近年来自然巨灾损失呈现高频高损态势，叠加俄乌冲突等"黑天鹅"事件影响，国际再保险市场承保利润不断受到侵蚀，再保险价格上涨是市场普遍诉求。其次，国际市场专业再保险公司更加关注风险对价，严控自然灾害的累计责任、严控部分特定领域的风险敞口、严控已过剩承保能力的进一步投放。最后，境内专业再保险公司在资本实力和承保能力上，暂未能与其所承保的风险同步增长，仍需要通过向国际再保险市场寻求转分保支持，而高涨的转分保障成本也必然提高其对分入业务的定价预期和报价水平。

第三章

3

2022年中国人身再保险市场回顾及展望

一、人身再保险市场规模

（一）人身险市场情况

2022年，中国人身险市场继续在调整中前行，长期储蓄类业务增长较快，保障类业务短期下降，人身保险公司经营压力和资本需求偏大，对人身再保险市场既有机遇也带来挑战。

业务规模方面，2022年，国内人身保险公司保费收入32 091.0亿元，按可比口径，同比增长2.8%。

业务结构方面，2022年，寿险保费收入24 519.0亿元，同比增长4.0%；健康险保费收入7 073.0亿元，同比增长0.1%，增速逐年放缓；意外险保费收入499.0亿元，同比下降14.4%，增速大幅放缓。

（二）分出保费规模

2022年，国内人身保险公司分出保费1 153.3亿元，同比增长15.8%。同期，人身保险公司原保险保费收入32 091.0亿元，按可比口径同比增长2.8%（见图1、表1）。总体来说，分出保费规模不同年份之间呈波动趋势。当前，宏观经济面临的需求收缩、供给冲击、预期转弱三重压力仍然较大，资本市场动荡下跌，直保市场面临发展转型，给人身再保险市场增长带来一定冲击和挑战。

2012—2022年，国内人身保险公司分出保费由140.4亿元增长至1 153.3亿元，年均增长率约23.4%，整体稳中有升。其中，2012—2014年，分出保费迅速增长；2015—2016年大幅回落；2017—2020年波动上涨；2021—2022年在稍有下降后有所回升。

图1　2012—2022年人身保险公司分出保费、原保险保费及增长率情况

（数据来源：《中国保险年鉴》、原中国银保监会）

表1　　2012—2022年人身保险公司分出保费、原保险保费及分出率情况

单位：亿元，%

年份	分出保费	增长率	原保险保费	增长率	分出率
2012	140.4		9 957.9		1.4
2013	298.8	112.8	10 740.9	7.9	2.8
2014	1 937.4	548.4	12 690.3	18.1	15.3
2015	555.6	−71.3	15 859.1	25.0	3.5
2016	435.9	−21.5	21 692.8	36.8	2.0
2017	722.4	65.7	26 039.6	20.0	2.8
2018	736.2	1.9	26 260.9	0.8	2.8
2019	673.9	−8.5	29 628.4	12.8	2.3
2020	1 043.7	54.9	31 673.6	6.9	3.3
2021	996.3	−4.5	31 223.7	−1.4	3.2
2022	1 153.3	15.8	32 091.0	2.8	3.6

数据来源：《中国保险年鉴》、原中国银保监会。

（三）分出率

2022年，国内人身保险公司分出率约3.6%，较上年上升0.4个百分点（见图2），连续第3年高于3%。当前，国内人身险分出率与全球趋同，基本稳定在3%左右。受业务结构及人身险市场变化影响，以风险保障为目的的传统再保险业务分出比例较大，储蓄型为主的人身险分出比例较低。境外存量市场业务变动主要受国际并购、年金业务等大宗交易业务影响，增长有限，整体格局稳定。

2012—2022年，人身保险公司分出率除个别年份外，整体呈稳中有升趋势（见图2）。其中，2012—2014年，分出率逐年提升并达到高峰；2015年大幅回落；2016—2022年，分出率逐步提升。整体来说，2022年分出率是2012年的2.6倍，高出2012年约2.2个百分点。这一变化很大程度上源于中国医疗险市场的高速发展，相较重疾溢额分保方式，医疗险多采用成数分保，人身保险公司分出需求有较大程度的提升。

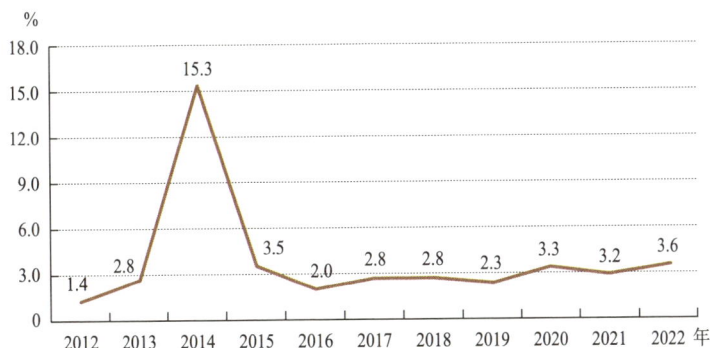

图2　2012—2022年人身保险公司再保险分出率情况

（数据来源：《中国保险年鉴》、原中国银保监会）

二、人身再保险需求侧分析

（一）人身保险公司分出保费分布情况[①]

2022年，分出保费规模超过50亿元的人身保险公司共10家，合计分出保费691.8亿元，占行业分出保费规模的60.0%；分出保费规模在10亿~50亿元的人身保险公司共19家，合计分出保费409.0亿元，占行业分出保费规模的35.5%；分出保费规模在1亿~10亿元的人身保险公司共35家，合计分出保费136.1亿元，占行业分出保费规模的11.8%；分出保费规模不足1亿元的人身保险公司共20家，合计分出保费6.9亿元，占行业分出保费规模的0.6%（见表2）。

表2　　　　2022年人身保险公司分出保费的规模分布情况

单位：家，亿元，%

规模	数量	合计分出保费	占全行业分出保费的比例
分出保费规模超过50亿元	10	691.8	60.0
分出保费规模在10亿~50亿元	19	409.0	35.5
分出保费规模在1亿~10亿元	35	136.1	11.8
分出保费规模不足1亿元	20	6.9	0.6

数据来源：原中国银保监会。

（二）人身保险公司分出保费变化情况

2022年，分出保费较上年增长的人身保险公司数量48家，占比为53.3%。其中，较上年增长超过50%的公司数量25家，占比为27.8%；较上年增长20%~50%的公司数量6家，占比为6.7%；较上年增长20%以

[①] 部分人身保险公司2022年分出保费规模数据为负数。

内的公司数量17家，占比为18.9%（见表3）。

表3 **2022年人身保险公司分出保费的增速分布情况**

单位：家，%

规模	数量	占比
分出保费较上年增长的人身保险公司	48	53.3
其中：较上年增长超过50%的公司	25	27.8
较上年增长20%~50%的公司	6	6.7
较上年增长20%以内的公司数量	17	18.9

数据来源：原中国银保监会。

三、人身再保险供给侧分析

2022年，在境内注册、经营人身再保险业务的专业再保险公司共10家。其中，市场份额超过50%的公司1家，市场份额10%~15%的公司1家，市场份额5%~10%的公司3家，市场份额低于5%的公司5家。中再寿险充分发挥国内再保险主渠道作用，市场份额排名第1位。其他主要参与者包括国际大型再保险公司，以及前海再、太平再（中国）、人保再等本土再保险公司。

（一）寿险业务

2021年，人身再保险市场中，专业再保险公司的寿险分保费收入587.1亿元，同比增长4.4%；2012—2021年，年均增长率约16.1%，整体呈波动增长态势（见表4）。从寿险业务逐年分保费收入来看，2013—2014年大幅增长，2015—2016年显著下降，从2017年开始稳步回升，除2019年外，2017—2021年中历年均保持正增长。

表4　　　　　2012—2021年专业再保险公司寿险业务分保费收入情况

单位：亿元

	2012	2013	2014	2015	2016	2017	2018	2019	2020	2021
中再寿险	125.7	142.2	166.0	178.1	252.9	368.5	404.6	390.0	464.8	443.7
慕再北分	4.0	20.4	23.1	30.3	9.3	6.2	4.2	5.0	7.9	6.1
瑞再北分	1.0	0.8	1.3	1.6	0.8	1.9	2.4	1.1	3.4	3.4
法再北分	0.3	10.6	19.0	10.8	2.1	3.8	10.1	7.3	8.0	40.0
通用再上分	2.3	2.6	3.1	3.8	4.0	5.1	5.6	7.1	8.0	9.8
汉再上分	19.7	120.7	586.9	96.3	16.7	9.3	12.5	17.6	18.8	16.4
RGA美再上分				0.1		2.1	2.9	2.0	2.4	2.5
太平再（中国）										0.1
前海再						33.3	42.2	29.0	49.1	62.5
人保再										2.4
合计	153.0	297.3	799.6	320.9	285.8	430.2	484.4	459.0	562.5	587.1

数据来源：《中国保险年鉴》、原中国银保监会。

从各市场主体寿险分保费收入情况来看，中再寿险位于行业第1位，2021年分保费收入443.7亿元，市场份额约为75.6%；其次是前海再、法再，2021年市场份额分别约为10.6%、6.8%，其中法再2021年寿险分保费收入增长迅速，同比增速达397.5%；其余公司的寿险分保费收入均在20亿元以下。

（二）健康险业务

2021年，人身再保险市场中，专业再保险公司的健康险分保费收入480.5亿元，同比增长12.3%；2012—2021年，年均增长率约28.4%（见表5）。近年来，健康险分保费收入增长较快，2021年健康险分保费收入为2012年的9.5倍，但2021年同比增速出现明显下降，增长呈放缓态势。

表5 2012—2021年专业再保险公司健康险业务分保费收入情况

单位：亿元

	2012	2013	2014	2015	2016	2017	2018	2019	2020	2021
中再寿险	16.2	26.8	25.1	32.5	37.3	50.6	97.6	139.3	175.6	212.3
慕再北分	10.6	10.8	10.8	17.3	24.5	28.5	26.3	36.4	44.3	37.5
瑞再北分	18.9	18.7	21.1	20.3	21.5	20.1	17.3	38.1	46.6	48.6
法再北分	1.5	2.0	2.5	1.4	1.2	5.0	13.7	21.8	30.7	26.3
通用再上分	0.5	0.4	1.2	2.1	2.9	7.8	23.4	37.0	40.9	41.7
汉再上分	2.9	4.8	4.7	38.2	12.7	19.7	28.8	41.6	51.9	58.4
RGA美再上分				0.4		3.9	7.8	8.5	8.2	8.9
太平再（中国）								0.6	1.4	2.4
前海再						0.4	2.1	12.2	27.8	39.8
人保再									0.4	4.6
合计	50.6	63.5	65.4	112.2	100.0	135.9	216.9	335.6	427.8	480.5

数据来源：《中国保险年鉴》、原中国银保监会。

从各市场主体健康险分保费收入情况来看，中再寿险位于行业第1位，2021年分保费收入212.3亿元，市场份额约为44.2%；汉再、瑞再、通用再、前海再、慕再、法再2021年健康险分保费收入在25亿~60亿元，其中前海再自2017年开展业务以来增长迅速，2017—2021年的年均增长率达211.8%。其余公司的健康险分保费收入均在10亿元以下。

（三）意外险业务

2021年，人身再保险市场中，专业再保险公司的意外险分保费收入65.8亿元人民币，同比增长4.5%；2012—2021年，年均增长率约11.8%，整体呈波动增长态势（见表6）。

表6　　　　2012—2021年专业再保险公司意外险业务分保费收入情况

单位：亿元

	2012	2013	2014	2015	2016	2017	2018	2019	2020	2021
中再寿险	17.1	13.6	18.3	18.1	22.2	23.0	21.5	25.1	24.6	37.0
慕再北分	2.8	1.3	6.2	3.8	5.5	8.3	11.5	12.6	13.0	11.6
瑞再北分	1.9	0.9	0.6	1.1	-0.6	0.5	0.9	1.5	1.7	1.4
法再北分	0.6	0.9	2.2	3.8	4.8	3.9	2.2	2.1	2.3	2.6
通用再上分	0.2	0.3	1.3	3.6	5.3	5.2	6.8	7.7	6.3	4.9
汉再上分	1.4	7.0	3.1	4.1	5.5	6.0	12.3	13.1	14.1	6.8
太平再（中国）								0.3	0.5	1.0
前海再						0.1	0.6	0.5	0.6	0.4
人保再										0.1
合计	24.1	24.0	31.7	34.6	42.8	46.8	55.7	62.9	63.0	65.8

数据来源：《中国保险年鉴》、原中国银保监会。

从各市场主体意外险分保费收入情况来看，中再寿险位于行业第1位，2021年分保费收入37.0亿元，市场份额约为56.2%；其次是慕再、汉再，市场份额分别约为17.6%、10.3%；其余公司的意外险分保费收入均在5亿元以下。

（四）全球人身再保险市场格局

从全球市场格局来看，AM.Best数据显示，全球再保险集团排名中，人身再保险业务至少占总保费收入的30%，整体格局较为稳定。2021年全球人身再保险公司排名中，加拿大人寿再超越瑞再，排名第1位；中再寿险超越法再排名第5位（见表7）。

表7　　　　　　2021年全球前十大人身再保险集团

单位：亿美元

排名	公司名称	毛再保费规模
1	加拿大人寿再	235.5
2	瑞再	160.7

续表

排名	公司名称	毛再保保费规模
3	慕再	142.3
4	RGA美再	133.5
5	中再	108.5
6	法再	106.1
7	汉再	96.7
8	伯克希尔公司	56.2
9	大西洋再	40.9
10	Assicurazioni Generali SPA	24.3

数据来源：AM. Best。

四、人身再保险市场机遇与挑战

随着中国经济增长和居民可支配收入水平提高，人身保险行业迎来高质量发展新阶段。目前，国内人身险市场步入深度转型期，人身险公司需要对原有的业务模式进行调整，以突破发展"瓶颈"，实现长期价值增长。

（一）人身险市场发展机遇

从宏观经济看，世纪疫情持续和复杂国际形势交织影响下，中国坚持"稳字当头、稳中求进"总基调，打好"宏观政策""扩大内需""改革创新""防控风险"四套"组合拳"，宏观经济将持续恢复性发展。国家在政策面持续推动三支柱养老保障体系建设，为保险业带来发展增量新机遇，养老产业融合也将同步加速。"三医"改革步伐加速，医药分家、社保医疗费用管控、医疗信息化等对商业保险经营环境产生深刻影响。粤港澳大湾区、海南等区域经济政策均提及保险，为保险科技创新、医养结合和跨境保险开展等提供了政策机遇。

从监管政策看，一是持续强化金融监管，防范化解重大经济金融风险。在顶层设计上，在原中国银保监会基础上组建国家金融监督管理总局，建立金融市场的统一监管体系；产品监管升级，积极推动负债成本下行，原中国银保监会发布《一年期以上人身保险产品信息披露规则》，取消"高中低"三档，分红险要披露红利；启动调研摸底，征求对监管部门或行业协会推动行业降低负债成本、提高负债质量的意见和建议。二是积极推动产品和服务的供给侧结构性改革。国务院办公厅印发《关于推动个人养老金发展的意见》，明确个人账户制和税优政策，促进第三支柱加速发展。原中国银保监会发布《关于开展人寿保险与长期护理保险责任转换业务试点的通知》，丰富寿险产品功能，努力提升长期护理保险支付需求和供给能力。

从人身险市场来看，2022年，人身险市场保费收入同比增长仅2.8%，触底信号尚未显现，但随着疫情防控措施优化、宏观政策叠加发力，头部保险公司转型成效渐显，将给人身险市场转型复苏带来正向影响。同时，新发展理念下催生行业新商业模式，对药品、医疗附加值服务需求显著上升，商业支付创新不断升温；新技术催生新竞争模式，互联网、区块链、大数据、人工智能等加速行业渗透，引发保险经营从理念到模式的加速升级。

（二）人身再保险产品创新机遇

近年来，健康中国战略持续深入推进，党的二十大报告要求"积极发展商业医疗保险"，监管部门也出台多个推动健康险发展的相关政策文件，为商业健康险带来巨大发展机遇。人身再保险行业将围绕健康险产品创新贡献专业价值。

1．重疾险

近年来，重疾险产品创新更多地体现在产品结构变化。人身再保险通过与直保公司合作，不断开发兼顾医疗费用报销、失能收入补偿等功能的重疾产品。产品结构创新主要包括模块化重疾设计以及"终身重疾+定期重疾"设计。模块化的产品设计较为灵活多样，既可以将不同险类的责任作为不同模块，也可以将重疾险的多个单独责任作为模块，客户根据自身需求进行灵活组合。在重疾险新业务规模萎缩的背景下，重疾型的护理险或失能险成为新的热点。此外，针对次标准体的重疾险也成为重疾险创新的方向之一。

2．医疗险

先进医疗一直是医疗险升级的一个主要方向，人身再保险借助在医疗产业领域的深耕和创新，提高患者对于先进治疗方式的可及性和支付能力，也可帮助先进医疗技术发挥其市场效应，增进客户对保险的感知度和认可度。此外，零免赔百万医疗险、税优医疗险等也成为医疗险下一步重要创新方向。税优健康险新规将于2023年8月1日正式生效，除医疗险外，长护险、疾病险等产品也被纳入税优范围。税优健康险产品设计更加强调社会性以及与基本医保的衔接性。在此背景下，人身再保险可借助自身产品研发和数据优势，支持零免赔、既往症人群可保可赔的税优专属产品设计，通过合理的产品精算机制，促进税优健康险长期可持续发展。

3．老年产品

为应对老龄化发展趋势，人身再保险积极推进老年保险产品体系建设，通过识别不同疾病状态、不同收入层次的老年客群需求，向保险行业推广了老年百万医疗险、老年护理险、老年防癌险、老年意外险等产品，满足中老年人群差异化的保障需求，对以往难以被商业保险承保的老年人群提供了风险保障，也为老龄化社会提供了保险解决方案。

4．消费医疗产品

人身再保险通过联动稀缺医疗资源，围绕癌症早筛、疫苗服务等场景设计保险产品，如针对结直肠癌的"肠安保"医疗险和针对女性特定疾病的宫颈癌产品。"肠安保"医疗险不仅为客户提供私立诊所的肠镜检查和息肉切除，同时保障未来罹患结直肠癌的特药费用。针对女性特定疾病的宫颈癌产品在为客户提供HPV疫苗预约接种的同时，还保障未来罹患宫颈癌的医疗费用支出。这些产品既满足了客户当下的医疗需求，又为客户提供了长期风险保障，提升客户对于保险保障的感知度（见表8）。

表8　　　　　　　　　　　人身再保险产品创新趋势

险种	发展方向	人身再保险支持方面
重疾险	产品责任创新	通过直保公司需求，开发兼顾医疗费用报销、失能收入补偿等功能的重疾产品。
	产品结构创新	模块化重疾设计以及"终身重疾+定期重疾"设计：既可以将不同险类的责任作为不同模块，也可以将重疾险的多个单独责任作为模块。
医疗险	先进医疗	借助医疗产业在不同领域的深耕和创新，提高患者对先进治疗方式的可及性和支付能力，增进客户对保险的感知和认可度。
	零免赔百万医疗险	借助自身产品研发和数据优势，支持零免赔、既往症人群可保可赔的税优专属产品设计，促进税优健康险长期可持续发展。
	税优医疗险	
老年产品	对既往难以被商业保险承保的老年人群提供可保性支持	识别不同疾病状态、不同收入层次的老年客群需求，向行业推广老年百万医疗险、老年护理险、老年防癌险、老年意外险等产品。
消费医疗产品	既满足客户当下的医疗需求，又提供未来远期风险的保障	通过联动稀缺医疗资源，围绕癌症早筛、疫苗服务等场景设计保险产品。

（三）人身险及再保险市场面临的风险挑战

一是受疫情、地缘政治冲突等多重影响，中国宏观经济面临需求收缩、供给冲击、预期转弱三重压力，经济恢复的基础尚需稳固。金融市场方面，全球滞胀风险上升，持续加息引发国际资本市场波动。二是国内人身险市场遭受需求端、销售端、资产端多重压力，保障需求短期下降，长期储蓄需求上升，销售人力大幅下降，代理人渠道新单销售和新业务价值深度下探，市场整体发展信心有待提振。三是国内人身险市场正在转型中，医疗支出提高，长期医疗险管理机制尚不成熟，健康险发展面临风险暴露增多、管理难度增加等挑战。

五、人身再保险市场发展展望

2023年，中国经济有望企稳回升，人身险市场发展将持续受益于宏观经济回暖与政策发力。从渠道端看，尽管市场发展存在较大挑战，但历经三年转型后，代理人渠道探底出清有望基本完成，增优提质将取得局部成效；在长期储蓄保险和税延养老金融的带动下，银保渠道将进一步发展；在共同富裕和普惠金融的时代背景下，团体或类团体业务的新模式以其高成交效率和低营销成本，或将为团险渠道的业务转型升级带来发展机遇，同时也为职域营销的发展带来新机遇。从产品和服务端看，市场利率稳中趋降，人身险产品凭借稳健较好的收益，形成较强的竞争优势；惠民保等普惠保险有望成为带动社商融合、三医联动的创新融合平台；重疾险与护理、失能等新型健康险产品有望融合发展；长期储蓄和年金产品仍然是市场主流。从资产端看，持续下行的资本市场有望走出阶段性行情，整体投资收益有望企稳回升。

预计人身再保险行业将继续深化直再合作，发挥数据积累、产品设计和平台生态优势，推动人身险行业加快转型升级。一是加强市场应变。寿险、传统意外险价格竞争激烈，利润空间收窄，健康险、新型意外险分出需求相对旺盛。以数据、技术为核心的产品开发和服务创新成为获取保障型新业务的重要方式。受人口老龄化和税收递延养老年金政策影响，长寿风险需求逐步显现。"偿二代"二期、IFRS17实施等，将使财务再保险等非传统风险转移方式呈现复杂化和多元化趋势，考验再保险公司创新应变能力。二是加快创新迭代。健康险是目前人身保险公司竞争的主要战场，直保公司对于再保险公司在产品迭代、定价支持等方面的反应速度要求越来越高。再保险公司在拓宽健康保险产品覆盖人群、保障责任的同时，将积极关注和研究特定医疗、特定疾病，如试管婴儿保险等领域的创新机遇，探索针对带病体、亚健康人群的保障产品。三是强调生态联动。再保险公司将拓展业务场景、延伸产业生态，加强与医院、医疗服务机构、健康服务机构合作，构建"保险+医疗服务/健康管理"服务保障体系，实现产品和服务的深度结合，为直保公司开拓健康险市场提供助力。四是强化科技赋能。再保险公司将利用大数据技术，整合再保险业务数据、直保公司数据、第三方机构数据等多方数据资源，建立健康险数据池，加强数据整合分析，协助直保公司降低成本、精选客户、优化决策、加强风控。

第四章

2022年中国再保险行业双向开放回顾及展望

中国改革开放四十五年来，保险业始终坚定不移落实国家对外开放基本国策，坚持"引进来"与"走出去"相结合，推动保险业发展不断取得新成效。得益于保险业高水平对外开放，外资（再）保险公司国内发展布局不断优化。在加快构建以国内大循环为主体、国内国际双循环相互促进的新发展格局背景下，中国再保险公司也持续推进境内和境外市场协同联动发展。

一、外资再保险企业在中国发展情况

（一）国际再保险市场概况

2022年，全球前50大再保险公司分保费收入为3 636.3亿美元，在2021年基础上上涨3%左右，约合25 054.1亿元[①]。2022年，中国再保险市场分保费收入2 250.2亿元，约占全球再保险市场份额的9.0%（见图1）。

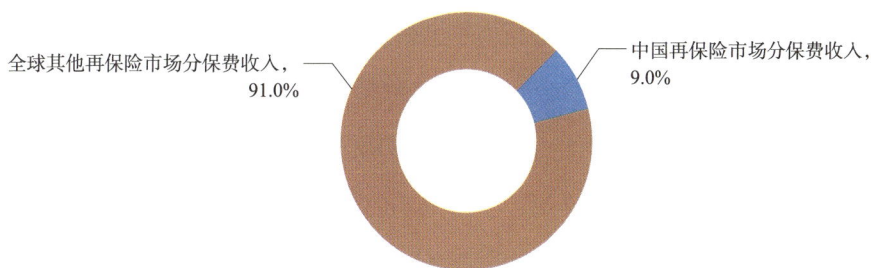

图1 2022年中国再保险市场分保费收入占全球份额

（数据来源：原中国银保监会、AM.Best 数据）

从险种结构来看，2022年非寿险再保险保费收入约占全球再保险毛保费收入的68%，寿险再保险保费收入约占32%（见图2）。

---

① 数据来源：AM.Best，Global Reinsurance-Segment Review 2022。按2022年12月31日银行间外汇市场人民币汇率1美元=6.89元人民币测算。

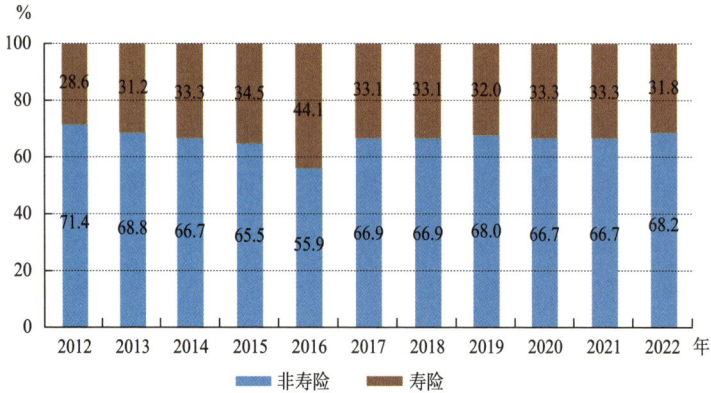

图2　全球前50大再保险公司业务结构情况

（数据来源：AM.Best，*Global Reinsurance-Segment Review*（2012-2022））

从市场竞争格局来看，根据AM.Best 2022年全球再保险公司排名（见表1），慕尼黑再保险集团位居第1位，再保险保费规模513亿美元，同比增长9.6%，保费增长主要来自财产险和意外伤害险。瑞士再保险集团排名第2位，再保险保费规模397亿美元，同比增长1.2%。汉诺威再保险公司排名第3位，再保险保费规模355亿美元，同比增长13.1%，保费增长主要来自财产险和意外伤害险。仅经营人身再保险业务的加拿大人寿再保险公司继续位于第4名。伯克希尔哈撒韦排名则提升至第5位。2022年，全球前50大再保险公司再保险保费规模为3 636.3亿美元，同比增长2.8%。

表1　　　　　　　　**2022年国际再保集团保费规模排名**

单位：亿美元

排名	再保险集团	2022年再保保费规模
1	慕再	513
2	瑞再	397
3	汉再	355
4	加拿大人寿再	234
5	伯克希尔哈撒韦	221

续表

排名	再保险集团	2022年再保保费规模
6	法再	211
7	劳合社	185
8	中再	169
9	RGA美再	138
10	Everest Re（百慕大）	93

数据来源：AM.Best，2022。

（二）外资再保险公司在华发展概况

自1994年国务院颁布《外资金融机构管理条例》以来，外资金融机构开始陆续来华展业。瑞再与慕再先后于1996年、1997年在上海设立代表处，是最早进入中国的国际头部再保险公司。2001年中国加入WTO之后，制定了金融业开放制度安排。中国再保险市场以此为起点，市场规模从小到大、发展步伐不断加快已成为全球最为开放、最具成长性的再保险市场之一。

截至2022年底，中国境内再保险市场专业再保险公司共有15家，其中7家中资再保险公司（含1家集团公司，即中再集团），8家外资再保险公司（见表2）。国际头部再保险公司通过在华设立分支机构参与中国市场，如瑞再、慕再近年来中国区毛保费收入占其集团整体再保险保费规模的10%左右，中国市场已成为其重要的业务市场。

表2　　　　2022年外资公司在华机构保费收入排名

单位：亿元

排名	在华外资机构	2022年分保费收入
1	瑞再北分	185.2
2	汉再上分	158.4
3	慕再北分	123.4
4	法再北分	87.9

续表

排名	在华外资机构	2022年分保费收入
5	通用再上分	46.4
6	RGA美再上分	14.1
7	大韩再上分	6.1
8	信利再	3.1

数据来源：各公司2022年度信息披露报告。

外资再保险公司根据其自身经营特点，制定了差异化的发展策略。比如，有的外资公司在中国聚焦政府与科技领域业务，一方面，注重与中国政府合作，对政府重点关注的医疗、"三农"、环境污染及食品安全等领域，重点发展相应的健康险、农险、责任险等险种；另一方面，拓展科技创新，与许多直保公司在车联网、物联网、数据挖掘等方面开展合作。再比如，有的外资公司更注重业务质量，强调在业务端实现可持续、有利润的增长，因而特别注重技术提升、市场研判和早期投入。还有的外资公司注重经营效益，强调业务端利润，同时善于通过精细化管理降低成本以维持高于同业的盈利能力。

（三）2022年外资再保险公司在华经营情况

2022年，外资再保险公司业务发展整体保持稳健，盈利能力不断提升，竞争力进一步增强，已成为中国再保险市场的重要组成部分。

1．业务规模情况

2017—2022年，外资再保险公司业务规模整体稳健。2022年，外资再保险公司分保费收入较2021年小幅下降，瑞再北分业务规模仍排名外资再保险公司首位，2022年分保费收入185.2亿元，汉再上分、慕再北分、法再北分紧随其后（见图3）。

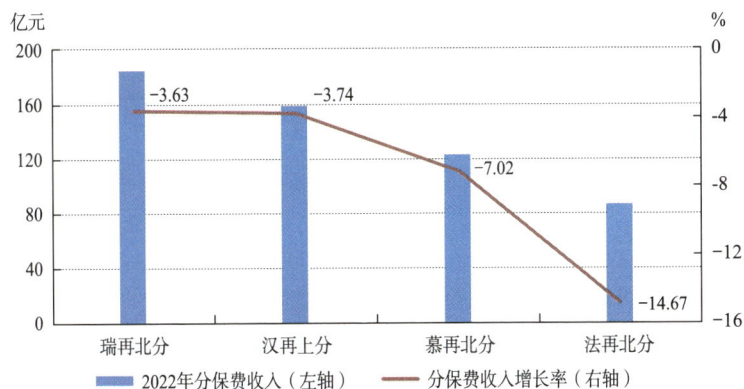

图3 2022年外资再保险公司分保费收入及增长率情况

（数据来源：各公司 2022 年年度信息披露报告）

（1）瑞再北分

从分保费收入看，瑞再北分作为外资再保险的龙头公司，2022年分保费收入185.2亿元，同比下降3.6%。近年来，瑞再集团的财产险业务增幅明显，瑞再北分的财产险业务贡献了其总保费收入的七成以上，远高于寿险和健康险。

从业务结构看（见表3），2022年瑞再北分财产险分保费收入占比70.6%，其中占比较高的为财产及责任险（43.8%）与车险（17.7%）。人身险分保费收入占比为29.4%。近两年，由于中国市场寿险及健康险发展前景广阔，且相关业务受疫情影响较小，人身险分保费收入呈现上升趋势。

表3 瑞再北分业务结构情况

单位：亿元，%

业务条线	2022年分保费收入	2022年分保费占比
人身险	54.5	29.4
寿险	6.0	3.2
健康险	48.5	26.2
财产险	130.7	70.6

业务条线	2022年分保费收入	2022年分保费占比
车险	32.8	17.7
财产及责任险	81.2	43.8
水险	12.4	6.7
其他	4.4	2.4
合计	185.2	100

数据来源：公司2022年度信息披露报告。

（2）汉再上分

从分保费收入看，汉再上分2022年分包费收入158.4亿元，同比下降3.7%。目前，汉再上分分保费收入规模仅次于瑞再北分，位居外资再保险公司第2位。

从业务结构看（见表4），汉再上分寿险业务占比六成左右，非寿险业务占比四成左右。寿险业务中占比最高的为健康险，占比为29.7%。非寿险业务中占比较高的有责任险，占比为13.2%；财产险，占比为11.3%；信用险，占比为11.2%；车险，占比为8.6%。

表4　　　　　　　　　　汉再上分业务结构情况

单位：亿元，%

业务条线	2022年分保费收入	2022年分保费占比
寿险	65.5	41.4
健康险	47.0	29.7
人寿险	10.2	6.5
意外险	8.3	5.2
非寿险	92.9	58.6
责任险	20.8	13.2
财产险	17.9	11.3
信用险	17.7	11.2
机动车辆及第三者责任险	13.5	8.6
农业险	8.1	5.1

业务条线	2022年分保费收入	2022年分保费占比
工程险	6.8	4.3
货物运轮险	3.5	2.2
健康险	1.6	1.0
船舶险	1.6	1.0
意外险	0.6	0.4
其他	0.6	0.4
合计	158.4	100

数据来源：公司2022年度信息披露报告。

（3）慕再北分

从分保费收入看，2022年慕再北分分保费收入123.4亿元，同比下降7.0%。其中，非寿险分保费收入为81.6亿元，同比上升5.3%；寿险分保费收入为41.8亿元，同比下降24.3%。

从业务结构看（见表5），2022年慕再北分非寿险业务占比66.1%，寿险业务占比33.9%。寿险保费收入呈现下降趋势，在分保费收入中占比减少，非寿险成为主要业务。

表5　　　　　　　　　　慕再北分业务结构情况

单位：亿元，%

业务条线	2022年分保费收入	2022年分保费占比
非寿险	81.6	66.1
寿险	41.8	33.9
合计	123.4	100

数据来源：公司2022年度信息披露报告。

（4）法再北分

从分保费收入看，2022年法再北分分保费收入87.9亿元，同比下降14.7%。其中，寿险分保费收入53.1亿元，同比下降20.0%；非寿险分保费收入34.8亿元，同比下降5.1%。

从业务结构看（见表6），法再北分近年寿险业务占比总体呈上升趋势，超过非寿险成为公司第一大业务险种。2022年法再北分寿险业务占分保费收入的60.4%，非寿险业务占比为39.6%。

表6 　　　　　　　　　　　法再北分业务结构情况

单位：亿元，%

业务条线	2022年分保费收入	2022年分保费占比
寿险	53.1	60.4
非寿险	34.8	39.6
合计	87.9	100

数据来源：公司2022年度信息披露报告。

2．盈利情况

2022年，外资再保险公司在华机构整体盈利情况较好（见表7）。部分外资再保险公司业务线均衡，互联网和中端医疗保险布局较早，重疾险业务占比较少，营利性较好。需要说明的是，由于外资再保险机构转分率较高，盈利水平会受到转分安排影响，因此净利润指标并不一定真实、全面反映其经营状况。

表7 　　　　　　　　外资再保险公司在华机构净利润情况

单位：万元，%

公司	2021年净利润	2022年净利润	净利润增长率
瑞再北分	8 069	27 617	242
汉再上分	-2 940	-84 973	-2 790
慕再北分	37 700	39 374	4
法再北分	18 113	24 129	33

数据来源：各公司2022年度信息披露报告。

3．偿付能力情况

偿付能力方面，上述4家外资再保险公司2022年偿付能力充足率较高，其中瑞再北分偿付能力充足率最高，达到了315%（见表8）。2022

年度，瑞再北分增资30亿元人民币，汉再上分增资15.25亿元人民币。外资再保险公司整体资本实力较强，有较大能力来承保高质量业务，为其深耕中国再保险市场提供了坚实基础。

表8　　　　　　　　外资再保险公司在华机构偿付能力情况

单位：%，亿元

公司	2022年底综合偿付能力充足率	2022年底营运资金	2022年底净资产
瑞再北分	315	43.6	85.3
汉再上分	233	72.5	70.3
慕再北分	254	16.5	47.0
法再北分	225	20.6	27.4

数据来源：各公司2022年度信息披露报告。

二、中资再保险企业国际化发展情况

在金融业双向开放过程中，以中再集团、太平再保险为代表的中资再保险企业也在积极"走出去"，为中资企业海外利益提供保险保障，参与国际再保险市场竞争，加快融入全球保险价值链，有力提升了中国再保险企业的国际形象与影响力。

（一）中再集团国际化发展情况

作为中国再保险业"走出去"的先行者和"排头兵"，中再集团多年来持续推进国际化战略并取得重大突破。1999年，中再集团在伦敦设立代表处，2008年和2013年又分别在香港和纽约设立代表处，建立了海外信息汇集与市场接洽的桥头堡。2015年在香港联交所成功上市，同年在香港设立中再资产香港子公司，打造海外资产管理统一平台。"十三五"期间，借助国家"走出去"战略东风，中再集团于2016年设立新加坡分公司，以"海上丝绸之路"枢纽新加坡为支点，着力拓展亚太地区国际再保险业务。2018年，中再集团把握市场机遇，成功收购百年老店、劳合社第一梯队公司英国桥社保险集团，国际业务运营实力得到显著提升。2019年，中再寿险在香港设立子公司，经营港澳及东南亚区域的国际人身再保险业务。2020年，中再产险设立马来西亚分公司，在当地经营财产再保险业务。

经过多年耕耘，中再集团境外机构已拓展到中国香港、新加坡、英国、爱尔兰、马来西亚、百慕大等10余个国家和地区，覆盖财产再保险、人身再保险、资产管理三大业务板块。2022年，中再集团国际业务保费收入302.1亿元，占集团合并保费收入的17.8%；其中财产再保险板块境外保费收入196.2亿元，占全部财产再保险保费收入的比重达32%。

（二）太平再保险有限公司国际化发展情况

太平再（中国）的母公司太平再保险有限公司于1980年9月在中国香港注册成立，是中国太平保险集团旗下专业再保险子公司，承保来自全球的财产及人身再保险业务，总部设在中国香港，并在北京、英国伦敦设有全资子公司，在马来西亚纳闽岛设有分公司，在日本东京和中国澳门设有代表处。

太平再保险有限公司依托其上市母公司——中国太平保险控股有限公司，以及战略股东比利时富杰保险国际股份有限公司的强力支持，坚持稳健、高效、灵活的承保政策和管理手段，财务实力雄厚，经营业绩良好，连续多年获国际评级机构标准普尔、贝氏和惠誉财务实力A评级。

太平再保险有限公司是亚洲地区知名的专业再保险公司，保持香港财产险专业再保险市场排名首位，业务范围覆盖全球五大洲的100多个国家和地区，服务客户达1 000余家。2022年，实现毛保费收入为25.9亿美元（约合202亿港元），总资产达79.3亿美元（约合619亿港元），境外业务占比在60%左右。

（三）中资再保险企业服务"一带一路"情况

中再集团于2020年在北京推动成立中国"一带一路"再保险共同体，担任主席单位和管理机构。目前，中国"一带一路"再保险共同体为30余个海外利益项目提供约190亿元风险保障。中再集团还在新加坡、英国分别牵头组建"一带一路"保险再保险行业性组织，发挥三地平台优势，构建遍及全球的保障服务网络，支持高质量共建"一带一路"，引入国内空白的政治暴力保险、恐怖主义保险，首创中国视角境外国家恐怖主义风险评估体系，为中资保险公司首单"海外工程保函"提供独家再保险支持，保障国内企业"走出去"面临的特殊风险保障需求。近三年，中再产险累计向"一带一路"沿线的40个国家和地区、上千个中国企业项目，提供稳定可靠的综合风险保障约4 000亿元。

人保再持续增强服务"一带一路"沿线客户的能力，创建国际中收业务模式，近两年先后完成阿根廷、智利离岸分出人资质注册，已累计为华为、金风科技、中铁建等重点客户和科兴疫苗支援拉美国家抗疫斗争提供风险保额106亿元，保费收入1 750万元，获得了良好的社会效益。

太平再（中国）积极参与粤港澳大湾区建设，参与超过40个项目，如粤港澳大湾区深圳都市圈城际铁路深惠城际、穗莞深城际前海至皇岗口岸等重大项目，提供超过78亿元的保险保障。

三、中国再保险行业国际化发展展望

（一）外资再保险企业对中国市场的发展展望

在市场潜力方面，中国市场规模巨大且具备持续的发展潜力。据瑞再研究院估计，中国在全球保险市场的份额将继续上升，中国市场仍将是未来全球保险业增长的重要引擎。未来10年，预计中国保险市场年均复合增速将达到8%，到2031年中国市场保费总额将比2022年翻一番。

在监管政策方面，中国市场持续对外开放、监管环境友好且可预期。近年来，原中国银保监会先后出台了涉及保险业的对外开放措施十余条。外资再保公司纷纷加大对中国市场的战略布局。以瑞再为例，中国市场最早被瑞再定位为新兴市场，后来被调整为高增长市场。

（二）中国再保险企业国际化发展展望

受益于疫情后经济复苏、商业险种费率大幅提高以及新兴市场增长等因素，全球保险市场或将逐步恢复增长。中国再保险企业将抓住机遇，进一步前瞻谋划国际业务发展战略，持续提升国际化经营管理水平与全球竞争力，加强境内外协同联动，加强与国家部委、行业主体的创新合作，以服务"一带一路"倡议为着力点，以优质专业的技术服务中国企业"走出去"，更好地参与国际市场竞争，为畅通国内国际"双循环"作出积极贡献。

受新冠疫情、地缘政治、气候变化等多种因素影响，全球再保险市场的发展仍面临诸多挑战。如气候变化导致极端天气事件呈现出频率升高、范围变广、强度增大和多灾并发的趋势，给再保险行业经营带来很大挑战。俄乌冲突导致地缘政治持续紧张、全球经济稳定运行信心受挫、国际货币汇率波动不断加剧、各主要经济体通货膨胀保持较高水平，也为再保险公司经营带来挑战。中国再保险企业在国际化发展过程中，将进一步加强风险研判，有效平衡发展与安全的关系。

2023年6月，国家金融监督管理总局与上海市政府共同宣布再保险"国际板"建设规划，依托数字化、科技化的国际再保险业务平台，着力打造透明、便利、高效的国际再保险交易市场，引导中国再保险市场由"单向开放"向"双向开放"转型升级，深度参与全球再保险产业合作，为全球风险保障和金融治理体系提供中国方案，助力维护多元稳定的国际风险保障格局和金融合作关系。中国再保险行业也将以此为契机，积极把握新机遇，不断提升跨境服务能力和国际化经营水平，更好地服务双循环新发展格局。

第五章

2022年中国再保险行业监管回顾及展望

2022年，中国再保险行业监管坚持金融工作的政治性、人民性，按照"疫情要防住、经济要稳住、发展要安全"的总体要求，积极贯彻落实高质量发展任务，陆续发布多项对再保险行业有较大影响的监管政策，有效防控行业风险，坚决支持稳住经济大盘，引导市场主体提升保险保障服务能力，监管工作取得积极成效。

一、再保险行业监管体系总体架构

（一）保险行业监管"三支柱"架构

中国保险及再保险行业经过数十年经营发展，行业监管目前已形成以偿付能力监管为核心、公司治理监管为基础、市场行为监管为抓手的"三支柱"监管架构。

具体而言，偿付能力监管是现代保险行业监管的核心，通过全面评价和监督检查保险公司偿付能力充足率、综合风险及风险管理能力等，确保保险公司偿付能力满足承保需求，维护保险市场稳定。2021年，原中国银保监会顺利完成"偿二代"二期工程建设，陆续修订发布《保险公司偿付能力管理规定》（中国银行保险监督管理委员会令2021年第1号）以及《保险公司偿付能力监管规则（Ⅱ）》（银保监发〔2021〕51号），明确第一支柱定量监管要求、第二支柱定性监管要求以及第三支柱市场约束机制的偿付能力监管"三支柱"框架体系，确定核心偿付能力充足率、综合偿付能力充足率以及风险综合评级三个有机联系的偿付能力监管指标，进一步收紧和细化对直保及再保险公司的偿付能力监管要求，提升对保险公司偿付能力监管的科学性、有效性和全面性，引导中国保险市场整体稳健发展。

公司治理是现代企业制度的基石，通过建立包括股东（大）会、董事会、监事会、高级管理层（以下简称"三会一层"）等治理主体在内的公司治理架构，明确各治理主体的职责边界、履职要求，完善保险机构风险管控、制衡管制及激励约束机制，助力提升公司治理水平，保障保险机构健康稳定运营。2006年1月，原中国保险监督管理委员会（以下简称原中国保监会）发布《关于规范保险公司治理结构的指导意见（试行）》（保监发〔2006〕2号），正式将公司治理监管引入中国保险行业监管体系。此后十余年，中国公司治理监管实践经验和理论水平逐步积累完善，监管机构陆续发布《银行保险机构公司治理准则》（银保监发〔2021〕14号）以及《银行保险机构大股东行为监管办法（试行）》（银保监发〔2021〕43号）等公司治理监管细分领域多项监管政策，细化明确保险机构"三会一层"组成设置、职责分工及运作机制，特色化地将党的领导融入保险机构公司治理各个环节，全面系统规范保险机构公司治理要求，不断优化完善保险行业公司治理监管体系。2022年，原中国银保监会修订发布《银行保险机构公司治理监管评估办法》（银保监规〔2022〕19号），吸纳近年来的监管评估经验以及监管政策发展，进一步优化保险机构公司治理监管评估机制，促进保险机构提升自身公司治理水平。

市场行为监管是保险市场有序运行的重要保障，主要包括对保险条款与费率制定、保险销售行为、保险中介行为、保险服务行为以及保险欺诈行为等方面的监管，以保险消费者权益保护为核心，强调通过规范保险机构市场行为维护保险市场正常秩序。市场行为监管具体政策措施与被监管主体的市场行为特点紧密联系，因财产保险、人身保险以及再保险行业在交易主体、经营模式、业务性质以及风险特征等方面存在一定差异，监管机构通常会采取分类监管方式，针对不同类型的保险机构和保险业务制定不同的监管政策。其中，针对再保险领域，原中国银保监会于2021年7月修订发布《再保险业务管理规定》（中国银行保险监督管理委员会令2021年第8号），加强对保险机构再保险顶层战略制定、再保险业务安全性管理及再保险业务经营管理规范等多方面的监管，强调保险公司应正确使用再保险工具，促使再保险回归"保险的保险"的核心定位。

（二）再保险行业监管政策体系

在法律层面，中国保险及再保险行业均由《中华人民共和国保险法》进行规范。

在行业监管机构发布的政策层面，国家金融监督管理总局对再保险行业的监管政策主要分为以下两类：（1）适用于保险行业整体的监管政策，如对偿付能力、公司治理以及保险资金运用等方面的监管政策。此类监管政策基于再保险和直保行业的共同特点制定，通常同时适用于再保险公司和直保公司，或者适用于直保公司，参照适用于再保险公司。（2）适用于再保险行业的特别监管政策，主要体现在再保险市场行为监管领域，以及针对再保险行业的国际化特征所做的特别监管，包括规范再保险公司的设立、明确再保险业务管理规范以及通过建立再保险关联交易信息披露机制、再保险登记机制、要求离岸再保人提供符合要求的担保等措施来加强再保险业务安全保障等。为保障上述监管政策的有效施行，国家金融监督管理总局将现场监管与非现场监管相结合，对保险机构采取制定管理标准、开展能力评估以及对违法违规行为实施行政处罚等监管方式，促使保险机构维持合理的偿付能力，提升公司治理水平，规范市场经营行为。

在其他相关监管机构发布的政策层面，中国保险及再保险行业除接受国家金融监督管理总局"三支柱"体系下的行业监管以外，在反洗钱、反恐怖融资、财务会计、国有资产管理及网络安全和个人信息保护等领域同时受到中国人民银行、财政部及国家互联网信息办公室等监管机构的专业监管。此外，党中央、国务院以及相关监管机构关于国家经济金融工作的指导意见和发展规划对中国保险及再保险行业的监管政策也会产生深远影响。

二、2022 年再保险行业重要监管政策出台情况

2022年，中国再保险行业相关重要监管政策主要涉及规范保险资金运用、加强关联交易管理、完善监管评估体系、明确资本补充和计量机制、完善网络安全审查机制以及健全数据出境监管制度等方面。

（一）进一步规范保险资金运用

1．优化保险资金投资金融产品的监管要求

金融产品投资是保险资金运用的重要途径之一。2012年12月，原中国保监会发布《关于保险资金投资有关金融产品的通知》（保监发〔2012〕91号）用于规范保险资金投资金融产品行为。但随着保险资金运用实践及保险资金运用相关监管制度的更新完善，该制度部分条款已不合时宜。因此，原中国银保监会于2022年4月修订发布《关于保险资金投资有关金融产品的通知》（银保监规〔2022〕7号），优化对保险资金投资非保险类金融机构发行的金融产品的监管要求。

新规衔接《关于优化保险机构投资管理能力监管有关事项的通知》（银保监发〔2020〕45号）等政策，规定：（1）保险机构投资金融产品应具备相应的投资管理能力，保险集团（控股）公司和保险公司投资

金融产品和单一资产管理计划、保险资金投资理财产品等金融产品应符合相应的要求。（2）保险集团（控股）公司和保险公司可自行投资或委托保险资管公司投资金融产品，但不得委托保险资管公司投资单一资产管理计划和面向单一投资者发行的私募理财产品。（3）保险机构自行或受托投资金融产品的，应做好风险评估、投后管理、关联交易管理、定期报告等工作；保险资管公司受托投资金融产品的，应承担主动管理责任。

新规的更新修订主要体现在：（1）删除保险资金投资保险资管公司发行的基础设施投资计划、不动产投资计划、资产支持计划的相关内容，该三类投资由《保险资产管理产品管理暂行办法》（中国银行保险监督管理委员会令2020年第5号）等政策进行规范。（2）新增理财公司理财产品、单一资产管理计划、债转股投资计划等可投资金融产品。（3）取消对保险资金投资信贷资产支持证券等金融产品的外部信用评级要求。（4）强化保险机构对所投资的金融产品的风险穿透监管。

2.完善保险资金委托投资管理监管机制

2022年5月，原中国银保监会修订发布《保险资金委托投资管理办法》（银保监规〔2022〕9号），进一步完善保险资金委托投资的资质条件、投资规范、风险管理及监管要求等方面的规定。新规纳入了最新行业实践与监管政策变化：（1）将保险资金委托投资定义为保险公司〔含保险集团（控股）公司〕将保险资金委托给保险资管机构，由保险资管机构作为受托人并以委托人的名义在境内开展主动投资管理业务。（2）将保险资金投资受托人限定为保险资管机构，删除旧规关于证券公司、证券资产管理公司、证券投资基金管理公司及其子公司等非保险资管机构可作为受托人的规定；将保险公司委托证券公司等非保险资管机构投资纳入单一资产管理计划范畴，由上文所述《关于保险资金投资有关金融产品的通知》进行规范。（3）明确开展委托投资的保险公司以及作为受托人的保险资管机构应符合的条件，规定保险资金委托投资资产限于国家金融监督管理总局规定的保险资金运用范围，直接股权投资、以物权和股权形式持有的投资性不动产除外。

（二）加强银行保险机构关联交易管理

近年来，中国银行业保险业快速发展，但同时银行保险机构通过隐匿或复杂的关联交易规避监管、套取利益的问题也不断显现，因此银行保险机构关联交易一直是金融监管的重点领域。此前银行机构和保险机构的关联交易监管主要分别由《商业银行与内部人和股东关联交易管理办法》（中国银行业监督管理委员会令2004年第3号）、《保险公司关联交易管理办法》（银保监发〔2019〕35号）进行规范。自2018年原中国银行监督管理委员会与原中国保监会合并为原中国银保监会以来，陆续启动银行业和保险业规章和规范性文件的集中清理工作，逐步统一银行业保险业的监管框架。

在此背景下，为进一步规范银行保险机构关联交易管理，原中国银保监会于2022年1月修订发布《银行保险机构关联交易管理办法》（中国银行保险监督管理委员会令〔2022〕1号），统一规范银行保险机构的关联方、关联交易、关联交易内部管理、报告和披露以及监督管理等方面的监管要求。（1）在关联方认定方面，统一银行保险机构的关联方范围，延续直接认定与实质重于形式认定相结合的方式，列举了自然人关联方的5种情形、法人及非法人组织关联方的5种情形。（2）在关联交易认定及标准方面，分别明确银行机构、保险机构、信托公司及其他非银行金融机构等不同类型机构的关联交易类型、关联交易金额计算、重大关联交易标准、资金运用类关联交易比例监管以及禁止性规定等，将保险机构关联交易类型调整为资金运用类、服务类、利益转移类、保险业务和其他类，并总体上收紧资金运用类关联交易的比例限额。（3）在关联交易管理方面，对银行保险机构关联交易内部管理机制建设、穿透识别、资金来源与流向、动态评估、信息系统建设以及内部问责等方面作出了要求，取消对"控股子公司为上市公司或已受行业监管的金融机构的除外"的豁免，并衔接《保险集团公司监督管理办法》（中国银行保险监督管理委员会令〔2021〕13号），明确"银保监会对设立董事会下设专业委员会另有规定的，从其规定"。

（三）完善保险机构监管评估体系

1.优化银行保险机构公司治理监管评估机制

公司治理监管评估是国家金融监督管理总局近年来采用的主要监管手段之一。2019年11月，原中国银保监会发布《银行保险机构公司治理监管评估办法（试行）》（银保监发〔2019〕43号），设定合规性评价、有效性评价、重大事项调降评级三个评估步骤，重点评估银行保险机构党的领导、股东治理、关联交易治理、董事会治理、监事会和高管层治理、风险内控、市场约束以及利益相关者治理等八个方面的情况。该评估办法发布以后，原中国银保监会又陆续出台了《银行保险机构公司治理准则》（银保监发〔2021〕14号）等公司治理领域的重要监管制度，部分原来的评估指标亟待更新。

因此，原中国银保监会于2022年11月修订发布《银行保险机构公司治理监管评估办法》（银保监规〔2022〕19号），优化改进公司治理监管评估机制。（1）优化评估机制。新规根据银行保险机构公司治理水平差异化配置评估资源，原则上银行保险机构每年至少开展一次评估，但对评估结果为B级及以上的机构，可适当降低评估频率为每两年一次。评估采取非现场评估和现场评估相结合的方式，其中现场评估新增"每三年实现全覆盖"的要求，并进一步细化现场评估和非现场评估的工作方式和要求，督促机构更为严谨扎实地开展公司治理基础工作。（2）更新评估指标。新规聚焦大股东违规干预、内部人控制等问题，新增"股东与银行保险机构开展严重影响机构资本充足率、偿付能力充足率真实性的违规关联交易"应被直接评为E级机构的情形，进一步丰富党的领导、股东股权、关联交易、董监高提名和履职等方面的关键指标，并调整指标权重、精简指标数量。（3）强化评估应用。新规将评估等级为D级及以下的银行保险机构列为重点监管对象，对其存在的重大公司治理风险隐患进行早期干预、及时纠正，坚决防止机构"带病运行"，并对E级机构新增限制其相关关联交易并可进行现场检查的监管措施。

2．建立健全保险公司非现场监管体系

非现场监管是保险监管的重要手段，机构监管部门通过非现场监管全面跟踪、评估保险公司的经营情况和风险状况。为建立健全保险公司非现场监管体系，原中国银保监会在既往非现场监管工作经验以及当前监管工作职责划分的基础上，于2022年1月发布《保险公司非现场监管暂行办法》（中国银行保险监督管理委员会令2022年第3号），统一规范保险公司非现场监管的职责分工和工作要求、信息收集和整理、日常监测和监管评估、评估结果运用以及信息归档等工作流程和机制。（1）强调机构监管主导。机构监管部门是非现场监管的牵头部门，负责研究制定非现场监管的制度规定、工作流程和工作标准。（2）明确分类监管原则。《保险公司非现场监管暂行办法》确定非现场监管工作流程和机制后，相应的机构监管部门另行制定下发财产保

险公司、人身保险公司和再保险公司的风险监测和非现场监管评估指引，以兼顾不同类型保险公司在业务经营以及风险特征方面的差异。（3）突出协调监管原则。非现场监管应与行政审批、现场检查等监管手段形成有效衔接，与公司治理等重点监管领域实现合作互补。

（四）补充明确保险公司资本补充和计量规定

1. 允许保险公司发行无固定期限资本债券补充资本

为进一步拓宽保险公司资本补充渠道，增强保险公司风险防范化解和服务实体经济能力，中国人民银行、原中国银保监会于2022年8月联合发布《关于保险公司发行无固定期限资本债券有关事项的通知》（银发〔2022〕175号），允许除保险集团（控股）公司以外的保险公司发行无固定期限资本债券。该通知规定了保险公司发行无固定期限资本债券的定义、发行申请、减记或转股条款、赎回、信息披露、信用评级以及补充资本等事项。（1）要求无固定期限资本债券应当含有减记或转股条款，并列举将触发减记或转股条款的事项。（2）当赎回无固定期限资本债券或支付无固定期限资本债券利息会导致保险公司偿付能力充足率不达标时，保险公司不能赎回或支付利息，同时无固定期限资本债券的投资人不能因保险公司无法如约支付利息而申请其破产。（3）允许保险公司通过发行无固定期限资本债券补充核心二级资本，前提是无固定期限资本债券余额不得超过核心资本的30%。

2. 完善非寿险业务准备金监管制度

针对非寿险业务准备金（以下简称准备金）监管，原中国银保监会于2021年10月修订发布《保险公司非寿险业务准备金管理办法》（中国银行保险监督管理委员会令2021年第11号），与会计准则和偿付能力监管规定的口径实现一致。2022年3月，原中国银保监会针对该办法发布配套的《保险公司非寿险业务准备金管理办法实施细则（1~7号）》（银保监规〔2022〕6号），具体包括未到期责任准备金、未决赔款准备金、风险边际和折现、分支机构准备金、准备金回溯分析、准备金评估报告以及准备金工作底稿等7号细则。（1）解释、说明并补充《保险公司非寿险业务准备金管理办法》尚未细化明确的事项。（2）针对目前存在的保险公司人为调整分支机构准备金、通过准备金调节利润等问题，修订此前发布的已不适应新情况的关于准备金监管的系列规范性文件。（3）消除关于准备金风险边际和折现、准备金有利发展、分支机构准备金等方面的监管空白和盲区。

（五）健全网络安全监管及数据保护机制

1．完善网络安全审查机制

网络安全审查是确保中国关键信息基础设施供应链安全、保障网络安全和数据安全、维护国家安全的重要措施。2021年底，国家互联网信息办公室等13个部门修订发布《网络安全审查办法》[①]，自2022年2月15日起施行。与旧规相比，除"关键信息基础设施运营者采购网络产品和服务，影响或者可能影响国家安全"外，新规明确"网络平台运营者开展数据处理活动，影响或者可能影响国家安全"的，也应当进行网络安全审查，同时"掌握超过100万用户个人信息的网络平台运营者赴国外上市"的，必须向网络安全审查办公室申报网络安全审查。网络安全审查的重点为评估相关对象或情形的国家安全因素，包括对关键信息基础设施的影响（如被非法控制干扰或者破坏的风险、

---

① 国家互联网信息办公室、中华人民共和国国家发展和改革委员会、中华人民共和国工业和信息化部、中华人民共和国公安部、中华人民共和国国家安全部、中华人民共和国财政部、中华人民共和国商务部、中国人民银行、国家市场监督管理总局、国家广播电视总局、中国证券监督管理委员会、国家保密局、国家密码管理局令第8号。

对业务连续性的危害）和对核心数据、重要数据或者大量个人信息的影响（如被窃取、泄露、毁损、非法利用、非法出境的风险）等。

就保险和再保险公司而言，若本公司相关信息系统被认定为"关键信息基础设施"，或者本公司被认定为"网络平台运营者"，应高度关注本公司的网络和数据合规管理，特别是本机构掌握的个人信息、重要数据和核心数据的安全管理，按要求开展网络安全审查。

2．健全数据出境监管制度

2022年，随着《数据出境安全评估办法》（国家互联网信息办公室令第11号）、《关于实施个人信息保护认证的公告》（国家市场监督管理总局、国家互联网信息办公室公告2022年第37号）和《个人信息出境标准合同规定（征求意见稿）》[①]的出台，中国初步构建了"出境评估+标准合同+认证"的数据出境监管机制，与其他国家或地区数据出境监管方式基本一致。

（1）数据出境评估。中国限制出境的数据包括重要数据和个人信息。对于重要数据出境，必须开展数据出境评估。对于个人信息出境，达到以下标准方须进行出境评估：一是因主体性质需要评估。包括关键信息基础设施运营者和处理100万人以上个人信息的数据处理者。该类主体无论向境外传输何等数量的个人信息，均应开展数据出境评估。二是因个人信息传输达到一定数量后需要评估。包括自上年1月1日起累计向境外提供10万条个人信息或者1万条敏感个人信息的。数据出境评估包括数据处理者的自评估和省级网信部门的监管评估，通过评估后数据方可出境。（2）签订数据出境标准合同。除上述情形外，数据处理者可以通过与境外接收方签订数据出境标准合同的方式

---

① 2023年2月，国家互联网信息办公室已正式发布《个人信息出境标准合同办法》（国家互联网信息办公室令第13号）。

合法向境外传输个人信息。但签署出境标准合同并不意味着"一签了之、一劳永逸"，数据处理者还需至少履行以下义务：开展个人信息保护影响评估；向所在地省级网信部门备案标准合同和个人信息保护影响评估报告；确保合同的实际履行。（3）通过跨境处理认证。根据《个人信息保护法》的规定，"按照国家网信部门的规定经专业机构进行个人信息保护认证"也是向境外提供个人信息的合法方式。根据相关认证规范，个人信息跨境处理活动认证主要适用于跨国公司或者同一经济、事业实体下属子公司或关联公司之间的个人信息跨境处理活动。

就保险和再保险公司而言，在国际业务经营和境外机构管理过程中都有可能涉及数据出境。各保险公司和再保险公司应梳理本公司在业务和管理中涉及的数据出境场景，识别本公司出境数据的类别和主体性质，选择恰当的数据出境方式，确保数据出境合规。

三、再保险行业监管趋势展望

2023年，中国再保险行业发展形势稳中向好，再保险市场需求增加，但同时也面临全球地缘政治形势紧张、自然灾害频发、宏观经济增长疲软、金融市场波动加剧以及信息科技风险上升等客观挑战，再保险行业监管在严格防范系统性风险发生的同时，也将结合行业发展最新情况不断优化政策环境，助力再保险行业高质量发展，更好地服务经济社会建设。

一是将继续推动再保险服务经济社会发展。保险再保险行业作为金融重要领域，在调动社会资源、提升经济抗风险能力、支持社会发展以及提高人民生活水平等方面发挥着重要作用。2022年，原中国银保监会陆续出台一系列政策，引导保险业从战略高度推进绿色金融，促进经济社会绿色发展转型，支持城市建设和治理、保障性租赁住房发展和公路交通高质量发展。未来，监管政策将进一步引导保险机构聚焦经济社会发展需求和国家重大战略，在产品供给、服务支持、风险防范以及资金融通等多方面积极发力，更好地发挥再保险"减震器"和"稳定器"作用，提供更高质量、更加全面的风险保障和保险服务。

二是将进一步鼓励再保险创新发展。增强对电子信息、先进制造、生物医药、现代农业、智慧交通、新型能源、航空航天等高精尖技术领域风险及其他大中型风险、特殊风险的定价、承保、理赔和管理能力，为中国保险再保险行业进一步提升核心竞争力、打造世界一流企业提供创新动能。

三是将进一步关注保险再保险行业的科技能力建设及相关风险防范。2022 年，原中国银保监会发布《关于银行业保险业数字化转型的指导意见》（银保监办发〔2022〕2 号），要求银行保险机构加强数字化转型的顶层设计、统筹规划以及日常经营管理能力。未来，行业监管将继续推进保险机构的数字化建设，提升保险机构的信息科技风险识别和应对能力。为应对保险行业信息科技快速发展以及日益复杂化的金融风险，行业监管将不断提升监管工具的科学化、标准化和流程化程度，提高监管资源配置效率和监管科技水平，在保障业务依法合规开展、维护市场正常秩序的同时，推动再保险行业更高效率地发展。

专题报告

全球人身险市场经验及中国人身险
转型发展趋势展望

近年来，在新冠疫情反复冲击、需求收缩、渠道转型等多重压力下，我国人身险市场整体增速明显回落，各人身保险公司纷纷启动转型，但转型更多聚焦个体经营层面。为助力行业从更加宏观的角度认识和把握人身险市场发展规律、研判发展方向、找准转型关键，对跨市场、长周期的全球人身险发展经验进行研究梳理，分析影响市场发展的底层因素，为中国人身险市场的高质量发展和转型提供参考借鉴。

一、中国人身险市场发展新形势

一是外部环境发生深刻变化。从国际看，中美关系、世纪疫情、俄乌冲突等交织演变，全球面临百年未有之大变局。从国内看，中国带领14亿人口整体性脱贫，社会已迈入深度老龄化阶段，共同富裕和长寿时代正在到来。劳动力红利逐渐消失，经济进入新常态，市场利率步入下行，低利率环境下，以利差为核心的传统盈利模式难以为继。科技发展和应用深刻改变客户需求和服务内涵，对保险商业模式、销售及服务、运营管理等产生影响。

二是内部流量扩张时代结束。过去40年人身险的快速增长，发展模式本质是跑马占地、流量扩张。无论是早期的机构铺设、网点扩张、代理人扩容，还是后期的互联网平台流量模式，本质是扩大投入、追求规模。随着新时代的到来，机构、网点、人数的简单扩张模式已不具备原来的发展条件，行业被迫转型。中国市场过往的发展历程和经验支撑明显不足，必须从更长周期、更多市场的发展历史中深刻理解人身险市场发展的内在逻辑，结合中国市场自身特点，依靠不断创新，才能走出一条符合发展规律、符合自身特点的高质量转型发展之路。

二、全球人身险市场发展的规律与启示

（一）研究基本框架

为研究全球人身险市场发展的一般性规律，建立起人身险市场发展"双层次、八因素"的GCED-TIFS研究框架，分析了美国、德国、日本等成熟人身险大市场和中国香港、中国台湾地区两个文化相似的地区性市场。在现有分析框架中，决定人身险发展的因素主要有两类：一类是对保险发展有直接影响的因素，称为直接因素，包括：财税政策（T）、利率环境（I）、资本市场发达程度（F）和社会保障水平（S）四项；另一类是对保险发展具有长期影响但无直接作用的因素，称为基础因素，包括：社会治理特征（G）、社会文化特征（C）、经济发展特征（E）和人口结构特征（D）四项，它们的作用是长期、根本性的。研究表明，不同市场在百余年的发展演进过程中，既表现出了具有普遍意义的共性规律，也体现了具有浓厚个性色彩的差异特征。

	维度	代表指标	指标意义
基础因素	G 国家和地区治理特征	分析国家和地区治理理念在经济体制和立法体系上的体现，特别是在个人福祉与集体利益、社会公平之间的权衡关系	
基础因素	C 社会文化特征	质化分析文化特征溯源及其对社会化、商业化人身风险保障意识和“自给自足”式的个人储蓄意识的影响	国家和地区居民在人身风险保障方式上的偏好和对保险机构功能定位的认知
基础因素	E 经济发展特征	人均名义GDP及名义GDP增速	人均可用于消费、储蓄及投资的收入水平以及人均收入增长的趋势和潜力
基础因素	D 人口结构特征	65岁以上老龄人口占比、生育率、老年抚养比等	社会老龄化程度以及由老龄化衍生的养老、医疗保障需求
直接因素	T 财税政策特征	保费/养老金所得税税前抵扣最大额度	说明财税政策对保障需求释放的激励力度
直接因素	I 利率环境特征	十年期国债利率	说明人身险市场所处的长期利率环境
直接因素	F 资本市场特征	核心股指水平以及社会直间接融资占比	说明资本市场发展状况及长期投资价值
直接因素	S 社会保障特征	社会养老金人群覆盖率、社会养老金净替代率、社会医保支出占总医疗卫生费用水平等	分别说明一支柱养老金和社会医保的定位和保障水平

图1　人身险市场“双层次、八因素”的GCED-TIFS研究框架

（二）全球人身险市场发展的共性规律

一是人身险市场增速与宏观经济发展周期高度正相关。宏观经济发展是人身险市场发展的基石条件，宏观经济发展水平影响企业和居民的商业人身险购买能力与意愿。

另外，寿险保费支出呈边际消费递减特征，在经济发展和人均收入达到一定水平后，寿险规模进入平台期，人均保费支出（寿险密度）很难出现大幅提升。美国在人均名义GDP到达30 000美元、德国到达27 000美元、日本到达26 000美元时，寿险市场规模开始遭遇瓶颈。目前，中国人均GDP刚突破12 000美元，寿险仍处于加速发展阶段，未达到市场饱和的平台期。近年来增速放缓是宏观经济、市场结构转型和人力队伍等多因素叠加导致。随着宏观经济回暖、市场结构性改革，预计寿险将呈恢复性增长。

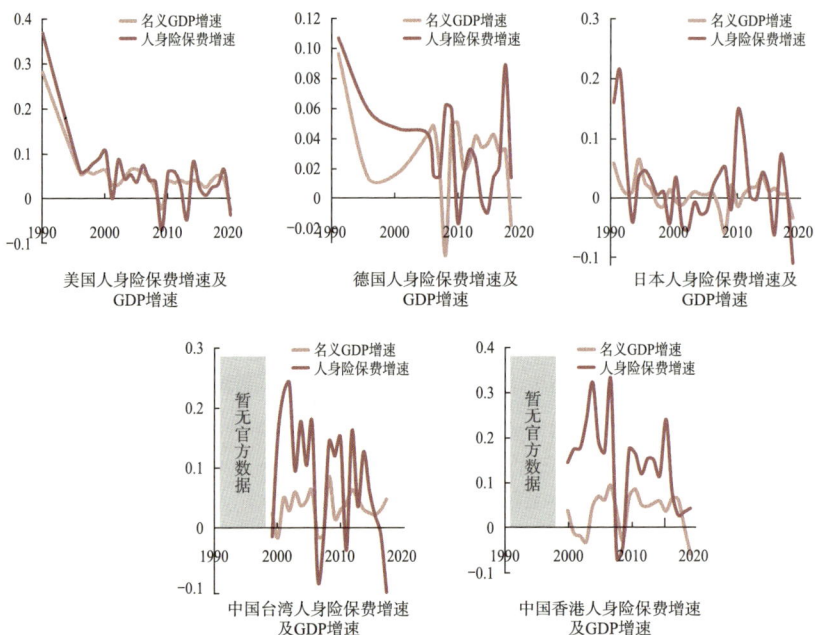

图2 商业人身险发展与宏观经济周期具有强正相关性

（资料来源：五个国家和地区寿险行业协会，Wind）

　　二是人口结构的变化深刻影响着人身险市场的发展空间。人口老龄化引发的社会医养保障负担加重，政策引导企业和个人承担更多责任，为商业人身险发展创造了市场空间。人口老龄化也同步带动人身险险种结构转型，保险机构顺应政策变化和居民需求推出商业养老年金险、健康险产品，人身险呈现险种多元化、产品长期化与综合化的发展趋势。

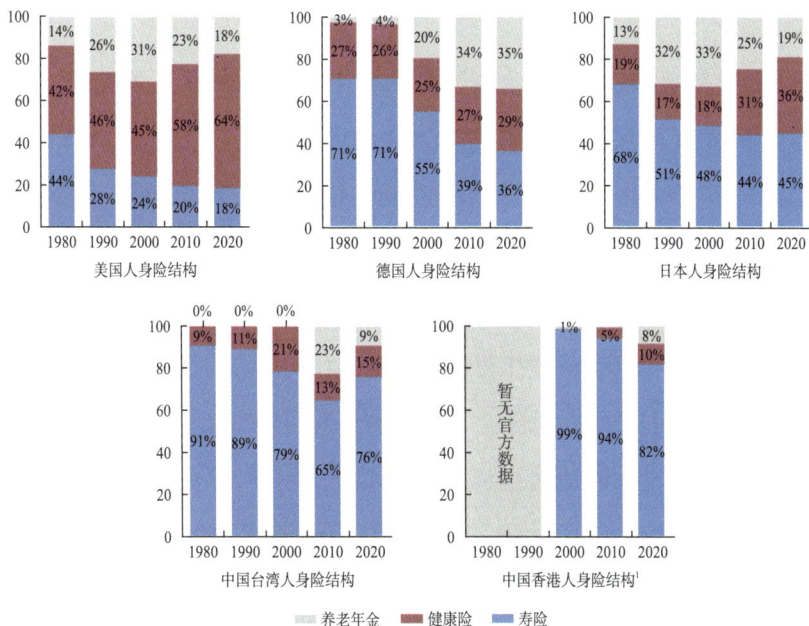

注：1. 官方未披露各险种占比数据，此处为估算值。

图3 年金险和健康险占比逐渐提升，人身险险种结构呈现多元化态势

（资料来源：五个国家和地区保险行业协会，公开数据搜集及行业访谈）

例如，美国在20世纪80年代，人口老龄化率达到12%，人身险产品结构向多元化发展，养老年金险与商业健康险占比逐步超过传统寿险。同样的情况发生在德国1995年左右、日本1990年左右。目前，中国65岁及以上人口占比已跨过14%的门槛，进入老龄化社会。民众对健康风险、养老保障等多元化的需求日益增强，商业人身险在多层次的医疗养老保障体系中将会发挥更大的作用。

三是税收政策是人身险发展的催化剂。资本利得税税惠等针对商业人身险的税优政策出台，使其相对其它金融产品具备财务比较优势，推动人身险行业整体发展和结构转变。美、德、日等国针对商业人身险都有力度较大的配套税惠政策，极大地推动了人身险规模发展和产品结构转型。近年来，中国在养老险和健康险领域不断探索税惠政策，2022年开始正式对政策支持、商业化运营的个人养老金实行个人所得税优惠。相信更为丰富有力的税收政策必将发挥杠杆作用，引导中国的养老金市场得到进一步发展，推动人身险长期化、综合性转型发展。

四是资本市场的繁荣发展是新型人身险产品发展的土壤。以美国为例，在二十世纪80年代中期，伴随其资本市场的快速发展，新型人身险产品得到了极大的发展，规模占比达到40%以上。日本、德国、中国台湾、中国香港地区也经历过新型人身险产品的发展，但对比美国独一无二的资本市场优势，这些国家和地区的新型人身险产品占比明显更低。当前，随着中国低利率时代的到来，资本市场在注册制下走向规范有序，新型人身险产品有望迎来新一轮的发展。

（三）全球人身险市场发展的差异特征

全球人身险市场发展具有四项普遍共性规律，同时各国家和地区在保险深度和密度、险种特征、分业经营程度、新型产品规模和渠道结构上存在较大差异，其底层原因在于社会治理理念与社会文化特征的不同，形成了四项差异性特征。

一是社会治理理念影响经济体制及社保定位与水平，决定国民剩余保障需求，即留与商业保险的市场空间，从而进一步体现在人身险市场的深度和密度上。

二是社会治理理念和经济体制影响下的社会医保覆盖方式决定了商业健康险的主体形态、健康险与寿险分业经营态势以及产业融合深度。

社保替代型主导的市场，以美国和德国为代表，社会医保仅覆盖部分人群，剩余人群需通过商业健康险获取医疗保障，商业健康险发挥社保替代功能，产品形态以费用补偿型为主。由于健康险运营体系复杂，经营逻辑与寿险产品不同，因此健康险和寿险由不同主体进行专业化经营，且保险与医药产业融合程度较高。

社保补充型主导的市场，以日本、中国香港和中国台湾地区为代表，社会医保覆盖全人群，但覆盖水平有限，需一定自付比例，因此留与商业保险的空间较小，主要在于补齐自付部分和社保无法覆盖的高水平医疗服务。产品形态主要是定额给付型，与寿险逻辑类似，因此无需分业经营。

表1   替代型主导和补充型主导两类市场的形态差异

国家和地区	替代型主导类		补充型主导类		
	美国	德国	日本	中国台湾	中国香港
社保支付/医疗卫生费用总支出	51%	78%	84%	60%	53%
社保覆盖人群	老弱病残群体	中低收入人群	全民	全民	全民
社保覆盖度	<40%	>90%	100%	100%	100%
社保覆盖水平	中高	高	中高	中	中
商保支付/医疗卫生费用总支出	36%	13%	3%	8%	18%
商业健康险核心产品特征	团体费用补偿型医疗险	个人费用补偿型医疗险	个人定额给付类健康险	个人定额给付类健康险	个人定额给付类健康险为主；同时政策驱动针对中高收入人群的全替代型私立费用补偿型医疗险
健康险/寿险分业经营	是		否		
保险+健康的产业融合程度	高	较高	较低		

资料来源：Wind，OECD，五个国家和地区保险行业协会。

三是社会治理理念与立法体系影响资本市场发展进程、繁荣程度和长期投资价值，进而影响新型人身险产品出现时间和规模化程度。

四是社会文化特征影响保险保障意识和个人储蓄意识之间的强弱

对比关系，进而体现在对保险机构的功能定位认知上，并进一步作用于人身险规模对GDP的相对增速以及人身险市场的深度和密度上。倾向保险文化的社会中，居民普遍具有较高的风险认知和相对低的储蓄意识，更倾向于通过社会化、商业化方式获取风险保障，因此保险支出的目的中保障成分相对较高，支出水平相对受限。倾向储蓄文化的社会如东亚社会，民众对人身险的保障功能理解和接受度低，更倾向通过个人储蓄来抵御风险，也更愿意把人身险产品当做类储蓄产品来配置，这类市场的储蓄型产品占比会更高，造就的市场保险深度也会比倾向保险文化的市场相对更高。例如，中国香港、中国台湾地区市场的人身险深度均达到了15%以上的水平；而GDP类似情况下，德国市场仅为4.3%，更为发达的美国市场也仅为8.7%。因此，具有强烈储蓄文化意识的中国人身险市场在发展到成熟阶段时，保险密度和深度会高于偏重保险文化的欧美市场。

表2　　　　　　　　社会文化特征不同造就市场差异化发展

国家和地区	保险文化倾向			储蓄文化倾向	
	美国	德国	日本	中国香港	中国台湾
文化特征	与不确定性和风险共存，分工协作，勇于创新			确定性强，自给自足	
保险文化相对储蓄文化的强弱程度	较强			较弱	
对保险机构的功能定位认知	较强			较弱	
人身险增速/名义GDP增速	同时期增速较为接近			增速显著高于同时期GDP增速	
人身险密度	5 508	2 017	2 275	8 823	4 490
人身险深度	8.7%	4.3%	5.6%	19.1%	16%
养老年金险+健康险占比	82%	64%	55%	约19%	24%

资料来源：五个国家和地区保险行业协会。

三、中国人身险转型发展趋势展望

（一）人身险转型关键

基于对全球人身险市场发展规律的总结分析，结合党的二十大明确提出的2035年社会主义现代化远景目标，到2035年，在中国式现代化发展理念指引下，中国将从发展中国家步入中等发达国家行列，影响人身险市场的八大外部因素将会发生跃迁性变化，中国人身险市场在"三新一高"整体要求下，将完成六大关键转型。

一是规模增速从"高速发展"向"中速提质"转变。受GDP增速渐缓和传统发展模式增长动力下降影响，中国人身险保费规模增速在中长期将切换至5%到10%的中速发展区间。

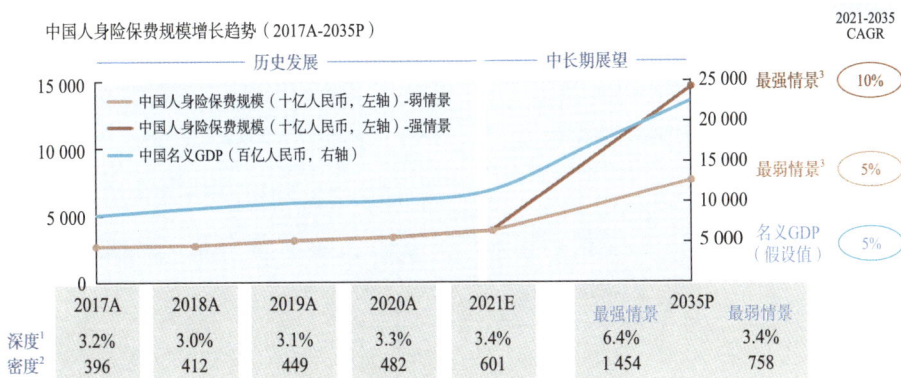

注：1. 深度计算方法为人身险保费规模 / 名义 GDP。
　　2. 密度计算方法为人身险保费总规模 / 人口，其中保费以美元计。
　　3. 在保险文化最强情景下，假设保费增速与 GDP 增速持平，在保险文化最弱情景下，假设保费增速是 GDP 增速的两倍。

图4　中国人身险市场规模增速将从"高速发展"向"中速提质"转变

（资料来源：《中国保险年鉴》，公开信息整理分析）

二是险种结构从"寿险主导"到"丰富多元"。随着老龄人口占比提升，国家治理现代化不断完善，在以公平优先、广覆盖、保基本为核心的社会保障体系之上，高质量、多层次的商业保障体系将进一步发展。在税优政策和监管政策推动下，商业健康险和养老年金险或将加快覆盖，成为市场增长新动能。

三是产品特征从"中短单一"到"长期综合"。随社会财富增长，围绕健康、长寿、富足三大主题，人身险的长期化、综合化特征更为突出，以补充养老为目的的储蓄型寿险以及年金产品期限延长，以补充医疗保障为目的的健康险更为多元，保险支付和医养服务的融合更加深入，针对不同人群的综合解决方案更加凸显差异化价值。

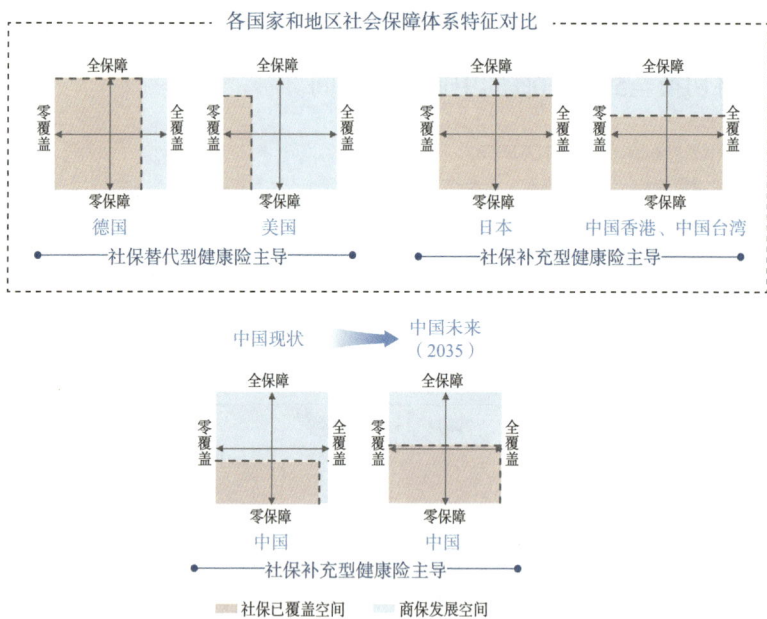

图5 中国商业健康险属于社保补充型主导类

四是金融融合从"相对有限"到"适度提升"。长期低利率环境下金融融合动力增强，万能、投连等新型产品在资本市场改革深化推动下具备潜在增长动力，监管政策、销售能力等将共同决定实际增长空间幅度。

五是渠道结构从"粗放发展"到"专业制胜"。产品多元化促使渠道结构更为均衡，代理人由"人海战术"转向专业化职业化发展，银保渠道在储蓄养老领域具有综合优势，在养老金政策的推动下价值凸显，产品综合化将促进专业经代渠道的进一步拓展。

六是价值来源从"投资牵引"到"利源多元"。随着社会经济发展阶段变化，利率及投资收益水平下降，利差驱动的高利润模式难以持续，人身险行业价值来源也将趋向多元化。

（二）趋势展望与相关建议

展望中国人身险市场未来发展趋势，从中短期来看，中国经济在恢复过程中，民众的消费在减弱而储蓄在增强，储蓄性寿险仍是现阶段行业增长的核心动力。从中长期来看，基于对全球人身险长周期市场规律的总结及对中国市场特点的深入分析，中国人身险市场未来发展空间巨大。一是具有极强韧性和较大潜力的中国经济发展对人身险市场形成强有力的支撑；二是中国深度老龄化带来的商业健康险和养老年金险新需求创造新的发展空间，商业健康险和养老年金险有望成为人身险市场的核心增长驱动力；三是中国极强的储蓄文化意识会使保险深度上限高于欧美市场。

寿险当前处于加速发展期，中长期随人均GDP走高，将逐渐进入稳定发展状态

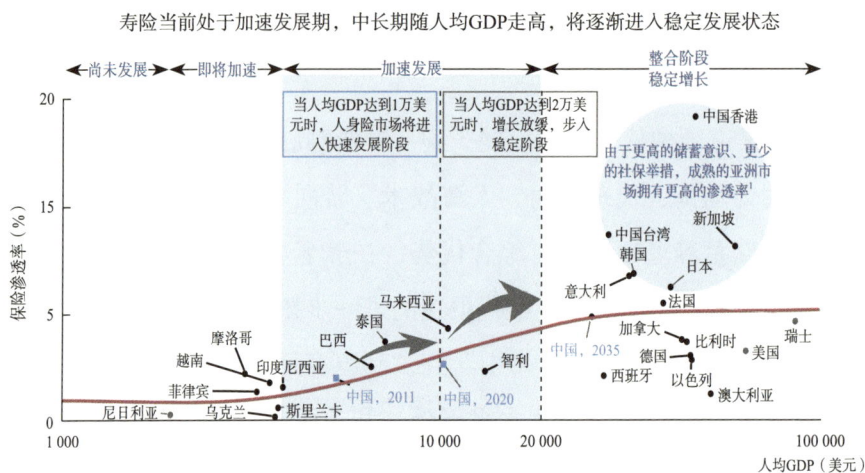

注：1. 保险渗透率 = 保费 / GDP，2020 年数据。

图6 中国人身险市场未来发展空间巨大

（资料来源：Swiss Re Sigma 2020）

从当下到中长期目标的实现将是一个充满挑战的过程，推动中国人身险市场走好高质量发展之路，必须保有战略发展信心，加快结构性改革，不断提升运营和管理效率。

一是要从战略上坚持资产与负债双轮驱动模式。中国极强的储蓄文化意识使得中国人身险产品拥有很强的储蓄特征，简单地依靠负债端改革无法实现新时期人身险的高质量发展，必须双管齐下。负债端要围绕人身风险保障和财富管理需求开发销售长期的、多元综合的产品；资产端要围绕负债特点打造专属投资能力，提升长期收益；同时建立资产负债联动的协同管理机制，资负匹配、协同发展，推动长期健康可持续发展。

二是要积极推动负债端结构性改革。对标成熟市场，中国人身险市场的产品类型并无明显缺失，但需加快结构性改革，提升产品、场景与需求的匹配程度，满足新时代下人民对健康风险、养老保障等多

元化的需求。首先，产品要结构性改革，责任结构实现从简单到多元的优化，改变储蓄险单纯比拼收益、保障型业务比拼价格的现状；实现产品不同期限的覆盖，做到从短期到长期的期限优化；实现"保险+服务"的优化，真正帮助客户解决问题。其次，渠道要结构性改革，针对意外险、惠民保、中端医疗等责任简单、客户易于理解的产品，降成本、提效能，选择政府、团体、互联网等渠道，节省成本让利给客户。针对投连、万能、高端医疗等责任复杂、在购买使用中需专业讲解和频繁互动的产品，在渠道建设上应重视服务、优化体验，选择代理人、经纪渠道等高附加值的专业渠道。

三是投资端要提升收益、风控、创新三种能力。投资能力建设应围绕负债的长期性、多元化发展特点展开，从收益获取、风险管控和丰富创新三个方面加以提升。长期看，投资端面临利率中枢下行、投资盈利空间收窄的挑战，提升资产收益满足负债成本和盈利需要是核心要求。资本市场波动较大，债券市场面临较高信用风险，要强化风险能力建设，推动投资资产多样化，牢牢守住风险底线是基本要求。未来，资产的创新能力和负债的结构性改革相辅相成，共同构成人身险高质量发展的关键内部因素。

四是要通过管理创新和模式创新，推动盈利结构多元、稳定。海外成熟市场的人身险经营均依靠多元化盈利。中国人身险公司若想实现盈利结构的多元、稳定发展，应注重做好四方面工作：一是提升死差贡献，做好精准定价，利用反欺诈等强化事前核保和事后理赔，以健康干预改善发生率；二是提升费差贡献，避免佣金战，利用AI、新技术等降本增效；三是稳定利差贡献，风险可控情况下获取长期期望收益水平；四是加强盈利创新，构建PBM、HMO等模式，形成新盈利点。

　　中国人身险市场是一个规模巨大、需求丰富、层次多样的超大型市场，正在经历广泛而深刻的市场变革。唯有将市场发展的普遍规律与基于自身国情的中国特色相结合，将人民日益增长的养老和健康风险保障需求与人身险转型发展方向相结合，全面、系统地提升负债端与资产端专业能力建设，在运营管理过程中守正创新，融合发展出新的商业模式，才能够真正推动人身险行业实现高质量发展。

专题二

中国农业再保险发展情况及展望

　　党中央、国务院高度重视农业保险发展。习近平总书记多次作出重要指示，强调"农业保险一定要搞好"，在2022年底召开的中央农村工作会议上首次提出"要健全种粮农民收益保障机制，完善价格、补贴、保险'三位一体'的政策体系"。2019年5月，中央深改委审议通过的《关于加快农业保险高质量发展的指导意见》把农业保险放在了推进现代农业发展、促进乡村产业振兴、改进农村社会治理、保障农民收益的重要地位进行统筹部署，农业保险进入高质量发展阶段。中国农业保险发展迅速，在稳定农业生产和保障国家粮食安全中发挥了越来越大的作用。农业再保险是助力农业保险高质量发展的重要保障。经过多年探索实践，农业保险大灾风险分散机制与现代农业风险管理体系逐步建立，农业再保险发展取得积极成效。

一、农业灾害和农业保险市场发展情况

（一）农业灾害发生情况

　　近年来，受人类活动和自然因素共同影响，全球变暖趋势不断持续，极端天气气候事件呈多发、频发、重发态势。世界气象组织2021

年发布的报告指出，受气候变化等因素影响，与天气、气候和水有关的灾害数量在过去50年间增加了5倍。中国地势西高东低，大陆东濒太平洋，西部为世界地势最高的青藏高原，形成复杂的陆海大气系统，是世界上受农业自然灾害影响最严重的国家之一。据国家应急管理部等部门统计，近十多年来中国每年因自然灾害造成的直接经济损失都在2 500亿元以上。从近几年情况看，2020年东北地区连续遭受三场台风影响；同年，长江中下游发生极端降水事件，降雨量较常年多1.2倍，为1961年以来最多；2021年河南省遭受了历史罕见的特大暴雨灾害；2022年中东部地区出现1961年以来最强高温过程。气象灾害对农业生产的影响明显加重，造成的损失程度不断增加。同时，根据国家发展和改革委员会统计数据，2021年三大粮食作物每亩产值达到1 274.0元，同比增长9.2%，较2016—2020年均值增长19.4%；2021年三大粮食作物生产总成本达到每亩1 157.2元，同比增长3.4%，较2016—2020年均值增长5.3%，农业生产成本和产品价值不断提高，一旦遭受自然灾害冲击，将会加重损失程度。

（二）农业保险市场发展情况

自2007年以来，中国农业保险发展迅速，从6个试点省份扩展到全国所有省份，已建成了覆盖全国、基本涵盖各类农产品品种的农业生产风险保障体系。据原中国银保监会统计，2022年农业保险延续快速发展良好势头，保费收入约1 219.4亿元，保额为4.6万亿元。2022年农业保险深度增加到1.4%，密度达到688.9元/人。农业保险保额从仅覆盖直接物化成本提高到将地租成本、人工成本和种植收益涵盖在内。完全成本保险保额一般为传统物化成本保险保额的2倍以上，如2022年黑龙江省小麦、玉米、水稻完全成本保险每亩保额分别为628元、1 405

元、911元，分别为物化成本保险的2.9倍、2.8倍和2.3倍；另外，蔬菜、花卉、水果、中草药等地方特色农产品和养殖业保险有较大的风险保障需求。目前，行业整体面临的风险敞口仍然较大，风险保障需求仍然较强。

（三）农业再保险需求情况

近年来，国内市场对农业再保险的需求不断增加。首先，农业再保险是直保公司业务经营的"稳定器"。受费率、保险金额和业务量等因素的影响，农业保险业务经营年际间波动较大，直保公司需要向再保险公司寻求风险分散途径。随着气候变化加剧、完全成本保险实施范围推广以及农业生产的集约化、规模化和高价值化趋势，农业保险自身风险也在快速积累，直保公司愈发需要再保险发挥风险分散作用，以助力其稳定业务经营。其次，受地缘政治局势、高通胀和气候变化等因素的影响，全球市场对于风险保障的需求显著提升，再保险市场需求也随之不断增加，再保险市场费率呈明显增长趋势。中国通货膨胀相对温和，但受中美利率区间收窄以及"偿二代"实施等因素影响，部分再保险公司资本金减少、供给能力小幅下降，市场对于再保险的需求也在不断上升。最后，直保公司可通过再保险有效分散风险，保障合理的偿付能力水平。中国"偿二代"监管制度体系以风险为导向，由于农业保险业务风险较大、波动性较强，对最低资本的要求相较其他险种更高，直保公司特别是专业经营农业保险的公司在资本管理和偿付能力管理上压力更大、要求更高。再保险降低了直保公司自留业务的资本占用水平，为其偿付能力水平维持合理区间、有效扩大承保能力、保障业务稳健经营提供了积极助力。

二、农业再保险发展情况

（一）市场规模情况

据统计，2022年中国农业再保险分保费收入超过370亿元，较上年增加超过80亿元，同比增长约28.2%（见表1），超过同期农业保险保费收入24.9%的增速。

表1　2021—2022年中国农业再保险业务主体分保费收入情况

单位：亿元，%

公司	2022年	2021年	增速
中资（部分）	359.2	279.4	28.6
外资（部分）	18.5	15.3	20.9
合计	377.7	294.7	28.2

注：表1根据8家再保险公司的分保费收入统计形成。其中，中资再保险公司（4家）：中国农业再保险公司、中再产险、前海再、人保再；外资再保险公司（4家）：汉再上分、慕再北分、瑞再北分、信利再。

从市场主体来看，中国农业再保险公司市场规模占比最大，逐步成为中国农业再保险市场的重要主体。2021年中国农业再保险公司分保费收入191.7亿元；2022年分保费收入240.8亿元，同比增长25.6%。对于2021年河南特大暴雨等灾情，向主要业务在当地的农业保险承保机构全年摊回赔款1.3亿元，为灾后恢复生产发挥了积极作用。中再产险农业再保险业务规模居市场第2位，2022年分保费收入109.3亿元，同比增长35.3%。

近年来，外资再保险公司业务规模不断扩大、竞争力不断增强。如慕再北分2021年农险业务分保费收入约3.4亿元，2022年约6.3亿元，同比增长约85.3%；汉再上分2021年农险业务分保费收入约7.8亿元，2022年约8.1亿元，同比增长约3.8%；瑞再北分2021年农险业务分保费收入约3.7亿元，2022年约3.9亿元，同比增长约5.4%。

（二）保险分出率变化情况

随着农业保险保费收入规模不断扩大与农业再保险市场的不断发展，农业保险对于再保险的分出率整体呈现上升趋势。如图1所示，2015—2020年，分出率从21.1%上升至28.0%；根据相关数据估算，2021年、2022年全国农业保险对于再保险的分出率分别为30.2%、30.4%，高于2020年及之前年份的分出率水平，农业再保险需求不断上升。

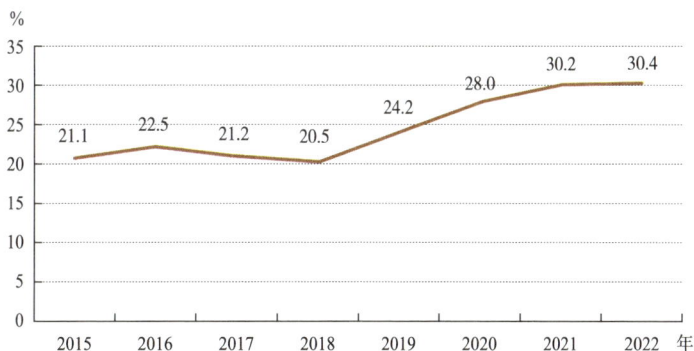

图1 2015—2022年农业保险分出率情况

（数据来源：《中国保险年鉴》及相关公开数据）

（三）再保险市场主体情况

目前，国内再保险市场专业再保险公司共15家，其中中资再保险公司7家，外资再保险公司8家。经营农业再保险业务主要为中国农业再保险公司、中再产险、慕再北分、瑞再北分、汉再上分、太平再（中国）、前海再、人保再、通用再上分、法再北分、信利再。

（四）服务国家战略创新举措

农业保险和再保险不仅是农业巨灾风险管理的基本手段，也是服务国家风险治理的重要工具。近年来农业再保险行业充分利用专业平台和技术优势，以服务国家战略为核心，推出诸多创新举措，为保障国家粮食安全、持续推动乡村振兴战略实施、助力农业绿色发展等发挥了重要作用。如中国农业再保险公司积极探索健全农业大灾风险分散机制。中再产险立足保险价值链，聚合行业资源，通过提高再保险业务质效、践行科技赋能等打造各类主体联动协同的合作共赢生态联盟，在推进农业农村绿色转型、促进行业"智能、高效"发展方面发挥了积极作用。

三、农业再保险发展趋势与展望

（一）将成为优化完善国家支农惠农政策的重要抓手

党的二十大提出了建设农业强国的新时代目标，"供给保障强"与"产业韧性强"是建设农业强国的重要内容，从国际经验和国内实践来看，农业强国建设离不开农业保险这一"防护堤"的保驾护航。习近平总书记在2022年中央农村工作会议上强调"要健全种粮农民收益保障机制，完善价格、补贴、保险'三位一体'的政策体系"，这不仅将农业保险提到了更高层面，也给农业保险工作赋予了更大使命、提出了更高要求。农业保险作为新时期重要的支农政策手段，具有政策性和准公共物品属性。中国政府高度重视发展农业再保险，中央一号文件多次提出要"健全农业再保险制度""积极发展农业再保险""完善农业保险大灾风险分散机制"，政策关注程度和推动力度不断提升。未来，随着中国农业再保险制度不断完善，大灾风险分散机制不断健全，农业再保险在提升国家灾害治理能力、服务保障农业强国建设等方面将发挥更大作用。

（二）将成为保障和推动农业保险高质量发展的重要力量

再保险作为"保险的保险"，在防范化解农业大灾风险、保障农业保险高质量发展方面发挥重要作用。首先，农业再保险是构建多层次大灾风险分散体系的重要一环，能够为直保公司提供风险保障支持。未来，随着气候变化加剧以及农业生产的集约化、规模化和高价值化趋势，农业保险风险敞口在逐步扩大，农业再保险体系将发挥更加重要的作用。其次，农业再保险的平台优势及专业技术优势将助力农业保险市场改革传统模式，加大科技投入，不断推动产品服务创新。如中再产险在农业农村部的指导和支持下，专门成立高标准农田保险创新小组，推动高标准农田保险产品服务的研发工作，目前已为辽宁、内蒙古等地高标准农田保险试点提供再保险支持。

（三）将在完善制度体系建设中发挥重要作用

从国际经验来看，美国、日本、西班牙、印度等都通过《农业保险法》等类似法规对农业再保险运行进行规范。2012年，国务院颁布了国内农业保险领域的首部法律法规文件——《农业保险条例》，对规范和推动中国农业保险发展发挥了重要作用。《农业保险条例》实施至今已超过10年，国内农业保险市场十年发展取得突出成就。2019年5月，中央深改委审议通过的《关于加快农业保险高质量发展的指导意见》，为农业保险高质量发展擘画了蓝图。新时期全面推进乡村振兴及加快构建农业强国等新发展形势与重大战略部署，对农业保险高质量发展提出了新要求。农业再保险作为农业大灾风险分散体系的重要一环，将在农业保险制度体系建设中发挥重要作用。

专题三

借鉴国际经验
加快上海国际再保险中心建设

国际再保险中心是再保险机构（包括总部、分公司、子公司）和其他保险市场参与者聚集的城市或地区，它能够提升该城市或地区在全球再保险领域的定价权和话语权，巩固提升其再保险市场的规模总量。目前，一些活跃的再保险市场依托完善的基础设施、充足的人才储备和便利的政策支持等多重因素，逐渐发展为国际再保险中心。

2021年10月，原中国银保监会和上海市人民政府联合发布《中国银保监会　上海市人民政府关于推进上海国际再保险中心建设的指导意见》，明确提出"推进上海国际再保险中心建设"。这是落实《中共中央　国务院关于支持浦东新区高水平改革开放打造社会主义现代化建设引领区的意见》的重要举措，也是中国再保险业的一件大事。2023年6月，国家金融监督管理总局与上海市人民政府在陆家嘴论坛共同发布《关于加快推进上海国际再保险中心建设的实施细则》，在上海开设面向全球的再保险交易市场（再保险国际板），对再保险中心的建设路径和配套支持进行固化明确，标志着上海国际再保险中心建设又迈出重要一步。

本文将通过剖析主要国际再保险中心的形成背景、建设经验和特征优势，为推进上海国际再保险中心建设找准着力点，为上海市因地制宜，扬长避短，建设成为一个成熟的国际再保险中心提供建议和启发。

一、国际再保险中心的形成

再保险起源于14世纪的海上保险，天然具有涉及范围广的特点，并且有进入国际市场寻求更大风险分散途径的需求，由此一些世界性的再保险公司或集团应运而生。早期的再保险集团不仅扎根于其总部所在地，而且积极扩张，在许多国家的重要城市设立分支机构，分入当地保险公司的再保险业务，逐渐形成了国际再保险市场。

自17世纪以来，商品经济和海上贸易的发展为再保险市场的形成创造了有利条件，德国、瑞士、英国、美国、法国相继成立了专业再保险公司，办理水险、航空险、火险、工程险以及责任险的再保险，形成了庞大的国际再保险市场。

在经历了20世纪80年代初期和80年代末期至90年代初期的两次行业危机之后，大型专业再保险公司进一步壮大了规模，市场交易更为集中。凭借市场条件，依托特定区域的再保险交易市场，全球逐渐发展形成了三大主要国际再保险中心，分别是伦敦国际再保险中心、新加坡国际再保险中心和百慕大国际再保险中心。

二、三大主要国际再保险中心概况与特征

（一）伦敦国际再保险中心

伦敦是大不列颠及北爱尔兰联合王国的首都，位于大西洋沿岸，是大西洋重要的港口之一，有着2000多年的历史沉淀。自17世纪以来，随着英国海上霸主地位的逐渐确立和资本主义市场的蓬勃发展，一批专业成熟的火灾、意外和人寿保险公司在伦敦建立，且其经营方式和规章制度一直被其他保险市场所参考或沿用，伦敦的保险业影响力和话语权辐射全球。伦敦国际再保险中心的发展和演进也与其历史积淀密不可分，其承保能力巨大，主要由劳合社和保险公司两个市场提供包括水险、非水险、航空保险、汽车保险等再保险业务，为"历史积淀型再保险中心"的代表。

1．宏观营商环境

伦敦的商业发展表现排名世界前列，经济竞争力和可持续竞争力较强（见图1），因此吸引了大量经济资源汇聚于此，也为保险及再保险业长期稳定发展提供了重要的经济环境。根据中国社会科学院与联合国人居署联合课题组出版的《全球城市竞争力报告（2020—2021）》的评定，2020—2021年伦敦的经济竞争力为0.939，排名全球第4位，仅次于纽约、新加坡和东京3个城市；其可持续竞争力为0.901，也位居世界前列，排名全球第5位。

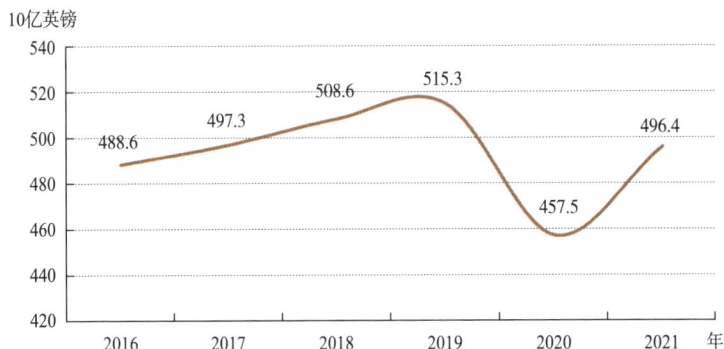

图1　2016—2021年伦敦GDP

（数据来源：Statista）

　　相较于整体经济发展水平，金融业发展水平更能反映保险业的发展情况。伦敦金融业发展水平高，2021年英国金融业增加值达1 383.74亿美元，其中伦敦占较大比重。伦敦不仅是保险中心，还是债券中心、股权中心和货币中心，其发达的金融业不但是推动保险业发展更直接的经济资源，而且为保险业发展提供了活力。基金经理、律师、会计师、银行家、经纪人等金融专业人士的存在为保险和再保险市场提供了重要的人才资源和业务保障，不同行业百花齐放也有利于保险公司多条线开展业务。

2. 保险市场发展

　　伦敦再保险的发展得益于英国发达的原保险市场，其原保险市场由两部分组成，一是商业保险公司，二是劳合社。这两个市场构成了伦敦原保险市场的强大承保能力。图2为2016—2020年英国原保险业发展情况。整体来看，2020年英国的保费收入为3 383.2亿美元，保险业发展体量较大。同样，英国保险深度整体呈上升趋势，到2020年保险深度达到11.1%，保险业在整个国民经济中占据较为重要的地位。从相对微观的角度来看，英国的保险密度也处于较高水平，2020年常住人口平均保险费达到4 523美元，反映了当地人民较高的收入和较强的保险意识。此外，发达的原保险市场也为再保险业务的办理提供了丰富的经验和大量的专业人才。

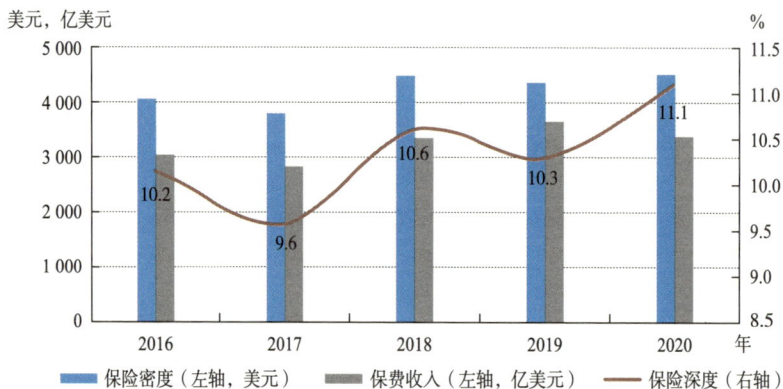

图2　2016—2020年英国保险深度、保险密度与保费收入水平

（资料来源：瑞再研究院）

英国是重要的国际风险集散中心和再保险交易中心，而英国的风险转移和再保险交易主要汇聚地之一便是伦敦。图3为2016—2020年英国再保险分保费收入水平，该指标近几年虽呈下降趋势，但整体水平仍较高。2020年，英国再保险分保费收入约730亿美元，约为当年保费收入的两成多。

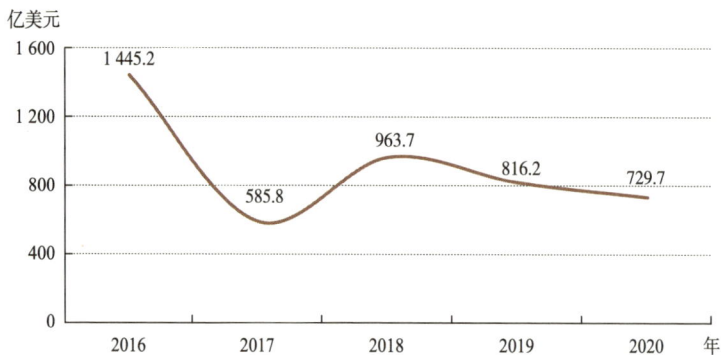

图3　2016—2020年英国再保险分保费收入水平

（资料来源：OECD）

伦敦国际再保险中心的又一特色及优势是其为水险、能源险和航空险等风险提供的完整承保方案。由于历史原因和专业能力的积累，目前伦敦是上述风险的重要集散中心，所有的这些特殊风险几乎都能在伦敦找到保险和再保险解决方案，可以说，这一业务是伦敦国际再保险中心的"品牌"之一。

随着现代保险业的发展，保险科技成为保险业发展不可或缺的工具。2021年，英国保险创新融资金额达到3.7亿美元，因此，其较好的创新前景为英国保险业及再保险业发展提供了巨大潜力，也成为强化伦敦国际再保险中心地位的力量。

3．政策条件

再保险起源于海上贸易，而英国作为一个海岛国家，其保险与再保险业有着深厚的历史沉淀，伴随保险立法与监管政策也一直走在世界前列，被各国广为借鉴。早在12世纪的英国就出现了关于海事行为的立法记载，《奥莱农法集》中记录了共同海损原则的相关事项。此后，在18世纪至20世纪中叶，英国又出台了一系列指导保险公司日常经营的法案，如《人寿保险法》（1774）、《保险公司法》（1958）等。在20世纪70—90年代，英国在之前立法的基础上，集中建立了范围更广、内容更为完善的保险监管体系，其中包括《保险经纪人注册法》（1977）、《保险公司法》（1982）和《劳合社法案》（1982）等。比如，由于英国绝大部分保险业务通过保险经纪人和代理人完成，英国通过出台《保险经纪人注册法》对保险经纪人的注册、培训、惩戒和用语解释等方面作出规范，这些法案对英国保险业务的开展以及世界相关法律体系的建设作出了巨大的贡献。同时，英国金融服务局和英国保险协会的共同监管也使英国保险与再保险市场变得更加高效。

英国长期实施保险契约自由化，在结果可控的范围内给予保险与再保险公司经营自由。保险契约自由化主要是指在相关法律和社会标准的底线之上，保险费率由市场决定，保险条款由保险公司的自身发展决定，而监管机构则主要监管保险公司的行为及经营结果，让市场竞争占据主导地位，这使伦敦再保险市场的费率更具竞争性，可保范围也更为广泛。

伦敦对保险经营主体准入的限制较小，市场进入门槛较低。伦敦市场上的保险公司，一般都是经过英国贸工部根据1982年《保险公司法案》批准注册的保险公司。此外，自1994年7月1日起，总部设在欧盟或者是在欧洲经济区的成员国持有本国颁发的执照的保险公司也可以进入伦敦保险市场。2020年英国正式"脱欧"后，英国和其他欧盟国家的（再）保险公司虽然不能再依靠通行证提供服务，但绝大多数公司已在2016年英国有脱欧计划后就开始制订和实施应急计划，比如建立新的授权公司、英国分支机构、重新选址等。

4．智力资源

伦敦国际再保险市场拥有完善的精算师和其他保险从业人员培养体系，并且保险从业者的平均薪酬也高于英国整体平均薪酬，这为促进保险业和再保险业发展的重要人力和智力资源提供了保障。

1848年，出于以数学理论进行寿险研究的目的，英国精算师协会（IFoA）正式成立，并且随着精算数学的发展，于20世纪中期开设了英国精算师考试，为协会成员提供阶段性的教育。英国精算师协会最初起源于伦敦，并且在伦敦高霍尔本中心设置了办事处，这使其在伦敦地区开办了更多的协会交流活动，也使更多伦敦的大学学院获得了英国精算师考试的豁免资格认证，为伦敦地区精算师人才的培养提供了强力的支撑。

此外，在非精算领域方面，英国高校将保险教育融入了人才培养体系，数量较多的英国高校都开设了保险学和精算学等相关课程，且英国特许保险学院开设了CII保险资质认证考试，提升保险从业人员的业务素质，该考试已与CPCU共同成为保险领域非精算资质的最重要执业资质认证。

据薪酬调查网站Salary Explorer披露，2020年英国保险行业从业者的平均月薪为5 930英镑，高于英国整体的平均薪酬，在世界主要再保险市场中也排名前列，这促使更多海内外保险人才纷纷涌入伦敦地区。

5．基础设施

基础设施是保证国家或地区经济活动的公共设施或系统，一般可分为生产基础设施、社会基础设施和制度保障机构三类。

生产基础设施包含道路交通系统、通信系统、环境卫生系统等公共建设。其中，由于再保险业离岸交易往来和实时信息获取的特点，道路交通系统与通信系统两类生产基础设施影响较大。

在道路交通系统方面，伦敦市内共有六个机场，其中，希思罗国际机场为英国最大的机场，也是主要的联外机场。即使在新冠疫情的影响下，2021年希思罗国际机场平均每天发送12.8万人次，其中有87.6%为国际乘客，充分起到了连接国内外交流的作用。此外，英国作为一个岛国，港口海运在经济发展中也起到重要的作用。2021年，英国所有港口共处理了4.5亿吨货物，其中伦敦处理的港口流量最多，占英国所有流量的12%。海运的发达不仅促进了对外交流，而且也带动了与衍生航运交易、融资、海事保险、海事法律和仲裁等航运相关服务产业集群的发展。

在通信系统方面，随着互联网时代的到来，网络通信已占据主导地位，图4为2016—2020年英国每百人宽带用户数。英国宽带普及率稳步上升，2020年，平均每一百人中就有超过40人为宽带用户。这一指标侧面反映了网络在英国的普及程度较高，具备开展再保险业务的基础设施条件。

人

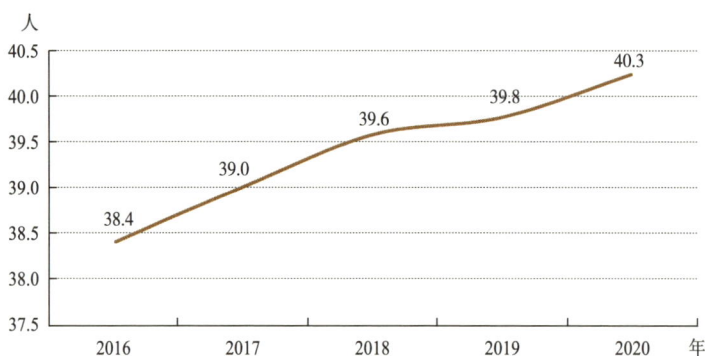

图4　2016—2020年英国每百人宽带用户数

（资料来源：世界银行）

社会基础设施主要是指服务于居民的各种机构和设施，与再保险业息息相关的即是各类保险机构的数量。英国有接近200家保险公司、近50家再保险公司和200家保险经纪公司，数量庞大的保险及再保险机构为其承载国际风险集散和再保险交易中心的功能提供了现实载体，这也是伦敦之所以成为重要的国际再保险中心的核心条件。

制度保障机构主要是指相关的建设规划与管理部门，其中比较典型的金融基础设施有金融资产登记托管系统、清算结算系统、交易设施等设施及其运营机构。除了上文中已提及的金融服务局和英国保险协会，劳合社也是保证伦敦国际再保险市场正常运行的重要机构之一，其300余年的历史吸引了世界各国的保险业代表云集于此，他们在劳合社提供的场所和服务的基础上便利地开展保险业务，这是伦敦市场迄今仍不失为国际保险市场重要中心的优势所在，也为其国际再保险中心地位的建立和巩固奠定了坚实基础。

（二）新加坡国际再保险中心

新加坡是位于马来半岛南端、马六甲海峡出入口的一个城市国家，由新加坡岛及附近63个小岛组成。一方面，新加坡经济的繁荣与其优越的地理位置息息相关，苏伊士运河的开通使身处要道的新加坡"乘上了发展的快车"。但由于国土面积较小，自身资源不足，新加坡高度依赖中、美、日、欧和周边市场，因此推动了其发展离岸金融市场。另一方面，新加坡金融监管机构—新加坡金融监管局（MAS）自2000年宣布全面开放保险业后，其根据本国特点因势利导，在国际再保险市场资金进出规定、所得税、离岸保险业务税收等方面发挥了关键的政策引导作用。因此，新加坡国际再保险中心可视为"政策驱动型再保险中心"的代表之一。

1. 宏观营商环境

与伦敦类似，新加坡再保险中心地位的基础条件之一是其优异的商业发展表现。2020—2021年，新加坡经济竞争力指数和可持续竞争力指数分别为0.947和0.959，两个指标都位列所有城市中的第2名。可以说，优渥的商业土壤为新加坡打造国际再保险中心提供了良好的环境。

作为一个发达国家，新加坡在整体经济发展水平较高的同时，仍保持高速发展。如图5所示，在疫情前新加坡的经济基本保持着7%~10%的正增长，在疫情开始后虽有所下滑，但在2021年却积极适应疫情常态，恢复了14.97%的GDP高增速。

10亿美元

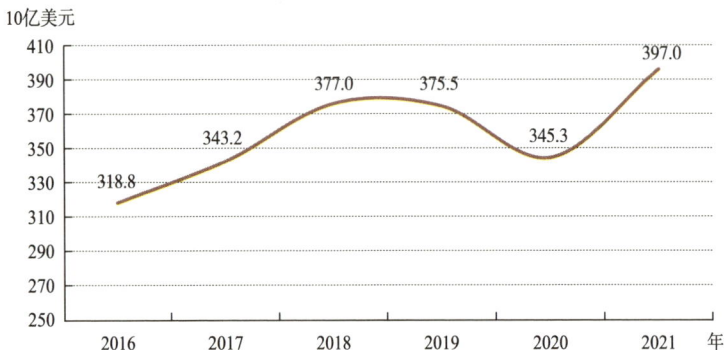

图5　2016—2021年新加坡GDP

（数据来源：iFind）

图6为2016—2021年新加坡金融业增加值，反映了新加坡金融业较高的发展水平及速度。新加坡金融业近几年均保持着稳定的增长，为保险业发展提供了良好的基础。

百万美元

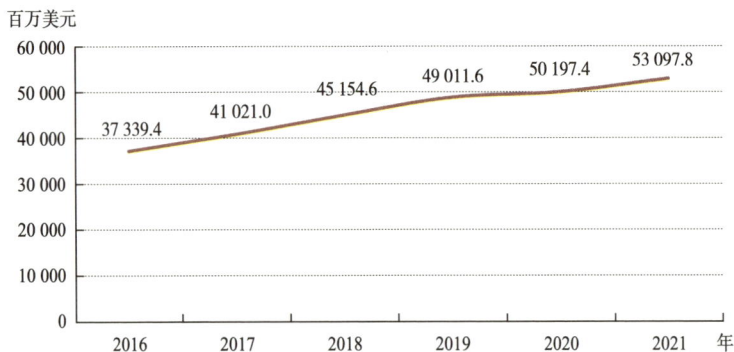

注：图中数值由1新加坡元＝0.72美元的汇率转换而来。

图6　2016—2021年新加坡金融业增加值

（资料来源：Wind）

另外，新加坡对研发较为重视。从20世纪起，新加坡就出台了多个推动科技发展的相关政策，如国家科技发展计划、国立研究基金和研发税收优惠等，其目的在于从实用主义出发，注重科技与产业经济的融合以及培养更多专业人才，而经济的协同发展也使保险及再保险行业从中获益。比如科技创新提高了企业的数字化能力，越来越多的直保与再保公司开始追求更为高效、准确的OA流程。再如研发的投入使制造业、生物医药行业技术更迭的速度加快，进一步拓展了保险公司的承保范围，提高了精算定价能力。图7为2016—2020年新加坡研发投入占比。虽然新加坡历年研发投入占比有所波动，但均保持在1.80%以上，且该比例自2018年起不断上升，说明新加坡对研发的重视程度在近几年有所提升。

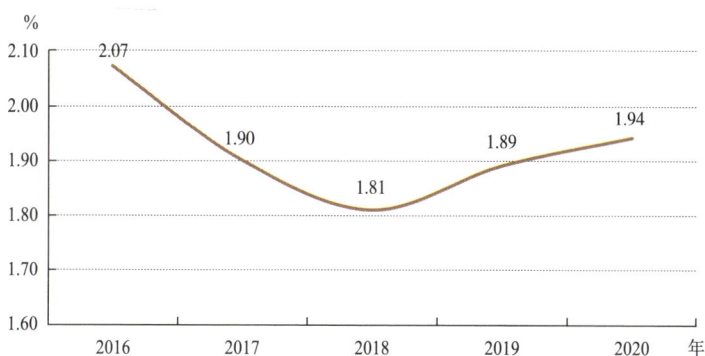

图7　2016—2020年新加坡研发投入占比

（资料来源：世界银行）

2．保险市场发展

发达的原保险市场为新加坡再保险市场发展提供了最基本的支撑。图8为2016—2020年新加坡原保险业发展情况。整体来看，新加坡原保险保费收入稳定增长，2020年原保费收入达到350.6亿美元；其保险深度略有波动但整体呈上升趋势，2016—2020年增长了2.3%，2020年达到9.5%；其2020年的保险密度高达5 638美元，甚至高于英国的4 523美元。

美元，亿美元

图8 2016—2020年新加坡保险深度、保险密度与保费收入水平

（资料来源：瑞士再保险研究院）

与伦敦类似，新加坡也是重要的国际风险集散中心和再保险交易中心。图9为2016—2020年新加坡再保险分保费收入水平。新加坡再保险分保费基本逐年增长，且近几年增速逐渐变快。2020年新加坡再保险分保费收入超过130亿美元，接近其当年保费收入的四成。

亿美元

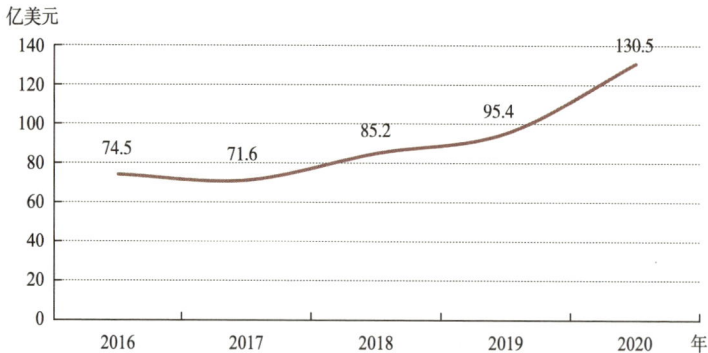

图9 2016—2020年新加坡再保险分保费收入水平

（资料来源：《中国保险年鉴》、经济合作与发展组织）

2021年，新加坡获得的保险创新融资金额为3.65亿美元，数值上与英国接近。创新融资将用于为行业配置保险科技，进一步提升行业发展效率。

3．政策条件

新加坡政府因势利导，实施了有利于保险业发展的政策。一方面，对保险业公司所得税、离岸业务所得税、个人所得税等给予优惠的税收条件；另一方面，在高标准监管的前提下，加大对非居民开办再保险公司业务条件、外资入股本地保险公司、保险经纪进场执业等方面的对外开放力度。

新加坡为再保险公司提供额外优惠税率。例如，2020年一般适用的企业所得税税率为17%，除了给予一般公司部分免税或退税的优惠政策，新加坡针对承保了认可专业保险业务的保险公司及再保险公司制订了发展总括计划，使其可享受10%的优惠税率。

新加坡金融服务业发端自银行业，其金融监管机构——新加坡金融监管局（MAS）自1990年以来对国内寿险业采取闭门政策，直到2000年才宣布全面开放保险业，同时撤销外国投资者在本地保险公司不能持有超过49%股权的限制，鼓励外资公司进入新加坡保险市场。自此，新加坡的离岸业务稳步上升，各家保险集团均在此设立区域业务中心。

资金进出规定方面，新加坡无外汇管制，资金可自由流入流出，企业利润的汇出无限制也无特殊税费，减少了国际再保险公司跨国业务的阻碍。

4．智力资源

新加坡有一套完善的人才培养和引进政策。首先，新加坡采用精英化的教育体系，该体系通过层层分流为不同特质的学生提供不同的发展方向，以培养专业性的人才。新加坡还设立了专门的人才引进机构"联系新加坡"，该机构成为沟通新加坡与海外人才的桥梁。此外，新加坡在签证、居留、子女教育、医疗等方面出台了一系列的措施，为引进的人才提供工作、生活方面的便利。

保险行业较高的平均薪资也吸引了大量人才流入新加坡。根据权威数据网站Salary Explorer显示，2021年新加坡保险从业人员的平均月薪在8 470新加坡元，其中风险管理经理的平均月薪甚至达到了14 800新加坡元，远高于人力部对于普通工作准证签发的薪资要求。

5．基础设施

在生产基础设施方面，由于新加坡自身国土面积较小，部分设施数量相比于其他大型国家或地区较小。从航运来看，新加坡全国只有两个民用机场，其中最大的樟宜机场在疫情影响基本结束的情况下，2023年4月平均每天向海内外发送15.3万人次。从海运来看，新加坡位于马六甲海峡的尖端，拥有优越的地理位置，处理了大约世界五分之一的集装箱转运吞吐量，自由港经济发展十分繁荣。从通信系统来看，如图10所示，2016—2020年新加坡的每百人宽带用户数略低于其他主要再保险市场，且增速较低。但据Speedtest发布的最新的（2023年4月）全球各国网速指数来看，新加坡高居固定宽带网速的第1名。

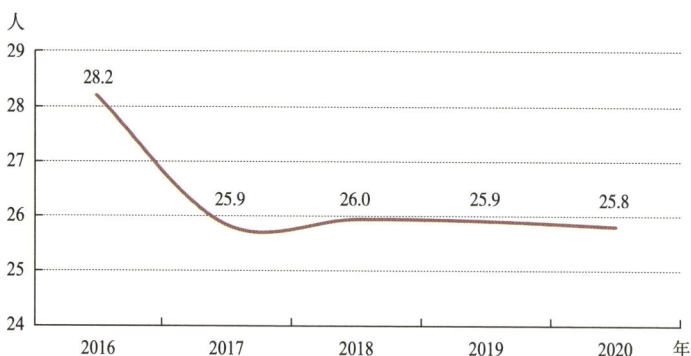

图10　2016—2020年新加坡的每百人宽带用户数

（资料来源：世界银行）

从保险机构数量上来看，新加坡保险市场包含丰富的市场主体，截至2021年，新加坡已有124家持牌保险公司和再保险公司，82家专属自保公司。

从制度保障机构上看，新加坡具有强大的金融基础设施。其中，新加坡金融监管局（MAS）主要负责银行、保险和支付领域等金融机构的监管，通过出台各种政策保障消费者权益与业态稳定发展。此外，新加坡还推出了由全球保险业者、监管机构和学术界三方联合建立的平台——全球亚洲保险合作伙伴组织（GAIP），共同提供保险洞察与研究见解。同时，行业自律也是新加坡保险行业稳定发展的重要原因之一。新加坡保险业按机构类别建立了健全的行业协会组织体系，分别成立了人寿保险协会（LIA）、一般保险协会（GIA）、再保险行业协会（SRA）和保险经纪行业协会（SIBA）等。

（三）百慕大国际再保险中心

百慕大群岛位于北大西洋，距北美洲900多千米，是自治的英国海外领地，沿用英国法律，政治稳定。其占地面积较小，人口密度不足，几乎所有商品都依赖于进口，因此该地区把发展重点转向了第三产业，金融和旅游业是百慕大的两大经济支柱。由于良好的交通以及在地理位置上靠近美国，百慕大天然拥有发展离岸金融的优势。而且由于该地区本身经济实力较弱，没有足以支撑其发展的本土企业，所以政府将目光转向海外，转而制定优惠的税收政策和营造宽松的监管环境来吸引大量海外金融机构，也是"政策驱动型再保险中心"的代表之一。

1．宏观营商环境

由于陆地面积与人口皆相对较小，百慕大整体经济总量不高，但人均生活水平远高于大多数国家或地区，并且离岸金融十分繁荣。由图11所示，百慕大整体经济总量较小，增速也较为波动。但百慕大

2021年人均GDP超过11万美元，这一数值远超发达国家的平均标准，甚至高于美国。

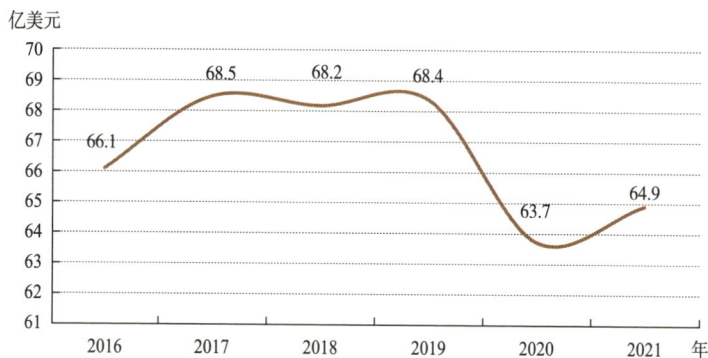

注：根据 2015 年价折合。

图11　2016—2021年百慕大GDP

（资料来源：iFind）

由于占地面积小和人口密度不足等区位因素，百慕大实体产业高度依赖进口，自身经济基础薄弱，缺少足以支撑其发展的本土企业。在此背景下，百慕大政府很早就将目光转向海外，意图打造有吸引力的离岸金融中心。目前，百慕大在岸金融业以及本地的实体经济仅占百慕大经济总量的5%，其离岸金融业在经济发展中扮演着中流砥柱的角色。

2．保险市场发展

百慕大再保险市场历史悠久，发展至今已有100多年的历史。近年来，在政府的支持和各种因素的加持下，百慕大再保险业更是获得了较快发展。2019年，百慕大再保险分保费收入928.3亿美元，这一数值在2020年增至1 489.3亿美元，占该地区所有保险公司毛保费收入的53.83%。这主要是因为21世纪初美国本土巨灾风险事件频发，包括2001年9月11日的双子塔遭受恐怖袭击导致巨额索赔，2005年美国遭遇卡特里娜（Katrina）、丽塔（Rita）和威尔玛（Wilma）飓风，给美国财险行业造成巨额损失，这些都使美国本土再保险价格飙升，再保险需求转向国外市场。而百慕大抓住了这一波再保险发展机遇，对再保险发展大力支持，同时政策上也比较宽松，加之拥有紧邻美国这一得天独厚的地理优势，从而吸引了源源不断的再保险需求和资本流入。由此，2001年与2005年有相当数量的保险和再保险公司在百慕大成立，包括2001年成立的Arch Capital、Axis和Allied World和2005年成立的Ariel Re、Flagstone Re和Validus Re等。据百慕大商业发展局（BDA）披露，截至2019年，百慕大市场上已有超过1 200家（再）保险公司。根据标准普尔《全球再保险要闻（GRH）：2022》的统计，全球排名前40位的再保险公司中有11家来自百慕大，这11家再保险公司的再保险净保费占前40名再保险公司净保费收入的12.63%。

作为离岸金融中心和国际再保险中心的百慕大，最早是以离岸自保中心的身份为人所熟知的，20世纪60年代百慕大即成立了第一家自保公司，稳定的政治环境、优惠的税收政策和宽松的注册监管制度在早期也吸引了一大批自保公司在此落脚。

"自保—再保"协同发展的模式让百慕大颇受风险资本的青睐，并持续推动百慕大的金融保险创新。相比于一般的保险业务，自保业务质量更高，自保的聚集带来了风险资本的大量流入，增加了再保险市场的买方主体，从而带动了再保险市场的发展，扩张了再保险市场的承保能力。同时，再保险公司、自保公司、资本市场等风险融资渠道的高度融合，淡化了金融保险产品之间的界限，金融一体化趋势得到进一步增强，保险市场的系统性风险得以降低，优质的市场环境反过来推动百慕大再保险市场的深度发展。

总体来看，数量充足且承保能力强大的再保险机构使得百慕大成为重要的国际风险集散中心和再保险交易中心。

3．政策条件

百慕大发达的再保险业离不开政府的大力支持。政府支持保险和再保险业发展的一个重要表现是实施有利于保险机构经营的税收政策。在百慕大经营保险业务无须缴纳增值税，只需缴纳营业税，后者在2021年税率为15%。优异的税收环境降低了再保险开展业务的交易成本，极大助力了市场发展壮大。

此外，百慕大有适合交易的政策环境，不存在外汇管制，资金可以自由进出，注册公司管理程序便利、设限少，严格遵守金融保密法，再加上稳定的政局和可观的市场前景，为离岸金融和国际再保险业务的开展提供了十分有利于交易的环境。除了直接提供稳定有利的交易环境，百慕大的政策环境还能够以较低的成本吸引国际资本参与国内保险市场的风险转移，其获取资本市场支持的能力也间接促进了保险业、再保险业的发展。

4．智力资源

保险及再保险行业对专业人才的需求高，而百慕大的保险行业有较多岗位的薪资高于平均薪资，从而吸引了大量人才从事于保险及再保险行业，为其提供充足的专业人才资源。表1为2022年百慕大保险行业部分职业平均每月薪资。与所有劳动者的平均月薪相比，表1中列举的保险职业月薪均较高，风险管理师的月薪甚至接近平均月薪的两倍。

表1　　　　2022年百慕大保险行业部分职业平均每月薪资[1]

单位：美元

职业	平均每月薪资
风险管理师	3 080
风险建模师	2 970
保险规划师	2 850
保险销售经理	2 610

职业	平均每月薪资
战略企划师	2 490
保险审计师	2 370
损失预防师	2 330
索赔估价员	2 250
精算师	2 140
保险项目经理	2 090
百慕大平均每月薪资	1 590

资料来源：Salary Explorer。

5．基础设施

在生产基础设施方面，由于陆地面积和人口较少，百慕大面临着和新加坡一样的问题。在航运方面，百慕大仅有一个国际机场，并且其每日航班数量也较少。在海运方面，百慕大有四个主要港口，最繁忙的为汉密尔顿港，每年约有400艘载有13.6万吨货物和1.5万个标准箱的船只到访港口。在通信系统方面，2020年，百慕大每百人就有近37人为宽带用户，这一指标甚至高于同年的美国，完善的网络设施为现代保险、再保险业务交易提供了便利。

在保险机构数量方面，百慕大积极的政策激励与税收优势，许多（再）保险机构在该地注册。据百慕大商业发展局披露，截至2019年，百慕大保险市场由1 200多家（再）保险公司组成，持有的总资产超过8 000亿美元，承保保费总额约为1 500亿美元。

在制度保障机构方面，百慕大为保险人、再保险人开展业务提供了专业化和规范化的制度环境。百慕大的保险许可和监管制度主要由《1978年保险法案》和相关条例来规范；此后又于1995年修订了《保险法》，首次对自保公司按照经营第三方业务的比例与风险性设立了多执照制度；2016年，百慕大进一步修改其法律，为达到相当于偿付能力标准Ⅱ（Solvency Ⅱ）的水平，百慕大司法辖区采取了一些增强监管制度的措施（如要求在百慕大建立总部）。在偿付能力和资本监管方面，百慕大金融管理局（BMA）引入了基于风险的资本模型，根据保险人和再保险人业务的独特性确定其监管资本要求。

三、加快上海国际再保险中心建设的建议

（一）宏观营商环境：保持经济平稳增长，促进金融业合力发展

上海再保险业虽相较于伦敦等老牌市场起步晚，但其发展迅速、繁荣开放的宏观营商环境为国际再保险中心的建设提供了良好机会和有力支撑。因此，保持宏观营商环境持续繁荣、经济连年平稳增长是国际再保险中心建设的基石。

目前主要国际再保险中心同时也是国际（区域）金融中心、证券交易中心和期货交易中心等，几乎没有依靠单一金融业态成为国际再保险中心的先例。金融业中各领域联系紧密、交易频繁，建议整合金融行业资源，积极补足再保险业发展短板，降低再保险业交易税费和作业成本等，将再保险的发展融入金融中心整体建设中去。

（二）保险市场发展：促进原保险市场增长，拓展再保险产品供给，加速保险科技建设

中国经济快速发展，已经连续多年成为全球第二大原保险市场，但保险深度与保险密度相较于欧美等发达国家仍然较低。再保险是保险业的内生需求，保险市场越大，再保险需求越大；保险市场发展程

度越高，再保险越重要。中国保险市场的巨大体量和高质量发展，必然需要规模更大、保障范围更广、专业程度更高、产品更丰富的再保险市场与之匹配。

积极建立大型风险和特殊风险的数据交换机制和资源整合机制，拓展再保险产品承保范围，提高承保能力，为科技创新、实体经济的发展保驾护航。此外，国内虽然已有若干家中资再保险机构，但总体规模与实力皆与世界级再保险机构有一定差距，因此建议鼓励再保险机构积极参与国际大型再保险项目，根据项目规模、参与程度等给予人才与经费支持。

聚焦保险"新理念引导、新科技应用、新服务升级"，依托临港新片区先行先试的制度优势和产业优势，积极推动网络安全保险、智能网联汽车保险等新兴保险产品的落地，积极创新数字化平台与新兴科技的融合，进一步发挥保险科技创新的支点作用。

（三）政策条件：构建新发展格局，贯彻陆家嘴会议精神，促进再保险业双向开放

近年来，中国再保险业通过业务分出分入和金融机构"走出去"的方式，积极参与全球再保险市场分工，但与全球再保险市场进一步双向融合仍需加强。因此，建议以第十四届陆家嘴论坛发布的《关于加快推进上海国际再保险中心建设的实施细则》为基础，在上海构建面向全球的富有竞争力的国际再保险交易市场，通过建立中国规制、标准，引导中国再保险市场由"单向开放"向"双向开放"转型升级。

为此，建议借鉴目前主要国际再保险中心如新加坡、百慕大等的经验。比如，这些国际再保险中心虽然整体经济总量和保费规模不如其他大型国家，但提供了较为优越的税收优惠政策，使它们在再保险

市场中极具吸引力，可见税收是吸引再保险机构入驻的重要条件之一。上海作为一个经济体量很大的国际化城市，在其他商业条件优渥的基础上，建议对（再）保险机构提供一定的税收优惠，以促进国际再保险中心建设。

（四）智力资源：加强再保险行业的宣传、人才培养与人才引进，建设属于上海的保险智库

近年来，伴随中国保险市场的飞速发展，从业人员专业素质大幅提升，但也存在参差不齐的问题。一方面，建议在高等教育发展和金融保险业高素质专业人才培养等方面加大力度。鼓励高校开设课程以及科研经费向再保险领域倾斜，重视再保险学科建设。2017年，中国精算师考试停考，直到2023年才重新恢复，对精算人才培养产生了一定影响。建议加快完善精算和非精算保险专业人才培养体系，持续更新相关教材，提高精算人才的留存率。另一方面，完善人才政策保障措施，提升中国再保险市场的人才吸引力。中国再保险业的发展晚于很多国外再保险市场，因此对国外再保险人才的引进至关重要。建议为专业再保险人才实施更为开放的住房、签证和用汇等政策保障。适度提高从业人员的薪酬，吸引国内外人才流入上海再保险市场。

（五）基础设施：促进生产基础设施开放，增加再保险机构数量，加速金融基础设施建设

加强生产基础设施建设，为离岸金融发展打好基础。上海的基础设施十分发达，在主要再保险市场中位居前列，建议充分利用现有完善设施，加强国内外航班、海运往来交流，适当放宽国际人员入境政策。

　　增加社会基础设施数量，鼓励保险集团、保险公司和再保险公司在上海设立再保险法人机构、分支机构。截至2022年，国内仅有15家专业再保险公司开展业务，相较于其他主要再保险市场，机构数量仍有待提高。建议进一步出台政策，以租房补贴、税收优惠等政策鼓励再保险机构在上海设立再保险法人机构、分支机构等。

　　加快金融基础设施建设，促进制度保障与国际接轨。中国互联网发展迅速，十分有利于金融基础设施建设。建议优化金融资产登记托管系统、清算结算系统、交易设施等基础设施，使其变得更为便捷透明。另外，建议建立仲裁、诉讼的境内外对接机制，遵循国际惯例，在语言使用上提供更大便利。

专题四

2022年全球自然灾害概况与长期变化趋势

一、2022年全球自然灾害回顾及长期损失趋势

（一）2022年全球自然灾害损失概况

2022年与自然灾害相关的损失依然保持高位。受极端天气事件的影响，巨灾造成的全球经济损失预计高达2 750亿美元，其中保险损失将达到1 250亿美元，连续两年超过1 000亿美元，远高于此前5年（1 100亿美元）和10年的平均水平（810亿美元），是自1970年以来第四高的水平（见图1）[①]。保险再保险行业承担了45%的经济损失，由此表明巨灾保障缺口仍然很大，但比过去10年平均61%的保障缺口比例有所缩小。2022年受主要自然灾害风险影响的地区保险深度相对较高，充分体现出提高家庭、企业和机构保险韧性的行业价值。

---

① 如无特别说明，本文有关巨灾保险损失的数据均来源于瑞士再保险Sigma数据库。

图1　全球自然灾害保险损失

（资料来源：瑞再研究院）

飓风"伊恩"是2022年损失最严重的自然灾害，初步估计保险损失达500亿~650亿美元[①]。这场4级飓风于9月下旬在美国佛罗里达州西部登陆，伴随着强风、暴雨和风暴潮，造成了巨大的灾难性破坏。这是Sigma数据库记录中继2005年飓风"卡特里娜"后导致第二高保险损失的热带气旋天气事件。这显示出即使是在飓风季较为温和的年份，仍然存在个别极端飓风天气事件对人口密集的沿海地区的潜在威胁。

此外，2022年的情况也再次证实了次生灾害的破坏性。全球强对流风暴造成的保险损失超过了330亿美元，主要是发生在美国的雷暴及伴随而来的冰雹和龙卷风，也高于前期的平均水平（见图2）。除了美国，法国也经历了有史以来最严重的一系列雹暴灾害，保险损失达50亿美元。全球洪灾造成的损失略高于平均水平，2—3月暴雨导致澳大利亚发生大面积洪灾，造成了43亿美元的保险损失，这是该国有史以来保险损失最大的巨灾事件。4月南非德班的洪水，估计造成15亿美元

[①]　包括美国"国家洪水保险计划"（NFIP）的理赔金额。数据为初步估计数，并可能随着后续索赔和评估过程的继续而进行调整。

的保险损失。

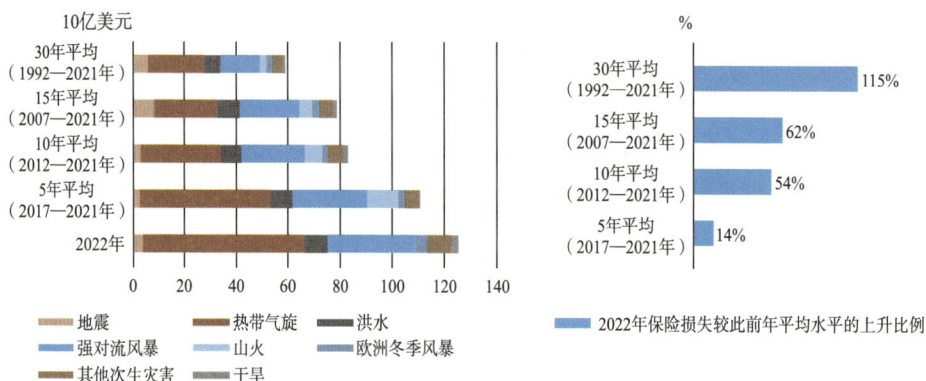

图2 按灾害分类，2022年全球巨灾保险损失

（资料来源：瑞再研究院）

冬季风暴在最近几年造成的损失严重程度相对较低，但2022年2月，欧洲西北部受到连续性冬季风暴侵袭，导致了41亿美元的保险损失，约为此前10年平均水平的2倍，使这一关键风险再次受到保险业的关注。尽管冬季风暴的风力不如热带气旋严重，但一场风暴就能影响欧洲大部分地区，不同地区的损失加起来可达数十亿美元。

2022年天气变化和异常的大气环流条件在世界各地造成了严重的干旱和热浪。在欧洲，2022年夏天成为有记录以来最热的夏天[①]。摩洛哥的炎热和干燥天气与北大西洋降雨不足相吻合[②]。在巴西，季风降雨低于前期平均水平[③]。高温和干旱导致许多地区的农作物减产，尤其是

---

① *Summer 2022 Europe's Hottest on Record*, Copernicus, 2022年9月8日；*Trockenheit in Europa 2022*, Deutscher Wetterdienst, 2022年7月。

② 2022年2月地中海西部干旱，欧洲委员会，2022年3月22日；请参见国家气象服务气候预测中心。

③ 参见"南美季风系统的不同阶段"，国家气象服务气候预测中心。

大豆和玉米受到的影响最大[①]。2022年成为美国本土地区有记录以来第三干旱的年份，农作物产量低于2021年[②]。在中国，长江流域的极端高温和干旱以及微弱的季风降雨影响了夏季作物的产量[③]。农作物减产加剧了全球粮食价格上涨的压力，进而增加了农业保险的损失。表1显示了部分市场以美元计价的农作物损失情况。

表1 部分市场因干旱导致的农作物损失情况

单位：亿美元

国家/地区	经济损失	保险损失
巴西	130	10
欧洲	62	6
中国	47	8
摩洛哥	2.5	0.4

资料来源：CAN、PSR、应急管理部、瑞再研究院。

（二）长期损失趋势

过去6年间，自然灾害造成的保险损失持续上升，预计未来这种趋势还将延续。自1992年以来，自然灾害保险损失年均增长率为5%~7%（见图3）。经历了2012—2016年损失较温和的阶段后，2017年开始保险损失再次显著上升，年均超过1 100亿美元，是2012—2016年平均520亿美元的2倍多，且过去6年已重返5%~7%的历史长期增长率。尽管存在年度波动且短期因素（比如高通胀率）的影响将逐步淡化，保险损失预计将延续增长趋势。

[①] 参见*Crop Explorer-World Agricultural Production Briefs: Brazil*，Foreign Agriculture Service，美国农业部USDA。

[②] 2022年创纪录的干旱席卷了美国大部分地区，美国国家海洋和大气管理局，2023年1月10日；2022年玉米和大豆产量下降，美国农业部报告玉米库存量下降，大豆库存量较上年同期下降，2023年冬小麦种子增加，USDA，2023年1月10日。

[③] "长江流域严重干旱的科学解释"，*Journal of Arid Meteorology*，2022年。

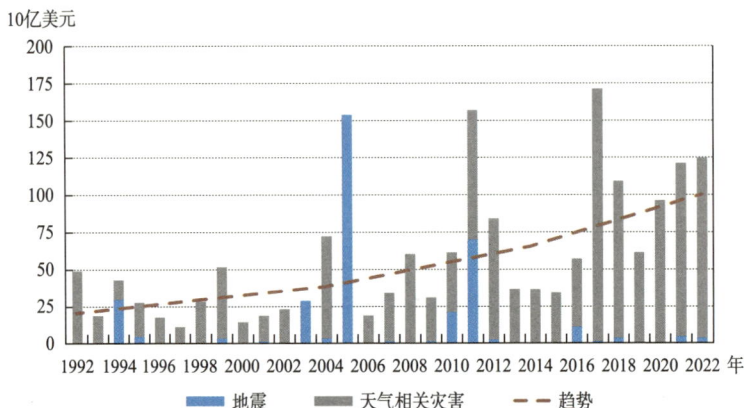

图3 全球巨灾保险损失变化

（资料来源：瑞再研究院）

具体而言，基于Sigma数据和近年自然灾害发生情况，归纳了全球巨灾的几个主要长期发展趋势：

在过去40年间，热带气旋和强对流风暴两大天气类型对全球保险损失的贡献平均各占30%，基本保持稳定（见图4）。原生灾害热带气旋给美国东海岸地区带来的飓风是对居民和企业的主要威胁[1]。虽然数量不多，但当一场较大飓风来袭时，损失可能非常严重。强对流风暴被归类为次生灾害风险，发生频率更高，在世界各地分布较广，年均损失金额的波动性较小[2]。通常情况下，由强对流风暴造成的损失低于原生灾害损失，但在个别情况下，单个强对流风暴事件造成的保险损失与中等飓风过后的保险损失相当。与此同时，在过去10年中，强对流风暴引起的保险损失占所有巨灾保险损失的比例显著上升。

---

[1] "原生灾害"是指损失规模更大的灾难，尤其是热带气旋、地震和欧洲冬季风暴。事件发生的频率较低，但造成的损失可能是巨大的。

[2] "次生灾害"是一些自然灾害的总称，这些自然灾害通常会造成低到中等规模的损失，但这种损失可能会相对频繁地发生。包括如强对流风暴（包括雷暴、冰雹和龙卷风）、干旱、山火、降雪、山洪暴发和山体滑坡等。

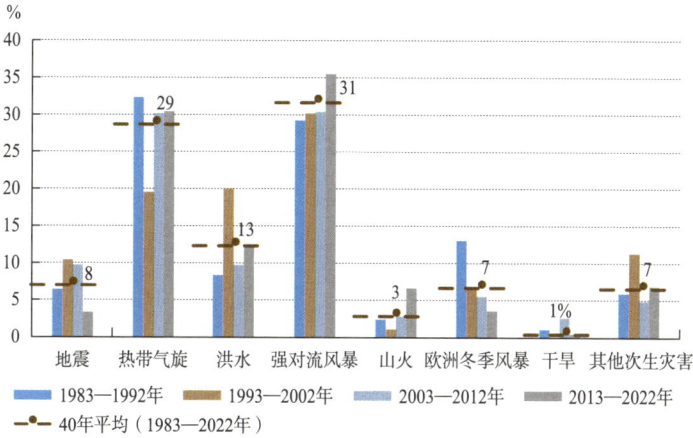

图4　不同灾害类型占巨灾保险损失的份额

(资料来源：瑞再研究院)

　　在过去30年间，森林火灾占巨灾保险损失的比例翻了一番。尽管与森林火灾相关的损失在2022年比较低，但近年来，尤其是在北美（2016年在加拿大，2017年、2018年和2020年在美国加利福尼亚州），山火造成了巨大的破坏和损失。这些事件反映了在荒野和城市交界地带不断增加的人口规模所带来的风险与日俱增，尤其是在加利福尼亚州。这一趋势也可能表明，随着全球变暖，极端高温条件为山火的形成提供了条件，风险不断加剧。预计未来几十年，气候变化和持续的热浪很可能会增加大型山火和干旱天气出现的频率，损失严重程度也会上升。

　　另一个长期趋势是，在过去10年间欧洲冬季风暴和地震等原生灾害造成的损失占巨灾保险损失的比例有所下降。在没有重大灾害出现的情况下，自1990年（冬季风暴"达莉亚"和"薇薇安"）和1999年（冬季风暴"洛萨""马丁""阿纳托尔"）以后，欧洲冬季风暴在巨灾保险损失中所占的比例一直在下降。同样，过去10年中与地震相关的损失也相对较低。虽然地震是罕见的，但与其他原生灾害一样，如果一场大地震发生在人口密集的城市地区时，造成的损失可能是前所未有的。因此，不应低估这种低频率、高破坏性的原生灾害风险。

原生和次生灾害造成的损失程度不断升级，是巨灾保险损失居高不下的主要原因。在各种灾害中，保险理赔金额已经向更高损失的灾害事件集中。按损失严重程度划分，中等损失（10亿~50亿美元的保险损失）和严重损失（超过50亿美元）事件占了大部分的保险损失（见图5）。同时，与极低损失（低于5亿美元）事件相比，这类事件的损失增长速度更快，尽管极低损失事件发生得更频繁。2013—2022年，平均每年发生70起低损失程度的灾害事件，累计造成的保险损失总额为117亿美元。然而，在同一时期内，平均每年仅发生两起严重损失灾害，累计造成的保险损失达344亿美元。

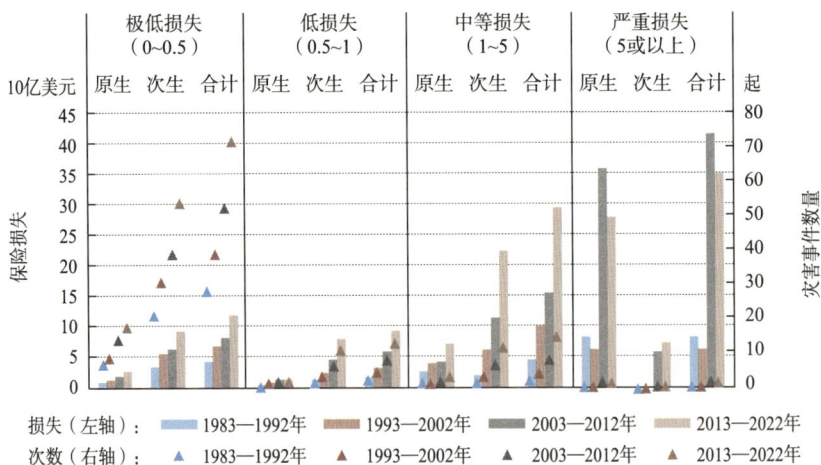

图5　按损失严重程度分类，10年平均巨灾保险损失

（资料来源：瑞再研究院）

二、2022 年中国自然灾害损失情况

2022年，中国自然灾害以洪涝、干旱、风雹、地震和地质灾害为主，台风、低温冷冻和雪灾、沙尘暴、森林草原火灾和海洋灾害等也有不同程度的发生，但全年自然灾害发生情况较往年相对较轻。全年各种自然灾害共造成农作物受灾面积约12 071.6千公顷，因灾死亡失踪554人，倒塌房屋4.7万间，直接经济损失约2 386.5亿元（见图6）。与近5年均值相比，因灾死亡失踪人数、倒塌房屋数量和直接经济损失分别下降30.8%、63.3%和25.3%。

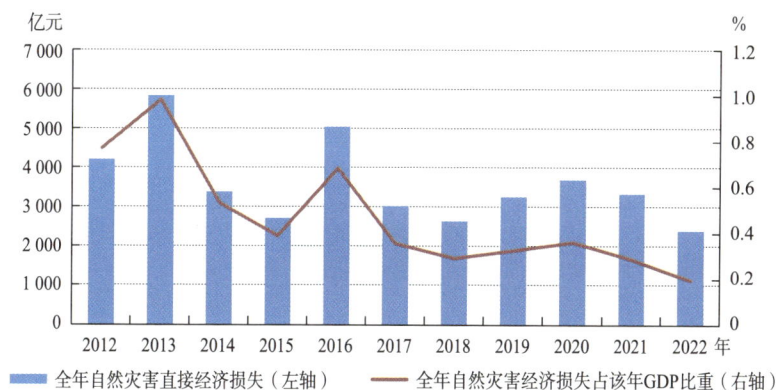

图6　中国自然灾害直接经济损失及占该年GDP比重

（资料来源：应急管理部、瑞再研究院）

典型灾害事件方面，受极端灾害天气影响，2022年发生了珠江流域性洪水、辽河支流绕阳河决口、青海大通及四川平武和北川山洪灾害、长江流域夏秋冬连旱，以及南方地区森林火灾等重大灾害，四川泸定6.8级地震造成重大人员伤亡。从时间分布来看，全年自然灾害主要集中于夏秋季。

洪涝灾害仍然是造成直接损失最大的自然灾害类型（见图7），2022年珠江流域连续形成两次流域性较大洪水，北江出现自1915年以来最大洪水，辽河发生自1995年以来最大洪水，黄河、淮河、海河汛情总体平稳。全年洪涝灾害共造成直接经济损失约1 289亿元，占全年自然灾害直接经济损失的54%。

2022年干旱同样造成较为严重的直接经济损失，约512.8亿元，占全年自然灾害直接经济损失的22%，相较2021年增长1.5倍，其中长江流域发生历史罕见夏秋冬连旱，影响范围广、造成损失重，是有完整实测资料以来最严重的气象水文干旱。

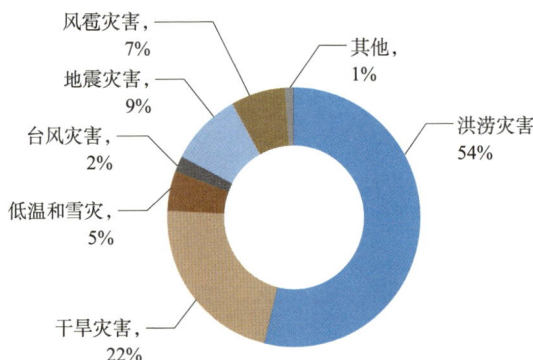

图7 各类型自然灾害占2022年自然灾害直接经济损失的比重

（资料来源：应急管理部、瑞再研究院）

近年来，中国自然灾害保险损失呈现出的一个趋势是单次自然灾害事件造成的保险损失均较为严重。例如，2021年的河南暴雨造成125亿元保险损失，2020年的长江洪水造成150亿元的保险损失。在灾害严重程度相对较轻、直接经济损失数额相对较低的2022年，这一趋势仍有延续，2022年长江流域的夏秋冬连旱造成的农业保险损失高达55亿元以上。

保险再保险业在提供自然灾害保障方面不断发挥积极作用。根据中国保险行业协会相关数据统计，2022年保险业涉及重大自然灾害的赔付约635.52亿元，投入防灾减灾资金约2.34亿元，投入防灾减灾人力约13.61万人次，预计减少灾害损失约22.77亿元。在灾害救援方面，保险再保险业协助救援受灾人员约14.49万人次，协助救援受灾机动车7.13万辆次，捐赠资金约705.43万元，捐赠物资折算金额约2 186.83万元，捐赠保险的保额约4 736.64亿元。总体而言，保险再保险业在自然灾害相关的赔付和援助方面承担了重要的社会责任。

同时，再保险行业在自然灾害风险量化建模研究、综合防范风险方面也有突出成就。2022年，中国洪涝巨灾模型1.0正式发布，这一模型突破多项前沿技术，首次实现全国范围洪涝损失的量化计算，填补了国内洪涝巨灾模型的空白，完善了中国巨灾模型体系建设。信瑞智农农业风险管理平台2.0版本，通过提供实时风险评估报告，为各级政府、农户和保险公司防灾减损、灾后救援和风险管理提供量化参考。2022年，在充分考虑巨灾保险多样化需求的基础上，再保险公司自主研发了集定价和产品设计于一体的"禹志"巨灾保险定制平台，将自身累积的指数保险产品设计经验融入先进的算法模型，不仅能够为保险公司提供定价指导，也可以为使用者提供自动化的巨灾保险产品设计建议。

三、自然灾害长期风险驱动因素对中国保险和再保险行业的经验启示

（一）自然灾害损失的风险驱动因素

自2017年以来，因自然灾害导致的年均保险损失超过1 100亿美元，较前5年平均水平（520亿美元）增加1倍以上。自然灾害事件及相关保险损失不断上升，需重新审视驱动长期趋势的影响因素。表2显示了整个保险价值链上的主要风险驱动因素。总体而言，过去两年巨灾保险损失上升并非由于自然灾害物理事件本身的异常表现，更大程度上是由于风险敞口价值不断增加、通货膨胀上升和风险经验（数据）不足等因素的综合影响。

表2　　　　　　　　　　　**2022年保险损失的驱动因素**

风险	脆弱性	风险敞口	社会经济影响
• 两类重大灾害的影响（热带气旋和强对流风暴） • 拉尼娜（ENSO模式）现象的影响 • 气候变化对天气灾害的影响	• 过时的和/或已更新的建筑规范 • 防洪基础设施不完善 • 新型基础设施（如屋顶太阳能电池板）	• 风险敞口地区的经济发展和资本累积 • 城市化和城区扩张	• 高通胀（尤其是建筑成本高企） • 利益分配（AOB）规则的不当使用

资料来源：瑞再研究院。

近年来人口快速增长、建筑区域迅速扩大、有形资产价值不断累积，导致重大天气灾害造成的损失显著上升。例如，尽管2022年北美飓风季飓风表现相对温和[①]，但飓风"伊恩"在人口密集的佛罗里达

[①] 2022年北美飓风季处于历史"平均水平"，一共发生14个有命名的风暴，符合1991—2020年年均14.4个的平均水平，仅发生2个严重飓风（三级或以上），与保险相关的风暴活动低于预测水平，也低于历史年均3.2个严重风暴的平均水平。资料来源："大西洋飓风展望和摘要档案"，《背景信息：北大西洋飓风季节》，国家天气局气候预测中心。

西部登陆就造成了估计500亿~650亿美元的保险损失。飓风"伊恩"9月底登陆佛罗里达西部时为4级风暴，袭击的地区近年来人口迅速增长、建筑区迅速扩大、有形资产价值迅速累积。自1970年以来，该风暴登陆地区人口增长了620%，大幅高于佛罗里达州（+217%）和全美（+65%）的人口增长率。防洪基础设施的不完善也是导致巨额损失的因素之一。飓风"伊恩"登陆地点的周边地区同样遭受了大规模风暴潮的袭击，尽管很多建筑能够抵御大风，但针对高水位潮水的防范措施不足导致风暴潮造成了更大的损失。此外，近年来佛罗里达州较为宽松的诉讼环境，尤其是保险金转让规则引发的社会性通胀，也是导致财产险理赔增加的主要因素之一[①]。

　　大坝蓄水量和土壤渗水能力饱和加剧了洪涝灾害的发生风险。大城市土壤封闭面积的增加是洪水损失上升的主要因素。例如，2022年2—3月，发生在澳大利亚东部的一系列洪水造成43亿美元的保险损失。过去20年，澳大利亚洪水导致年均损失预计上升约7%，城市化、人口增长、防洪基础设施不完善和土壤封闭面积的增加导致洪水相关保险损失呈上升趋势。

　　2022年因全球供应链中断及持续的疫情管控措施导致的高通胀也造成了建筑重建成本上涨，使灾后重建费用高于预期水平。2022年发达市场的平均通胀率为7%，新兴经济体达9%。在新冠疫情暴发初期，供应链中断和各国大规模刺激政策引发高通胀，而俄乌冲突导致的食

---

① 佛罗里达州的诉讼环境，尤其是保险金转让规则引发的社会性通胀，同样加剧了佛罗里达的保险损失。保险金转让规则是将保险权利转让给第三方，使该方有权在无须原保单持有人参与的情况下，提出理赔请求、作出维修决定和收取理赔金的约定。在飓风"艾尔玛"中，保险金转让规则导致理赔金额增加10%~20%。该规则导致财产险市场承压，佛罗里达的个人财产险保费是全国平均水平的3倍。参考"飓风'伊恩'凸显了佛罗里达存在的保险金转让规则问题：是否会作出改变？"Verisk，2020年；"极端欺诈和诉讼导致佛罗里达的个人财产险市场停滞"，保险信息研究院，2022年6月23日。

品和能源价格暴涨进一步加剧了通胀压力。价格上涨导致建筑物、车辆和其他可保资产的名义价值上升，进而推高了巨灾引起的保险理赔金额。该影响在建筑业尤其明显，因材料和熟练工人短缺导致的成本上升，进而推高了与建筑维修费用相关的保险理赔。在美国，2022年的建筑成本预计比2020年初上升了40%。

缺乏对风险敞口的（数据）经验可能导致灾害风险被低估。2022年，南非德班地区连续数天的暴雨引发了洪水和山体滑坡，预计造成15亿美元的保险损失。损失包括作为国际供应链环节之一的工业区被损坏所引发的保险理赔，但灾前该风险并未被考虑在内。该事件表明风险敞口相关数据不足可能导致保险公司低估风险并导致超出预期的损失。当今世界的商业和工业运营都实现了全球化，不同领域之间的关联日益错综复杂。为提升风险评估的准确性，保险再保险公司需要充分了解企业在生产场所和内部流程方面的具体状况，增强建模能力，以覆盖全球供应链所涉及的越来越多的地区，以及这些地区面临的不同风险。

（二）自然灾害损失给中国保险和再保险行业的经验与启示

2022年全球自然灾害经验再次表明，保险再保险业在应对快速变化的风险格局时依然面临严峻的挑战。过去10年，自然灾害风险建模能力取得了显著进展，但仍存在进一步提升的空间。2022年的保险损失经验为我们提供了一些启示（见表3）。虽然全球各地区巨灾风险特征和管理存在差异，但由此吸取的经验教训同样值得中国保险再保险行业学习。

表3 2022年发生的灾害事件和吸取的教训

事件	地区	估计的保险损失	吸取的教训
飓风"伊恩"	北美洲	500亿~650亿美元	一场风暴足以产生严重的后果
澳大利亚洪水	亚太地区	430亿美元	风险敞口增加和通胀推动损失上升
南非洪水	欧洲、中东及非洲地区	150亿美元	数据缺乏透明度影响风险评估
强对流风暴	北美洲	260亿美元	财产损失上升的趋势仍将持续
法国冰雹	欧洲、中东及非洲地区	50亿美元	需要重新评估市场回归期假设
欧洲冬季风暴	欧洲、中东及非洲地区	41亿美元	更大的风暴将会到来

资料来源：瑞再研究院。

1．分享特定灾害的细化风险敞口数据是关键

与现有风险敞口相关的全面数据是所有承保流程的基础。收集和传输颗粒度充分的风险敞口数据仍有改善的空间，尤其是有关次生灾害，特别是洪水和冰雹的数据。保险再保险业长期关注原生灾害，这方面的建模能力很强。就特定灾害的风险敞口和模型结果共享而言，次生灾害并未得到同样的重视。这有时会阻碍保险公司承保这些风险。次生灾害导致的保险损失多年来呈上升趋势，有时甚至达到中等原生灾害事件造成的损失水平。为确保风险评估的完整性以及掌握次生灾害可能导致的重大潜在损失，如2022年南非布里斯班洪水，保险业需要为这些风险敞口制定与原生灾害相同的监控管理措施，并分享风险敞口数据和模型结果。

2．在高通胀时期，最新的风险敞口数据至关重要

另一点是要确保更新风险敞口数据，以了解最新的通胀形势。例如，过去两年通胀飙升，导致房屋重建成本随之上升。通胀是导致2022年2—3月澳大利亚洪水造成严重损失的因素之一。重建成本之所以高于保险再保险行业预计的水平，是因为风险评估并未完全考虑全

球供应链持续中断以及与疫情相关的限制措施引发的通胀影响。

3．风险评估应及时反映快速变化的风险格局

模型和风险评估需要反映所有风险驱动因素，比如土壤封闭、用于缓释风险的新的基建资产、建筑规范的更新、气候变化影响和社会性通胀。重要的是了解所有相关风险驱动因素的变化，并且前瞻性地考虑这些因素。如果根据短期影响（比如通胀上升或预期通胀上升）调整模型结果，承保决定就能够确保充分的风险评估。

4．选择合适的观察窗口并消除历史损失数据偏差

过往的损失经验是自然灾害风险评估的重要依据。选择的观察窗口应当针对特定的灾害，既限于最近的历史时期，又要具有前瞻性，以掌握重要的发展状况，如天气情况的变化。此外，需要对历史数据进行转换，以反映当前的风险环境。仅仅根据通胀和经济增长趋势进行调整可能导致低估风险程度。对于历史损失更加全面和代表性的趋势分析和去偏，还应考虑重建和维修成本的增速，这通常高于消费价格的上涨幅度，且有形资产价值的增速通常高于经济增长率。将所有灾害和地区特定风险相关的驱动因素考虑在内，包括城市发展的变化、向易遭受极端天气事件影响的地区迁居以及风险减量基础设施的完善，可以有效地消除历史损失数据的偏差。

5．有时作出大胆改变是必要的

定期更新模型持续改善风险展望。所有模型输入值和/或承保决定的更新对于应对迅速变化的次生灾害（比如，山火和强对流风暴）尤其重要。大多数自然灾害事件会留下经验教训，需要行业将它们运用到风险评估的实践中。在理想情况下，这些经验学习是小幅度和易于消化的。但是，有时作出大胆改变也是必要和适当的。例如，2022年

法国冰雹和澳大利亚洪水提供的损失经验表明有必要重新评估相关回归期假设。

6．2022年灾害事件损失的严重性是由气候变化以外的因素所导致的

从科学角度看，将气旋、冰雹等极端天气归因于气候变化的说法缺乏依据。当前，自然灾害导致损失上升的主要驱动因素是风险敞口的上升、风险暴露的地区城镇的集中，以及最近高通胀加剧了脆弱性。极端天气自身的异常表现比是否归咎于气候变化更重要。尽管如此，财产险核保人员应当持续关注气候变化影响以及风险模型对这类风险的反馈程度。

四、总结

近六年来，自然灾害保险损失的持续上升，再次印证了近30年来巨灾损失年均增长5%~7%的长期趋势，预计未来仍将持续。单一巨灾事件造成的损失严重性日益上升，是驱动这一趋势的主要原因。对于暴露于自然灾害风险的地区，经济增长、城市化和人口增长导致风险敞口持续上升。自2017年以来，灾害活动日益频繁推升了巨灾保险需求，是驱动当前保险再保险市场走强的因素之一。再保险费率自2018年以来呈上升趋势，且势头在2023年1月的续转中有所强化。过去两年，通胀上升至40年以来的高位水平，成为近期再保险续转价格上涨的催化剂。通胀将推升可保资产的价值，进而使理赔金额进一步增加。此外，由于现有模型是否能充分反映风险仍然存在不确定性，投资者风险偏好有所下降。2022年发达市场央行快速收紧货币政策，大幅上调利率导致资金成本上升，再保险行业和相关投资者因而进一步

减少了资本供给。风险敞口上升与风险偏好下降共同作用，导致费率上涨、自留比例上升以及承保条件更加严格。

保险再保险业是巨灾风险的管理者，并已经为多种风险搭建了先进的仿真模型。需要加强对灾害的监控，同时加强对风险敞口、理赔数据及模型结果的收集、更新和分享。保险行业长期以来一直对原生灾害进行监测，但对次生灾害风险的关注度还不够高。近年来，洪灾和冰雹等次生灾害的发生日益频繁，相关损失一直在上升，保险业需要对灾害模型和数据可得性进行升级和扩容，在应对所有灾害风险时应保持前瞻性。同时，在评估次生灾害风险时，作为核心基准的历史损失数据需要系统性消除偏差，以体现实时的、针对特定地点的风险变化状况，从而反映出相关因素互相影响的复杂性及其变化趋势。这意味着风险定价还需要考虑到诸多不断变化的变量对风险格局的影响，如通胀对灾后重建成本的影响、社会性通胀、城市化、土壤封闭以及人口向风险地区流动等情况。因此，保险行业需加强承保纪律，使定价能够准确反映风险敞口的长期发展状况，从而增强保险作为社会稳定器的重要作用。

专题五

中国保险科技发展情况及展望

一、中国保险科技发展背景

（一）中国保险科技发展的三个阶段

第一阶段是2000—2013年的信息化阶段。中国加入WTO，中国经济和中国保险业高速发展，保险企业面临激烈的市场竞争与管理手段滞后问题。该阶段的主要特征是保险公司通过承保、理赔、财务、OA等信息化系统建设，实现了手工处理方式向信息化管理手段的迭代。

第二阶段是2013—2022年的互联网或在线化阶段。该阶段的主要特征是保险业全面拥抱"互联网+"，关键词是"移动""在线""流量"。保险业用10年时间基本完成了在互联网上实现保险交易、理赔、运营的全流程在线化。大型保险公司和科技类保险机构多已完成核心系统的"云"化。同时，互联网保险交易已渗透到社交工具、媒体、航旅、视频内容等各种移动互联网场景。该阶段也是中国保险科技创业创新最火热的时期。

第三个阶段是2022年开始的数字化阶段。党的二十大报告指出，要加快建设网络强国、数字中国。2022年1月，原中国银行保险监督管理委员会印发了《关于银行业保险业数字化转型的指导意见》，旨在加快数字经济建设，全面推进银行业和保险业数字化转型。在数字经济和大数据、云计算和人工智能等科技应用的推动下，数字化、智能化成为保险行业科技发展方向。保险企业加快向以客户为中心转型，通过数据、智能赋能前端销售、运营、服务等各业务环节，强调科技数据与业务应用的深度融合，支持全业务流程的数字化、智能化再造升级。

（二）中国保险科技发展的驱动力

1．政策、技术、资本

一是国家宏观政策、保险行业相关重大改革和监管政策为保险科技发展指明了方向，也明确了窗口红利和监管红线，对保险科技发展起到决定性影响；二是技术成熟度是影响保险科技发展的核心因素，保险科技是保险业与新兴技术的组合，日臻成熟的技术与保险结合效果更好，比如很多保险企业在移动互联网、媒体内容上取得了成功；三是资本市场和更为市场化的投资运作是保险科技发展的加速器，适当的资本助力是抢抓红利的推进器，但过度资本化和短期利益为目标的资本化也会伤害创业者。

2．效率、成本、体验

过去，效率提升、成本降低、用户体验改善是一个"不可能三角形"，难以有效协同，但在保险科技加速应用的背景中，一些优秀的保险科技企业实现了三者的共赢，这为保险行业发展提供了巨大价值。2015年既是移动互联网技术走向成熟、高度繁荣的一年，也是互联网投融资最活跃的一年，更是保险业政策红利释放最集中的一年。中国保险科技快速发展，催生了数百家保险科技创业公司，也沉淀出第一批互联网保险头部科技公司。

二、中国保险科技创新发展概览

（一）财产险科技创新

1. 车险

2014—2015年，资本市场围绕"互联网+汽车"生态开启了投资热潮。而在保险领域，以平安财险为首的保险公司车险网销发展逐步成熟，中保信公司成立后，车险的标准化体系逐步建立。2015年3月，商业车险改革试点启动，点燃了互联网车险创业的热潮。这一时期，车险比价平台、UBI等产品开发型企业成为热点。但是，第一批车险创业者低估了中国车险改革的长期性、艰巨性和复杂性。随着车险费改红利预期下的竞争升级和汽车消费外部大环境受挫，车险费改放缓、车险监管升级，此轮创业的大部分公司已经消失在公众视野中。但围绕车险仍然沉淀出一些优秀的保险科技公司。总结这些优秀车险创业公司的特质，主要表现为以下几点：一是技术赋能型企业，创造价值而非单纯的销售或比价平台；二是把握了车险经营的实质（数据、风控、服务）和费改的趋势；三是坚持合规经营并适应车险经营的属地化特征；四是强大的运营和融资能力；五是快速应用移动互联网或AI技术。

随后，商业车险费改革深化开始催生了车险多个领域的创新。车险市场从增量转为存量，竞争日益加剧，以价值挖掘为核心和成本管理、数据和风控科技公司将大有作为。同时，车险的在线化能力逐步完善，从承保到理赔逐步形成线上化闭环服务能力，2B的能力积累也开始延伸到2C服务。随着各类互联网服务基础设施完善，更多便利化的车主服务也通过互联网方式连接优化，显著提升了用户体验，降低了成本，增加了保险公司与用户交互的频度。

（1）车险交易

车险是财产险品类中监管最严、体系化建设最完善的。由于车险产品、费率、预定费用率都有行业标准，是典型的标准化产品，最适合互联网交易。但实际上车险经营的属地化、多渠道和复杂的市场竞争，其本质是非标准化产品。此外，由于复杂、动态的监管政策、制度要求和核保政策，互联网车险想打通新能源智能车机，或在滴滴、百度地图、ETC、中石化易捷等场景中有良好的交易体验也有很大难度。车险科技从业者们前赴后继，用10年时间基本解决了互联网交易问题。

（2）车险风控

车险科技必须围绕车险本质，而保险的本质是经营风险和服务。凯泰铭科技、明觉科技等车险风控公司也成为过去几年车险科技领域的大赢家，他们根据数据、规则算法和延伸服务，将车险理赔风控带入数据化、智能化阶段，改变了过往静态看待风控的逻辑，实现了用户体验提升、效率提升、成本降低的共赢。

（3）车险理赔和后市场

在时代大潮下，汽车配件、维修等后市场企业也完成了信息化、在线化，同时保险行业理赔成本管理和服务品质管理深化，一些保险企业联合生态链伙伴，通过科技平台建设，将车险的保、修、配进行数字化集成，整合供应链，合理配置维修资源，优化理赔成本和客户体验。比如，由人保金融服务有限公司发起设立的邦邦汽服，利用科技创新与数智驱动，深度融合车后产业，建设"维修服务企业数字化连接平台"和"事故车配件供应链平台"，服务保险主业。

过去数年，车险科技围绕交易、定价、数据标准化、智能化风控等领域，均取得了显著的创新成果。新的挑战在于现有风险管理能力的上限受限于保险行业当前的数据维度和颗粒度，短期内难以出现质的飞跃。要想突破"瓶颈"或"弯道超车"，车险经营也必须完成"从车到人"的角色转变，比如车车科技提出的"科技·乘·人·致美"。在以人为本的逻辑下，经营、数据、风控、服务都会发生质变，而当车险产品本身突破传统思维框架，延展到用车相关服务，进一步发展至围绕用户的综合金融保险服务后，成本、风控均需要重新定义。另一个关键因素是互联网的发展。移动互联网的进一步发展将使世界变得更扁平、交互更高频，AI使人连接世界的能力变得更强，数据资产和社交资产的价值越发明显。伴随车险改革不断进展，互联网演变的特殊资产价值都将通过市场给予体现。

2．其他财产险

（1）房屋和家财保险

中国房地产发展经历高速期后已进入存量时代。不仅仅是房地产行业，地产建设、销售带动的大量产业链企业，如家具、装修、家电等，都面临严峻的生存问题。随着房屋年限增长，维修的需求量也在大幅上升。未来房产的价值，可能更多取决于物业管理和房屋的升级。近年来，围绕旧房升级改造、局部一体化定制、智能化升级、适老化改造等新兴业态快速发展，为客户体验更好的"服务型"家财险、"嵌入式"家财险提供了肥沃的土壤。以飞鸟鱼保险科技等为代表的科技企业，基于对物业、地产、商业等多类客户风险痛点的深度洞察和理解认知，凭借理赔与维修服务供应链的独特优势，致力于服务型家财险的创新升级。

（2）宠物和3C保险

以智能手机为主的3C产品和快速升温的宠物热也是数字化、媒体化时代的产物。虽然这两类业务总规模有限，但全球各地均不乏从事该领域的保险科技公司，国内如平安、大地、众安等头部险企和蚂蚁金服等互联网企业也高度关注该领域发展。因为智能手机和宠物与背后的使用者高度相关，其衍生的保险和商业价值都颇具想象空间。

（二）健康险科技创新

2019年12月1日，新版《健康险管理办法》正式实施，叠加国家医疗改革深化、老龄化不断加深、消费者健康保障需求觉醒等新形势，健康险面临重要的历史机遇。借助互联网和科技发展，健康险的快速发展更是如虎添翼。一系列医养健康重要文件连续出台的背后，是中国老龄化加速和巨大健康保障缺口的现实问题，同时也反映出健康险的供给侧从产品、风控、服务等方面，均无法有效满足日益增长的客户需求的现状，未来健康险领域具有较大发展机遇。

1．新型健康险产品开发

目前，中国已有5 000余款各类医疗、健康险产品。在保险科技与创新队伍中，有一批专注于健康险产品创新的研发企业，有些专注通过产品创新为客户提供更高性价比的保险产品，有些专注优质医疗服务网络和风险管理、创新用户体验的服务型健康险产品。互联网对中国健康险传播发展起到了放大器作用，数字化让健康险创新更有据可循，为增强与客户的互动性和产品设计的科学性提供了较大的支持。例如，英仕健康致力于百万医疗险、中端医疗险，爱选科技致力于长期健康险定价和数字化产品研发，都是这方面的突出代表。

2．健康险风控与交易

有效的风险管理是健康险高质量、可持续发展的重中之重。近年来，该领域出现了前海再保科技、深圳派氪斯科技、商涌科技等多家专注医疗、意外、健康风控与智能核保的保险科技公司。很多保险再保险公司也积极投入健康险智能核保和风控建设，已从早期的健康告知等发展为以数据和经验模型为核心的智能核保引擎，涵盖非标、慢病等过去无法定价和承保的群体。

3．健康险TPA和服务运营

近年来，保险客户和保险机构对健康管理和医疗服务的需求与日俱增。健康险TPA和服务运营整合方等为解决医疗服务资源分散、优质资源稀缺等问题，运用科技手段优化配置资源、连接保险与医药产业两端。代表性的科技公司如优加建康、镁信健康、圆心惠保等，提供"医—护—健—药—械—险"的"一站式"健康管理及保险产品定制开发服务，为健康险运营与服务管理提供重要支持助力。

4．健康险细分市场——数字化团体员工福利解决方案

在短期健康险中，企业补充医疗保险仍占据50%的份额。过去，优质团险业务集中于外企和国企，新兴科技企业和中小企业难以获得标准化的承保和理赔服务，导致团险的普及遇到阻力。在企业服务的数字化商保方面，以保险极客、鼎源万家等团险科技服务商为代表，主要服务国内高成长、创新型企业，保险服务已覆盖数万家企业、数百万员工及家庭。

（三）保险交易与保险中介科技创新

保险科技的核心就是要解决保险交易的问题，即解决交易信息不对称和风险识别颗粒度等影响交易效率和成本的问题。保险科技是保险行业经验模型与先进数字化技术的结合体。这也能很好地解释，为什么中国保险科技发展过程中涌现的大量公司，无论从单一体量、公司估值，还是总量占比，切入"交易"的保险科技公司都是规模最大、

占比最多的。那些热衷于解决交易端问题的科技公司，如互联网报价、智能核保、互联网保险产品研发、网络分销、数字化代理人交易工具、短视频等公司远比2B的信息化软件公司发展得更快。

1．互联网保险交易平台

2015年6月，保险代理人考试取消，激起了新一轮寿险业代理人增员热潮，代理人存量数量几年间由300万人增加至800万人。借助互联网创业大潮，最早一批以互联网技术和代理人融合的保险科技企业踏上了快速发展的道路，代表性公司如保险师、i云保、小雨伞等。随着互联网保险深入发展，产销分离、分工协作的数字化保险组织开始崭露头角，专业管理型代理公司（MGA[①]）快速发展。

2．保险科技赋能专业销售与AI在线化销售

专业化、职业化是行业主体未来发展的核心优势，在流量红利、产品红利、人口红利出尽，只有专业化和职业化才能带来边际效益递增，专职队伍的长尾效应日趋明显。以年青一代为代表的数字化原生保险销售人员将成为未来保险专业化、职业化的中坚力量，而当前保险公司、专业中介的主要组织模式都与未来解放劳动力要求和职业化队伍的诉求有显著差距，这也为未来专业中介市场提供了巨大的想象空间。服务于交易的保险科技创新也从服务代理人增员"人口红利"向赋能专业化、职业化销售人员转变。

[①] MGA，全称为Managing General Agent，即管理型总代理，是一种特殊的保险中介机构，指为保险人履行一部分管理和承保功能的机构。而后逐渐发展为一种特殊的代理模式，指保险人将其承保权限授权给一家代理人，代理人经授权后代理保险公司签订保险合同。MGA向保险公司提供产品管理、分销管理、精算、核保、理赔等服务，获得保险公司分配的承保额，进行产品配置后发放给保险经纪机构进行销售。

　　寿险业正在进行一场深刻的组织变革，依托大规模保险代理人销售的时代已经一去不复返。依托流量、用户经营和精准的数据标签、用户行为与偏好分析，以及企业微信等数字化工具，人身险在线销售率先在蚂蚁保、微保、水滴、谱蓝保等平台落地生根，组织架构更为扁平化，人均产能大幅提升，且在线交易全流程可回溯，显著降低了客户投诉、退保等问题。

3．保险内容平台

　　2015年，《互联网保险监管暂行办法》等政策发布，鼓励互联网保险和第三方平台发展。移动互联网的普及促进了网络媒体的演变，从微信公众号移动图文平台到抖音、小红书、B站等短视频平台，每个人都有机会成为保险UP主，直接或间接地从事保险活动。在这轮大潮中，为"保险内容创造者"提供技术、产品和运营支持的慧择网、蜗牛保险、小帮规划、多保鱼、深蓝保等保险内容平台发展迅速。

三、中国保险科技发展对再保险行业的启示

　　"再保险+保险科技"是再保险行业服务数字时代保险高质量发展的重要力量。

（一）"突破性"创新与背后的再保险力量

　　2017—2021年，金融保险监管逐步转向以防风险和风险处置为核心的阶段。互联网技术在应用端的发展也逐步走向成熟，互联网保险第三方平台发展进入成熟期，大型互联网平台大多涉足了保险业务，一些头部保险数字化中介创业公司也已有相当规模，保险品类涵盖了车险、意外险、医疗险、宠物保险、家财险、场景责任险和各类长期

人身险业务。这一时期保险科技的发展方向开始向垂直细分领域和产业端发展，特别是医疗健康领域是其中的突出亮点。

2016年，众安尊享e生在互联网正式推出并热卖，形成良好的用户口碑，带动了大量保险机构和互联网平台参与到"百万医疗"类产品的销售热潮中。在百万医疗产品研发和推向市场的启动阶段，再保险公司发挥了重要支撑作用。

另一个有代表性的健康险产品创新是特药险。2018年，中再寿险与镁信健康、华夏保险合作推出了国内首个含有特药责任的保险产品"华夏医保通"。2019年4月，镁信健康携手微保、泰康在线等推出"药神保·抗癌特药保障计划"，并迅速成为市场热销产品。此后，特药险迎来发展高潮，成为百万医疗险之后又一市场热销的健康险产品。2020年，中再寿险与镁信健康结成全面战略合作伙伴关系，以特药服务为亮点的惠民保新产品开始加速推广。截至2022年底，惠民保已覆盖29个省级行政区，保障范围约1.58亿人次，263款产品共纳入了300多种海内外特药责任，为更多人群送去重要的特药保障。

如今，百万医疗险与特药险的原型已演化为各种健康险形态，无论是百万医疗的普惠版、火遍全国的惠民保产品，还是长期医疗险、防癌险、中端医疗险，都以百万医疗险原型为基本逻辑，同时大部分产品均覆盖了特药责任。

在这两个重要的突破性创新中，有两个共性特点值得关注：一是产品创新均得到了再保险公司的大力支持；二是均通过专业保险科技公司与互联网保险平台的合作实现市场推广与热销。

百万医疗险和特药险的突破性创新已验证了再保险与保险科技、互联网保险合作创新的重要价值，也找到了一把打开数字时代保险增长大门的钥匙，用以高效弥合广大人民群众日益增长的保险保障需求与不平衡不充分的保险市场供给之间的矛盾。

（二）再保险与保险科技的全面融合

再保险公司积极拥抱保险科技创新，通过加强自身研发投入，与保险科技生态伙伴的深度合作，在核心市场及未来主要新兴市场持续发力，强化为保险行业赋能，深化保险科技创新与保险业务场景的全面融合。

在数字化转型与保险科技创新合作中，由于经营逻辑和发展目标差异化，再保险公司更关注专业与市场，直保公司则更关注内部的信息化升级与管理数字化。传统上认为，再保险公司距离一线业务和客户较远是一种劣势，但在数字化转型与科技创新过程中，再保险公司因不需要过度关注传统保险经营的销售逻辑和内部管理要求，在与保险科技公司的合作与创新中走在了前列。

由于技术变革和用户迁移，传统保险业发展中的诸多经验逻辑和管理要求正在重塑。互联网时代的特征是以客户为中心，产品逻辑、运营逻辑、响应速度、客户体验都对保险行业提出了全新的要求。再保险公司与直保公司相比更具优势也更为专注，更为聚焦科技创新与产业创新的生态蓝海。

（三）再保险与保险科技天然契合

再保险公司与保险科技天然契合，特别是在互联网、数字化时代，两者结合更加如鱼得水。一是再保险公司离交易更近，更符合技术的本质，例如再保险公司是最早参与区块链技术合作与可信交易平台建设的主体。二是再保险公司更关注风险，具备深厚的业务实践经验和专业风险管理经验，与保险科技企业有很好的互补性。保险经验积累、专业风险识别与管理技术、方法论和洞察力正是很多科技公司和大型互联网企业所缺乏的。三是再保险公司对保险行业整体和相关产业的发展有更宏观和整体的观察视角，可以从国家、产业发展层面把握未来的机遇与挑战。同时，再保险公司也在战略层面更加关注科技发展和新兴技术在各行业的应用前景。四是再保险公司了解与之合作的保险公司的经营情况，保持长期良好的信任与互动关系。保险科技公司通过与再保险的合作，可以更为高效地与众多保险公司建立合作关系并获得相关信息。五是再保险公司是多渠道数据的集成方，其多触角的平台属性和相对中立的第三方角色，可以成为数据源的有效整合方，通过与多家保险公司或科技公司的业务合作，数据产品可以得到快速反馈和改进。同时，这种一对多的平台可以降低数据和产品的使用成本，让更多中小保险机构和科技公司享受数据和算法的红利。

（四）保险科技发展加速再保直保化

近年来，再保险公司从专注于风险洞察逐步升级到对风险交易的高度关注，但再保险公司并不拥有直保公司庞大的销售、运营管理体系，产品研发、销售组织、理赔运营仍然高度依赖直保公司。伴随过去十年互联网保险和中国保险科技的全面发展，科技在各个保险交易环节广泛渗透，直保公司与再保公司的传统合作模式正在发生改变，再保直保化已呈发展之势。以近年发展迅猛的百万医疗险、特药险等为例，再保险公司与互联网科技公司、保险机构、互联网平台深度合作，研判洞察风险，积极尝试创新，在创新业务早期推动中发挥了至关重要的作用，在创新业务推向市场过程中承担了产品设计、尾部风险保障等核心职能。保障型、服务型健康险是保险业未来发展的大市场之一，在与保险科技公司、直保公司共创共建过程中，再保险公司逐步积累了丰富的产品开发与核保核赔经验，不断加强与科技公司的合作力度与科技投入的信心。

在互联网、数字化、智能化时代，传统保险公司庞大的销售组织和较长的管理链条正在成为转型发展的阻力之一。2022—2023年，保险行业数字化转型的呼声越发响亮，转型的动力也更为迫切。但相比于互联网公司和保险科技公司，传统保险机构轻装上阵仍然面临很多困难，例如用户的迁移、市场与渠道的变化，都使保险公司面临越发突出的成本和经营压力。数字化时代的机遇、保险行业整体转型的挑战，赋予再保险公司发展新的形势与任务。再保险公司需要加速再保直保化，依托长期积累的专业能力、品牌价值，积极拥抱创新，与拥有数字化基因、产业供应链交付能力的科技企业合作，在医疗健康、房屋住建、新能源等领域深度挖掘机会，为自身发展锻造新的优势。

（五）"保险科技+MGA"推动再保中介化

中国保险科技公司的核心组成部分是互联网第三方保险平台，或称数字化保险专业中介，他们是数字化保险时代和新兴保险市场发展的主要推动力量。虽然近年来保险公司互联网保险直营占比有所提升，但仍然难以撼动数字化保险专业中介作为互联网保险渠道的主体地位。相关机构预测，互联网保险保费收入到2030年或将超过2.85万亿元，比2022年增长近5倍，整体理赔金额也将接近1万亿元[①]。

从国际与国内趋势来看，近10年来再保险公司正在深化与具备MGA属性和能力的保险科技公司的合作。例如，RGA美再全资子公司RGAX于2022年3月参与了深圳派氪司科技有限公司Pre-A轮融资。派

---

① 数据来源：《2023年互联网保险理赔创新服务研究报告》，中国社会科学院金融研究所、中国社会科学院保险与经济发展研究中心，2023年5月发布。

氪司成立于2020年，专注于保险风控，主要针对保险领域四大风险构建风控服务体系，包括恶意欺诈、高额风险、健康风险和续期风险。又如保险科技Akur8成立于2018年，可服务于保险公司和MGA公司，合作伙伴包括AXA、Generali、Munich Re、Canopius和Tokio Marine Kiln等大型保险再保险集团。Akur8依托其"透明人工智能"技术改变保险定价，旨在通过自动化风险和需求建模来增强非寿险公司的定价流程，使精算师和定价团队能够做出更好、更快的决策。再保险公司与派氪司、Akur8等保险科技公司的合作，既可以借助科技公司的能力提升自身研发效率、把握更多市场机会，又能借助科技公司的合作网络和销售能力，将再保险技术能力迅速转化为再保险业务收入。

（六）科技能力加持下再保险业务创新解决方案

气候变化、城镇化发展带来的巨灾风险不断增加，集成电路、新能源、大数据、生物医药研发、网络安全等新兴风险日益凸显，需要再保险公司进一步创新，提供相适应的解决方案。

保险科技与再保险公司的专业合作，可以依靠对数据的深度挖掘和分析，识别出其中风险可控的部分，从而降低风险的不确定性。通过与专业TPA保险科技公司合作，引入相关智能设备，可以在事前、事中、事后更好地控制风险。再保险公司依托专业引领能力、资本实力和中立平台属性，可以牵头整合分散的承保能力、创新承保解决方案；同时，也可以借鉴国际市场经验，用风险证券化方式，通过资本市场为保险风险的有效分散提供助力。例如，2021年，中再产险在香港成功发行巨灾债券，为减少内地因台风造成的损失风险募资3 000万美元。

科技创新为再保险走向前台提供了重要助力。再保险与保险科技的深度合作、全面融合是双方在专业、品牌等方面历史积淀的不断延伸发展，未来必将创造出更为显著的商业价值与社会价值，为行业整体的高质量发展、为服务经济社会发展与民生保障作出更大的贡献。

专题六

再保险行业数字化转型洞察

当前，信息技术创新日新月异，数字化、网络化、智能化深入发展，成为推动经济社会发展、促进国家治理体系和治理能力现代化、满足人民日益增长的美好生活需求的重要变革力量。数字化转型已是大势所趋。再保险行业作为金融业重要组成部分，伴随新一轮科技革命和产业变革，也在加速商业模式和角色定位转型升级，积极培育数字化能力，重塑竞争优势，以数字化转型为驱动，加快实现高质量发展。

一、数字化转型的背景与动因

（一）数字经济发展势不可当，带动商业模式变革

在全球科技创新进入空前密集活跃期的新发展阶段，以区块链、人工智能、网络安全、物联网、云计算、大数据为代表的新一代信息技术呈现群体性爆发式发展，与传统产业加速深度融合，推动世界进入数字时代。数字经济也被视为撬动全球经济的新杠杆。据测算，数字化程度每提高10%，人均GDP将增长0.5%~0.62%。近年来，中国数字经济规模保持快速增长，2022年数字经济规模达到50.2万亿元，总

量稳居世界第二，同比名义增长103%，占GDP比重提升至41.5%[①]，成为稳定经济增长的关键动力。科技创新与数字经济快速发展正在改变全球企业的商业模式。对于保险再保险业而言，新技术正在深度融入产业端价值链，提升产业风险识别的分辨率，增强产业风险数字化认知能力，孕育风险管理模式发生根本变革，直接影响保险行业底层经营逻辑。一是风险精细量化识别可实现保险产品个性化设计，使保险保障更加精准，从"千人一面"发展为"千人千面"；二是风险数字化认知使保险行业从事后风险补偿向事前风险预防转变，从风险的等量管理向风险的减量管理转变。这将对保险行业的商业模式、服务模式、经营模式带来深刻变革。

（二）国家与监管政策要求，指明战略发展方向

《中华人民共和国国民经济和社会发展第十四个五年规划和2035年远景目标纲要》中明确提出，"稳妥发展金融科技，加快金融机构数字化转型"。自2020年以来，原中国银保监会先后下发《关于推动银行业和保险业高质量发展的指导意见》《关于推进财产保险业务线上化发展的指导意见》《推动财产保险业高质量发展三年行动方案（2020—2022）》等文件，鼓励和支持保险企业加强科技赋能、加快数字化转型。2021年底，中国保险行业协会下发《保险科技"十四五"发展规划》，首次从全行业的高度对保险业数字化发展予以梳理规划，并制定了一系列具有可操作性的具体落实目标。例如，在科技投入方面，规划提出推动行业实现信息技术投入占比超过1%、信息科技人员占比超过5%的目标；在服务能力方面，提出推动行业实现业务线上化率超

---

① 数据来源：《数字中国发展报告（2022）》，国家互联网信息办公室。

过90%、线上化产品比例超过50%、线上化客户比例超过60%、承保自动化率超过70%、核保自动化率超过80%、理赔自动化率超过40%的目标；在创新应用方面，提出推动行业专利申请数量累计超过2万个的目标，为保险机构制定自身数字化发展规划提供了指导和依据。2022年初，原中国银保监会出台《关于银行业保险业数字化转型的指导意见》，提出到2025年保险业数字化转型取得明显成效，并进一步在机制、方法等方面对数字化转型予以规范和指导。

（三）（再）保险业转型发展内在需求，塑造竞争新优势

在数字化不断加速大背景下，中国（再）保险业也正处于从高速发展向高质量发展的关键时期，行业发展面临深刻变革。一是客户需求不断升级，随着全球化数字化发展下消费市场的变化，保险公司客户的需求向随时随地在线化、个性化、无触感方向发展，消费者期望全渠道、"一站式"的服务体验，特别是新冠疫情进一步加速了这种变化趋势，传统保险公司不能及时获取消费者即时保险需求，这种"低频"的传统保险业务交易模式正面临着数字化保险需求的重大挑战。二是竞争格局正在重构，来自保险同业与跨行业的竞争压力不断增大，以保险科技公司为代表的新竞争者拥有客户、数据、技术等优势，利用数字化保险经营、提供主动式防灾防损服务的新业务模式，逐渐替代保险经纪人、保险公司和再保险公司在业务价值链中的传统角色，颠覆了传统保险产品和服务的供给方式，正在重构保险业务价值链，给传统保险机构带来新的数字化转型挑战。三是新兴风险不断涌现，全球气候变化、大规模疫情暴发、地区冲突加剧、恐怖主义和极端暴力事件、虚拟资产、传统风险演变等带来的新兴风险在对人类社会风险治理和韧性发展带来挑战，同时也蕴含着巨大的保险发展机

遇。新兴风险的认知和管理需要新的数字化技术作为支撑，用以有效识别和认知新兴风险，从而管理风险，开拓新的业务发展领域。总之，面对新的市场竞争环境，（再）保险业希望借助数字化转型，迎接挑战、寻求突破。例如，通过新技术应用，赋能业务发展，改变服务模式，优化内部流程，实现降本增效；通过数字化转型，打通行业内外价值链上下游，构建协同发展生态圈，形成竞争新优势；通过组织变革，成立单独科技实体，以期与自身业务深度融合，提升核心竞争力。

二、再保险行业数字化转型实践经验

从全球视角看，国际再保险公司的数字化转型起步较早、实践经验较为丰富，转型成效更为显著，对国内再保险业具有很好的参考借鉴价值。从国内实践看，中国再保险业的数字化转型仍处于初始阶段，但行业整体高度重视，近年来不断加速转型步伐，取得了一定的创新突破，在实践中探索走出了一条具有中国特色的再保险数字化转型之路。以下从典型案例的总结梳理出发，归纳和提炼全球与中国再保险业数字化转型的共性、特点与经验，为下一步深化转型发展提供有益启示。

（一）全球对标

1．制定明确战略，注重执行落地

国际上数字化转型较为成功的再保险集团主要采用内嵌式数字战略，即将数字化转型嵌入集团整体战略中作为重要组成部分，强调战略落地，明确实施路径。瑞再将自身定位为处于市场领先地位的"风险知识公司"，其数字化转型战略体系以集团总体战略为指引，以数字

化战略为驱动，注重将数字战略与业务战略深度融合，形成内部一致的体系系统，以推动实现整体战略目标。同时，将数字化转型作为长期目标，伴随内外部形势要求的变化，不断调整更新转型举措、细化实施路径，推动转型成效日积月累、逐步深化。慕再的数字化进程从集团整体战略出发，将"数字要素"嵌入整体战略中，作为重要战略目标之一，推动实现数字元素嵌入到创意提出再到产品开发的全过程提升。

2. 强化科技赋能，助推管理与服务数字化升级

国际再保险公司主要在智能承保、高效理赔、风险管理等方面加强科技赋能，推动研发新技术平台，提高内部管理效能。智能承保方面，慕再研发基于云服务的新一代智能核保Allfinanz系列平台，运用预测模型（Predictive Analytics）对历史核保数据展开深度学习，显著提高了全球寿险公司核保自动化比例，降低了核保师处理常规保险申请的时间。瑞再利用人工智能、大数据等技术，推出了一体化人身险智能核保解决方案Magnum，助力保险公司实现低成本、高效率的流程优化，统一风险评估尺度，大幅提高了核保运营效率。汉再联合保险与科技公司，研发自动化模块化核保平台hr|ReFlex，可直接在保险销售端提供即时、快速的核保决策，灵活性强，易于集成到保险公司新产品中，显著提高核保决策的一致性和准确性。RGA美再充分利用自身核保经验和数据分析的优势，建设数字时代的自动化核保和决策平台AURA Next，实现快速、灵活和可靠的自动化核保。高效理赔方面，慕再利用人工智能数据分析技术，通过MIRA Digital Suite的理赔模块CLARA plus解决失能保险理赔烦琐、效率低的问题，实现自动化理赔，显著提升理赔效率。法再利用人工智能、OCR等技术研发了核赔规则引擎SCOR Claims Rules Engine（CRE），通过数字化解决方案简化

保险公司理赔流程，优化理赔效率，提升客户体验。风险管理方面，慕再推出一系列自然灾害风险管理套件Risk Suite平台，为保险公司巨灾风险管理提供助力，平台覆盖自然灾害、气候变化、野火三个业务版本，并面向不同层次需求提供多种产品套件。瑞再推出CatNet®系列平台，运用有关气候变化、灾难性事件、人口密度等的地图数据来支持保险公司提升风险管理能力，推动产品开发，降低业务成本。

3．打造产业数字生态圈，培育新增长点

再保险利用数字化手段打造贯通产业价值链的生态平台，为客户提供高效便捷定制化的服务，拓展自身业务增长空间。2018年，瑞再推出高级驾驶辅助系统（ADAS）风险评分方案，不断在自动驾驶领域进行风险研究和产品创新，并逐步构建起由汽车生产厂商、直保公司、再保险公司组成的车险生态，为购车人提供全周期服务。通过将带有高级驾驶辅助系统的汽车与相关保险产品的捆绑销售实现深度合作与多方共赢，生产厂商汽车销量增加，车险消费者获得保费优惠，直保公司和再保险公司获得更多业务、积累更多数据。慕再积极联通汽车行业上下游，以数据为驱动、以"车企+保险"为中心，构建起涵盖车企、经销商、保险代理和汽修厂的新汽车产业生态圈。RGA美再与医疗技术创新者RoadtoHealth（RTHG）合作，发布了全面集成的数字健康生态系统HEIDI，为客户提供一站式医疗健康服务，并提供一系列预防式、个性化的医疗和福利服务，不仅帮助客户做好健康管理、降低保险公司赔付成本，而且在客户更高频次的系统使用过程中，帮助美再获得更丰富的数据。

4．强化战略性投资布局与合作，打造创新引擎

加大科技领域的战略性投资与布局已成为国际再保险公司抢占数字时代发展先机、拓展创新赛道的重要战略举措。瑞再通过设立加速

器、进行外部投资、与科技公司合作、成立专业子公司等方式加码前沿科技，获取业内最新动态，作为公司数字能力和科技能力的补充。参与多家保险科技初创企业的融资，增加在细分领域的数据积累，为产品创新与业务拓展打下数据基础。慕再旗下三大投资主体，Munich Re Ventures、HSB Ventures、ERGO Digital Ventures分别针对不同的新兴保险科技领域进行投资布局，关注领域包括将创新技术推向市场的初创公司；物联网、网络安全、人工智能和分析领域；AI保险、数字驱动、数字健康、互联汽车等。2016年，慕再设立Digital Partners，目标是投资于拥有一流技术的公司助其成为全球数字领导者，在国际市场非常活跃，特别关注工业技术和金融科技垂直领域的公司。2019年，汉再创建数字化平台hrlequarium，汇聚数字创新者、保险科技公司、保险公司，在保险业务价值链上提供多元化解决方案。平台目前提供多达百余个的综合保险解决方案，来自100多个国家的汉再客户通过在线平台获取服务。

5．优化组织机制，加强人才保障

建立与数字化转型相适应的组织架构，打造具有数字化专长的人才团队，是推动数字化转型的重要基础和保障。瑞再设立首席数字科技官（Chief Digital & Technology Officer）负责统筹推进数字化转型工作；成立瑞再研究院研判数字化趋势、输出数字知识、跟踪全球数字化应用最新案例；建立智能分析研究中心，侧重于数据洞察和风险评估，以提升内部智能分析能力；企业文化和职场设计对标科技公司，全面推行移动办公；构建更加扁平化的组织架构，弱化职能层级，进行集团自上而下技能轮岗。同时，瑞再重视引入具有科技背景和数字化转型经验的专业人才，包括高管、技术团队、理工背景应届生等；并与苏黎世联邦理工学院、瑞士圣加伦大学、新加坡国立大学等高等学府合作，增强研究能力并培养后备人才。慕再积极引入外脑，聘请行业专家，打造创新智库，为慕再提供前沿创新和数字化转型思路与建议。例如，聘请里特咨询公司数字化转型专家聚焦创新商业模式、平台生态建设提供策略建议，帮助构建创新能力。聘请柏林艺术大学电子商务学院专家顾问，利用其科技研究合作网络，探索前沿市场趋势、创新灵感和创新解决方案。

（二）中国实践

近年来，在国家与行业政策大力推动下，在市场竞争日趋激烈、客户需求不断升级的背景下，国内再保险公司数字化转型步伐明显提速，纷纷将数字化转型作为中长期战略发展的核心驱动力之一，持续加大科技投入，创新服务模式，加快战略布局，打造数字保险生态圈。

1．明确战略顶层设计，加大资源投入

国内再保险公司特别是龙头企业，已紧跟数字经济发展步伐，制定明确中长期数字化转型战略，并不断加大对科技创新与数字化转型的投入力度。2018年，中再制定"数字中再1.0"战略，开启数字化转型之路。2021年将"科技赋能"作为"十四五"规划中战略发展的重要支点，以创新驱动、科技赋能打造数字化驱动业务发展的新引擎。2021年底升级"数字中再2.0"专项规划，提出"以场景为导向、以客户为中心、以智能化为内核、以生态化为协同"的新发展理念，从传统轨、创新轨、组织变革三条主线描绘公司"十四五"时期数字化发展总体框架，加快推动业务与科技融合发展，更好助力业务创新、提升运营效率、赋能行业发展。在资源保障上，中再近年来持续加大数字化资金投入与人才培养，2021年科技投入近8.5亿元，组建了近400人的科技人才队伍，保障各项数字化举措具备充足的人力基础和技术

支撑能力。前海再提出实施科技赋能战略，在新渠道、新产品、新模式和新业态等领域加大保险科技的战略投入，围绕"再保+科技+生态"的规划加速推进保险科技创新和数字化转型，赋能再保险主业。人保再坚持数字化发展方向，坚定以数字化手段破解经营难题，持续提升科技运营支持效能。

2．加强数据资产整合应用，提升内部管理效率

再保险强化对数据作为新型生产要素的运用，使之成为发展的基础性、战略性关键要素。提升数据管理能力与应用能力，加强数据资产梳理，建立数据仓库、数据湖、企业级大数据平台，依托数据中台等加强数据可视化建设，探索数据在业务经营、风险管理、内部控制等方面的应用。中再面向服务内部经营管理，构建"业务+数据"双中台体系，持续深化业务线上化、智能化，进一步实现降本增效和风控能力提升。业务中台聚焦再保险核心业务流程自动化，全面提升业务处理效率和智能化水平，整体业务线上化率已超过90%。数据中台聚焦企业级数据能力建设，打造涵盖数据采集、存储、传输、消费等关键环节的治理体系，在数据质量和数据服务能力等方面实现飞跃，数据集中度已超过90%。中国农再以"约定分保业务信息系统"为起点，建设全国农业保险数据信息系统，探索推进农业保险数据治理，加强与农业保险相关参与方的信息共享，提升服务效能。

3．提供数字化风险管理服务，创新再保险解决方案

再保险立足自身中立性平台性属性，面向服务保险行业整体，打造行业性数字化基础设施为载体的客户赋能平台。中再研发智能核保引擎平台，融合大数据、人工智能等技术，解决了保险公司承保过程中核保难度大、流程复杂、资料难获取、核保过程缺少线上化和自动化、逆选择风险高和差异化风控难等痛点难点，已覆盖寿险、重疾

险、医疗险等多种保障性产品。区块链网络打通再保险和保险数据通路，与国寿财险打造财险行业首个再保险账务及结算联盟链，与中国人寿共同建设基于寿险行业的临分邀约联盟链，大幅提升流转效率，降低交易成本，初步形成行业基础数据设施。以区块链网络为底座的核保险"核·星"业务平台是基于区块链的保险行业第一个联盟链，实现了洽商、承保、理赔、账单结算全流程上链，营造开放共享的核产业生态。跨界数据融合网络推动保险与银行、交通、建筑、农业、应急、气象等多行业数据融合，探索数据要素流通规则，挖掘再保险数据价值，打造数据驱动的创新竞争力。与银行合作，充分挖掘银行和保险公司的多方数据价值，简化了客户投保审核流程，提升客户服务质量，实现国内首个"银行—保险—再保险"的全联通。与保险公司合作，合作网络基于联邦学习技术，确保各方数据的"可用不可见"，构建起数据安全的共享生态，全面捕捉客户画像，满足客户多层次、个性化的保险需求，开创了保险与再保险公司业务协同新模式。人保再推出移动端客户查询工具、客户管理系统等，以科技手段提升服务客户的能力，也进一步加深对客户需求的洞察，为优化产品服务提供助力。人保"再保险区块链运营管理平台"荣获中国人民银行"2020年度金融科技发展奖"，其基于区块链技术架构，构建了链条完整的再保险数字化交易平台，重塑了再保险业务交易方式，目前已支持200余家企业再保运作，平均每年交易资金超过300亿元，实现超过100万亿元保险风险的再保险交易处理。前海再研发"非标体"自动核保系统，针对带病人群的标准化风险评估规则，开发上线了在线自动化加费核保系统，为超过10亿亚健康人群解决投保难的痛点。

4．打造平台生态圈，推动业务创新发展

再保险以数字化推动商业模式转型升级，搭建起面向政府和产业

的服务平台，构建多元生态系统，从赋能走向资源融合贯通，有效提升服务实体经济和人民群众的能力水平。中再在巨灾、建筑业、大健康等多个领域拓展平台生态。巨灾领域，相继推出灾害风险数据服务平台"再瞰"、数据服务API SaaS平台"视界"、具有自主知识产权的中国巨灾模型"再型"、巨灾风险组合管理平台"再融"等系列产品，多次实现行业从"0"到"1"的基础性突破。建筑业领域，推出工程质量潜在缺陷保险（IDI保险）、建工安责险和建筑业质量手册平台等，产生显著社会效益和示范效应。大健康领域，推出天玑智能保险云平台，通过智能算法和业务深度结合，构建以被保险人为中心的产品模式，嵌入预测分析模型，多维量化评估客户情况，助力保险公司智能化业务构建。太平再（中国）积极布局汽车产业生态圈，与北汽安鹏保险经纪等三方合作，围绕新能源汽车动力电池相关提供风险管理解决方案。近期，与中汽数据合作，积极构建"产业+保险+科技"的新生态，服务汽车行业转型升级。慕再构建新汽车产业生态圈，已经与长安汽车进行合作，共同开发中国本土的创新保险服务生态体系。2022年，瑞再发布"信瑞智农"（SRAIRMP）农业风险管理平台2.0版本，通过提供实时风险评估报告，为各级政府、农户和保险公司防灾减损、灾后救援和风险管理提供量化参考。

5．加强战略合作与投资布局

近年来，保险科技在中国蓬勃发展，再保险企业在中国市场的战略性投资与布局也在不断深化。瑞再在中国市场有多笔保险科技领域投资实践，是平安好医生赴港上市引入的7家基石投资者之一，也是太平洋保险在伦交所发行GDR引入的基石投资者，还联合领投了保险科技独角兽水滴保险。2021年，法再在中国设立保险科技子公司—蜂科技，为直保公司提供科技服务，打通营销、产品、风控、理赔全流程。2015年，RGA美再成立全资子公司RGAX，是其数字化转型与创新的重要引擎，主要承担投资与创新孵化、加速新产品开发和业务方式创新的职能。RGAX在中国重点投资与保险相关的大数据、人工智能、生物科技等领域。2018年，中再成立国内第一家巨灾科技公司中再巨灾风险管理股份有限公司。2021年，前海再孵化并发起设立前海再保科技有限责任公司，应用大数据和人工智能等技术手段，致力于为行业提供包含基于数据驱动的人工智能实时风险评估与定价、风控分保及核保自动化引擎，成为数字保险新产品的开发、分发、聚合及创新孵化服务平台。

6．积极探索组织改革和机制创新

再保险公司在实践中不断探索和调整与数字化转型相适应的组织架构，推动跨领域、跨部门、跨职能联动融合的组织架构，如在管理层面新设立相关委员会或小组，工作层面增设或优化科技团队，积极探索市场化、灵活敏捷的组织形式推动科技创新。中再在"数字中再"战略的指导下，成立信息化工作委员会，后升级为数字化转型委员会，负责统筹部署数字化转型战略实施各项工作，确保有效落地。将信息技术部门的定位从单一的内部技术支持向对外发展创新和对内技术支持内外兼修转变，推动IT职能与组织架构调整。成立信息技术中心与创新孵化中心，引入算法工程师、架构师、开发工程师等科技紧缺人才。成立京东数科联合实验室、区块链创新工坊、创新实验室、与孵化器Plug & Play合作构建实验室，推动科技赋能创新。2022年，慕再成立中国创新研发中心，整合保险与科技资源，聚焦绿色能源、绿色科技等行业的风险解决方案。

三、主要启示与相关建议

（一）对保险业整体的启示与建议

1．数字化转型首先是认识和思维上的转型

一是企业内部要自上而下认识到数字化转型不仅仅是信息技术部门的事，都能够充分一致认识和理解数字化转型的重要性，要将数字化转型作为业务发展的一项基本且重要的支撑。二是要认识到数字化转型不是单纯地运用新技术，而是要将业务数字化，将数据转化为有价值的资产并加以利用，将数字化充分融入业务发展中，从而为企业创造新价值。三是要认识到数字化转型不仅仅是优化工作效率效能，更是商业模式的变革，要创新定义业务目标，实现保险产品创新、服务模式转型。

2．数字化转型要有战略决心与定力

一是从国内外实践经验均可看出，数字化转型是典型的"一把手"工程，制定明确战略后，需要公司高层亲自领导和推动规划实施，在暂时性的困难和问题面前展现强大的战略定力与执行能力，保障持续充足的资源投入。二是将数字化转型作为中长期战略目标的重要部分，长期坚持不懈，持续推动落实，明确重点举措以及相应的时间表路线图，严格执行，不受外部因素变化的影响。

3．数字化转型要坚持科技与业务深度融合

保险企业数字化转型的本质目的是利用数字技术赋能商业模式的创新与转型，落脚点是服务业务，支撑点是科技，因此转型的成功离不开科技与业务的深度融合，以确保在建设应用数据能力和数据资产

时，与业务价值有机联系、与业务发展相辅相成。一是服务公司内部，要深入剖析业务流程和经营模式，结合新科技新突破，改善经营效率和科技体验，打造更具竞争力和智能化的经营管理模式。二是要深入洞察客户与市场，深挖客户行为，抓住需求痛点，将智能风控、智能服务、生物识别、区块链、多方安全计算等科技手段深度融入承保、理赔、产品、客户、生态建设等各个层面，升级提供更具针对性和多样性的新型保险产品与服务，将事后、被动的理赔业务模式向事前、主动的防灾减损服务模式转变，进一步拓宽保险市场广度。

4. 数字化转型要有体制机制与人才队伍保障

一是科技创新孵化机制能够提供重要助力。瑞再、慕再、RGA美再等再保险公司均利用有效的创新孵化机制，快速响应市场变化，敏捷捕捉市场机会，在创新产品服务、孵化合作、股权投资布局等方面效率较高、能力较强。二是人才管理体系与数字化转型需求相匹配。国际再保险公司人才引进机制丰富多元，校企合作培养人才，社会招聘发现人才，中长期的人才梯队建设，都为公司数字化转型落地提供强大智力支撑。此外，较为完善的薪酬激励机制，较为畅通的晋升渠道，重视对核心人才团队资源倾斜、考核侧重，都成为吸引和留存人才的有效手段。

（二）对再保险业的启示与建议

1. 发挥行业平台优势，着力营造产业互联生态

再保险商业模式正从风险等量管理向风险减量服务转变，从事后评估与服务模式向事前可预测、定制化和生态化转变，要充分发挥自身资源与技术优势，加强内外部合作，利用科技手段积极打造平台生态圈。一是重视聚合多方资源，在数字化转型过程中聚合专家、数

据、服务、市场、客户资源，通过有效的资源整合和连接发挥最大价值。二是重视共商共建平台，集合多方力量共同建立数字化平台，发挥各方功能、促进沟通协同。三是重视营造开放生态，面向服务政府和"医、食、住、行、美"各行业，营造开放的产业互联网生态，打通生态系统各相关方，参与融入产业互联网生态。总之，再保险行业应站在经济社会发展宏观角度，深入对经济社会潜在影响巨大、风险管理需求最为迫切的自然灾害、绿色发展、社会治理、医疗健康、长寿风险等领域，与相关方携手打造垂直生态系统，嵌入风险管理与专业服务，形成综合风险解决方案，探索从生态参与者到主导者的商业模式转型。

2．建立以数据为核心驱动的转型体系，加强数据能力建设

从国际实践可以看出，数字化转型较为成功的再保险企业都基本实现了向数据驱动转型的关键一步，数据已不仅是一种资源或应用，而是成为企业发展依托的基础性、战略性关键要素。国内再保险企业要积极打造以数据为驱动的企业级架构，发挥再保险数据资源禀赋优势，特别是要加强数据能力建设。一是推动数据标准化建设，完善企业级数据标准体系建设，推进公司内部数据统一管理、数据融合融通。二是强化数据应用能力，加强与保险健康数据机构、头部互联网公司与金融科技公司的战略合作，利用创新平台、区块链和跨界数据安全合作等各种方式，丰富保险相关数据来源；加快数据平台建设，全面整合企业内外部数据，解决"数据孤岛"问题，提升数据分析对业务需求的快速响应能力，同时应用大数据分析、机器学习等技术手段，实现数据价值的深度挖掘。三是打造数据资产运营模式，以场景需求为根本，完成从数据原材料到数据产品、商业化输出的全过程驱动和管理，打通数据资产化、价值化通路。

3．探索组织变革与机制创新，加大资源投入保障

一是在体制机制上，科技创新日新月异，面对具有较大成长性、较好发展空间、对主责主业有较大促进作用的商业赛道或创新项目，国内再保险业要借鉴国际经验，积极探索体制机制创新，在孵化合作、股权投资等战略布局方面争取新的突破，如成立科技子公司在国内外已积累较为成熟的经验，再保险业也需加紧布局。二是在资源保障上，相较于保险业其他类型机构，无论是在资金投入规模还是专业人员投入方面，再保险公司在数字化转型上的投入都相对较少。数据显示，2020年国内再保险公司信息科技投入约1.03亿元，同比增长8.69%，增长幅度远低于直保公司的16.74%[①]。国内再保险业未来应进一步加大资源投入，在数据平台、创新技术应用、创新平台建设上增加资金投入；加快引进兼具金融、科技等背景的复合型管理人才与专业技术人才，通过专项能力培训计划等方式加强数字化人才培养，并不断完善绩效考核与人才激励机制。通过培养科技人才和扩大资金投入，有效支撑数字化转型的实施落地。

---

① 数据来源：《中国保险科技发展报告2021》，中国保险行业协会。

专题七

巨灾科技赋能保险业风险减量

为进一步建设更高水平的平安中国，以新安全格局保障新发展格局，2021年，原中国银保监会印发《关于推动财产保险专业化、精细化、集约化发展的指导意见》，鼓励保险机构积极运用物联网、人工智能等前沿技术，增强风险识别、监测、预警等风险管理专业能力，主动提供防灾减损服务，从源头上降低风险损失，推动行业由风险等量管理向风险减量服务转型。2023年中国银保监会印发《关于财产保险业积极开展风险减量服务的意见》，要求各保险机构通过完善制度建设、强化内控管理、加强人才建设、提升信息化水平、创新科技应用、推动基础研究等方式，夯实风险减量服务基础，提高社会抗风险能力，助力维护国家安全和社会稳定。风险减量逐步由企业自主服务上升为行业监管的新要求。面对新形势新变化，保险机构利用科技手段有效管理风险，巨灾风险减量面临新挑战，也迎来了新的发展机遇。

一、巨灾风险形势与巨灾风险减量背景

（一）国内外巨灾风险形势

近年来，全球自然灾害损失连年增加。2022年，全球自然灾害直接经济损失达2 750亿美元[①]，灾害风险形势不容乐观。中国是自然灾害频发国家，2011年至今，年均自然灾害直接经济损失超过3 500亿元，约占中国GDP的0.4%[②]，占全球灾害直接经济损失的近1/4。地质灾害、洪涝、地震造成的死亡人数分别居世界第1、第2和第3位[③]。"5·12汶川地震""7·20河南特大暴雨"等重特大自然灾害对中国经济发展、人民安居生活和社会安全稳定构成了严重威胁。

与2011年至今全球自然灾害直接经济损失呈现的增长趋势[④]相比，中国自然灾害直接经济损失自2011年以来出现一定程度的下降趋势[⑤]，在全球自然灾害直接经济损失中的占比也呈下降趋势。分析其原因，一方面或与中国近年来重特大自然灾害事件较少相关，另一方面或与中国自然灾害工程/非工程防御能力不断提升及各行业风险减量行动不断深入相关。

---

① 数据来源：2023年第1期Sigma报告"2022年自然灾害和通货膨胀：一场完美风暴"，瑞再研究院。

② 数据来源：中国自然灾害直接经济损失数据及GDP数据来源于国家统计局；2011—2022年中国年均GDP为817 428亿元，以此为基础计算。

③ 资料来源：徐锡伟等. 我国主要城市群自然灾害风险分析与防范对策［J］. 城市与减灾，2021（6）：1-6.

④ 2011年以来的全球自然灾害直接经济损失分别为：2 750亿美元（2022年，数据来源于2023年第1期sigma报告）、2 521亿美元（2021年，数据来源于2021全球自然灾害评估报告）、1 794亿美元（2011—2020年平均值，数据来源于2021全球自然灾害评估报告）。

⑤ 依据国家统计局数据，2011年以来的中国自然灾害直接经济损失为：2 386亿元（2022年）、3 340亿元（2021年）、3 683亿元（2011—2020年平均值）。

（二）国内外巨灾风险减量背景

国际上，联合国自20世纪80年代开始关注国际减灾战略及灾害风险管理。1987年，联合国通过大会决议，将1990—2000年定为"国际减少自然灾害十年"（IDNDR）。1994年，联合国举行第一次世界减灾大会并通过"横滨战略"及其行动计划，强调要从国家到社区各级逐步执行灾害评估与减灾计划。2005年，第二次世界减灾大会通过"兵库行动框架（2005—2015）"，指出要提升国家和地方灾害风险评估、预警和管理能力建设。2015年第三次世界减灾大会通过"仙台减少灾害风险框架（2015—2030）"，进一步明确要提升民众的灾害预警信息和风险评估结果的可获得性，建议优先"提高对灾害风险评估、预防、减缓、应急的认知"，优先"以资金投入促灾害风险减少及灾害能力提升"。在国际行动及国际政策的影响下，国际成熟保险机构非常重视风险前置管理。各保险机构在提供常规的产品保障服务之余，多通过自身能力建设及赋能客户风险管理来强化行业风险减量。例如，为客户提供在线自助风险评估工具、防灾防损培训、端到端定制风控解决方案等服务，在官网普及防灾防损、应急管理常识等。

国内保险机构目前正由"风险等量管理"向"风险减量管理"逐步转型。保险机构早期主要强调风险经济补偿及事后风险分散。近年来，随着社会风险保障需求日益提升，保险机构开始重视风险前置管理，纷纷主动参与社会风险治理与风险减量服务。本着"防重于赔，防赔结合"的理念，保险机构多措并举推进防灾减损及风险管控工作。一是广泛开展防灾减灾宣传教育，帮助投保人增强风险防控知识，及早发现潜在风险；二是组建专门的防灾减损队伍，配合政府、产业、民众进行风险处置，主动防控灾害损失；三是采用专业先进的科技手段，介入保险标的的风险管理流程，助力客户灾前风险识别、灾中风险控制、灾后复盘等，协助提升行业灾害风险管理能力。大数据、量化模型、区块链、"3S"[①]技术及云服务等科技手段，逐步应用到风险识别、风险评估、产品设计、风险预警、风险处置、查勘定损、组合风险管理等全流程风险减量服务。

二、保险业巨灾科技发展现状

国内保险机构早期巨灾科技主要以巨灾模型为核心，逐步扩展至使用遥感、物联网等科学技术。随着信息技术的迅速发展及广泛应用，当前巨灾科技泛指一切与巨灾风险管理相关的科学技术手段，主要用于解决保险业灾害风险长期"看不清、算不明、管不住"的难题。巨灾科技可分为巨灾数据库、巨灾模型、巨灾风险管理平台、巨灾组合风险管理平台等。巨灾数据、巨灾模型、巨灾风险管理平台在保险机构业务流程中的服务应用情况见表1。

表1   巨灾科技在保险业务流程中的应用

巨灾科技分类	灾前			灾中		灾后	
	风险识别	产品设计	风险定价	风险预警	风险处置	查勘定损	灾害复盘
巨灾数据	★	★	★	★	★	★	★
巨灾模型	★	★	★	★			★
巨灾风险管理平台	★	★	★	★	★	★	

注：★表示该项巨灾科技在对应保险业务环节具有显著的应用实践或前景。

---

① 3S是遥感（Remote Sensing）、地理信息系统（Geographic Information System）和全球导航卫星系统（Global Navigation Satellite System）的简称，是多学科高度集成的对空间信息进行采集、处理、管理、分析、表达、传播和应用的现代信息技术的总称。

（一）巨灾风险数据库

数字时代下的巨灾风险管理首要是"数据底座"建设。完善的巨灾风险数据是巨灾风险量化的重要前提，也是巨灾风险减量管理能力提升的关键支撑。为加强巨灾保险业务服务，大型保险再保险公司相继建设了覆盖自然灾害、气象、地理、遥感、社会经济等多维度数据的自然灾害与社会经济时空数据库。数据库从内容维度、时效维度、加工程度维度等多方面延伸，逐步体系化发展（见图1）。一是保险机构与国家气象、地震、国土部门合作，引入暴雨、洪水、台风、雷电、冰雹、雪灾、滑坡、泥石流等自然灾害数据，收集整理行业人口、GDP、农业、房屋建筑等社会经济数据，以及各类历史灾害损失数据，构建了相对全面的数据库底座框架；二是按照历史数据、实况数据和预测数据等不同时间维度，积累各灾害及社会经济数据，延长数据时间纵深，用于支撑保险风险评估、产品定价、风险预警、风险预估等防灾减损方案；三是联合科研单位研发网格风险地图，推进数据可视化，进一步提供自然灾害风险评级、风险区划产品，为保险机构风险管理和可视化决策提供依据。

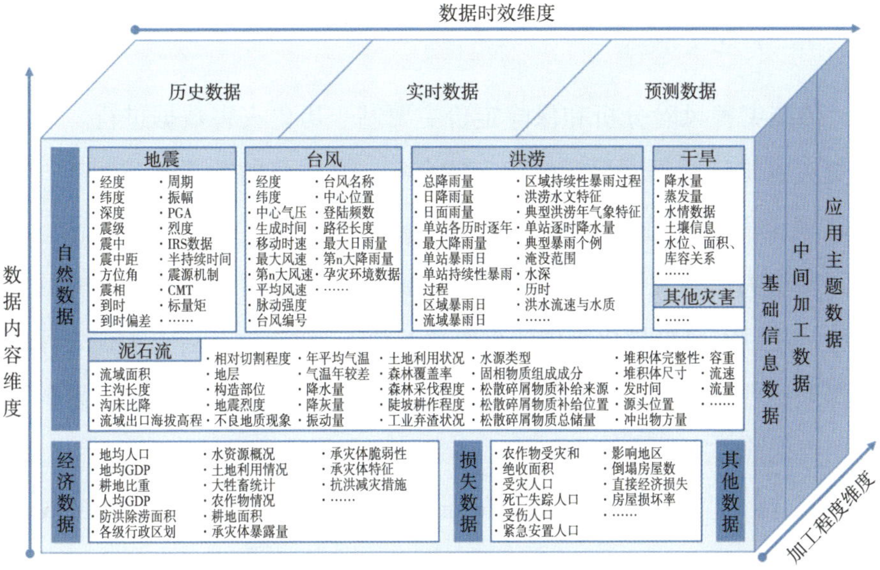

图1 保险业巨灾数据库建设体系

再保险公司在相关领域实践经验较为丰富。慕再建立了全球Nat Cat Service自然灾害损失数据库，该数据库包括历史自然灾害损失数据，如经济损失、保险损失、伤亡人数、房屋破坏数量等。基于该数据库，慕再定期发布各大洲及重点国家的损失数据报告，分享巨灾事故发展情况及趋势。瑞再搭建了全球CatNet风险地图数据库，数据范围包括气候变化、灾难性事件影响、人口密度等地图集和数据集；支持对单一风险标的和特定风险组合进行全球自然灾害风险评估，支持提供地震、热带气旋和欧洲冬季风暴的瞬时事件足迹分析。中再建设了中国区域范围的再瞰地图和视界地图数据库，数据库涵盖了历史自然灾害地图集，人口、GDP、房屋建筑及地理环境空间分布数据地图集；支持灾害数据调用和灾害风险分析，支持风险地图分析服务、气象预警服务、气象站点服务、风险指标服务等。

（二）巨灾模型

传统灾害风险分析和保险定价主要基于历史灾害数据进行。中国历史灾害统计数据详尽记录仅有70余年，高质量的数据不到50年，难以客观全面体现符合物理机制但低频高损的极端灾害事件信息。因此，基于灾害孕发机制、社会风险暴露及科学易损性曲线构建的巨灾模型，是巨灾风险量化管理的重要"芯片"，对支撑社会灾害损失评估及保险行业承保核保、费率厘定、防灾减损、灾后理赔、风险累积管理、再保险方案设计等业务核心环节具有重要科学指导作用。

国际上，VerRisk Extreme Events Solutions（原AIR Worldwide）、Moody's RMS（原RMS）和CoreLogic®（原EQECAT）公司是巨灾模型的主要研发单位。其开发的巨灾模型历经30余年发展，已覆盖多种灾害类型，辐射全球50余个国家和地区。2006年，人保财险开始试用AIR Worldwide公司的中国地震模型。2010年开始，中再逐步引入RMS的地震模型、台风模型，支持国际业务发展，巨灾模型开始正式应用于中国巨灾业务发展。

为解决模型基底高精数据的国别壁垒及模型标的标准体系的国别差异问题，2018年，中再集团成立聚焦巨灾模型研发和巨灾风险管理数字化的保险科技公司——中再巨灾风险管理股份有限公司（以下简称中再巨灾）。中再巨灾率先研发中国地震巨灾模型，并相继成功研发推出中国台风巨灾模型和中国洪涝巨灾模型，目前已基本完成具有自主知识产权、符合中国国情的三大巨灾模型研发。中国巨灾模型主要包括灾害危险性模块、工程易损性模块、风险暴露模块和金融模块四部分（见图2）。

（1）灾害危险性模块。主要分析巨灾事件的发生机理并评估灾害危险性程度。基于灾害孕发物理机制研发的万年/百万年虚拟灾害事件集是灾害危险性的核心，可客观反映灾害事件的发生规律，对极端灾害事件有良好体现。

（2）工程易损性模块。主要用于评估不同类型的承灾体（风险标的）在不同灾害强度下的损失程度。巨灾模型需针对不同类型的承灾体，采用调查研究、实验或计算分析手段，建立承灾体的易损性模型、构建易损性曲线，并利用该曲线，计算承灾体的损失情况。

（3）承灾体风险暴露模块。主要反映区域范围内各类保险标的的时空分布，如人口、房屋建筑、交通/通信/水利/电力等生命线工程的时空分布。中国巨灾模型底座嵌入了覆盖国内住工商房屋建筑风险暴露基础数据库，也可用于支撑聚合保单的精细化风险分析。

（4）金融模块。主要将灾害事件造成的财产或人员伤亡损失转化为可量化的经济损失和保险损失，并依据不同的保险条款设计特定的保险、再保险及减量管理方案。

目前，中国巨灾模型已逐步被国内保险、再保险及保险经纪等各类机构应用，支撑其保险业务定价和风险减量管理。同时，中国巨灾模型也开始延伸拓展应用到政府相关职能领域，发挥其短期灾害风险预警和中长期灾害风险评估作用，支撑政府机构的应急减灾。

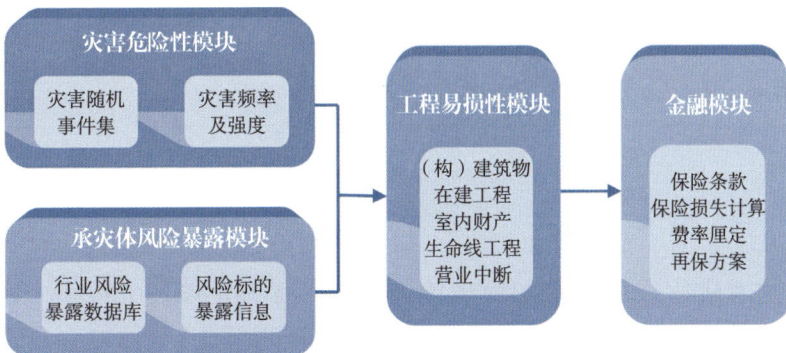

图2 中国巨灾模型功能模块框架

专栏：巨灾模型赋能风险减量案例——中国台风巨灾模型服务电网资产管理

作为生命线工程的重要一环，电网安全稳定运行关系到人民的生活质量和国家的安定发展。在南方区域，台风灾害引起的线路故障已严重影响到电网，尤其是配电网的安全稳定运行。鼎和财险从保险为产业服务角度，量化分析电网资产风险，快速预评估台风灾害造成财产损失，开展针对性防灾减损服务。中再研发的中国台风巨灾模型助力鼎和财险建立了业内首个电网资产台风巨灾模型，通过对电网资产、地理、灾害、气象、保险等大数据的精准分析，提供电网资产台风防灾减灾的综合解决方案，保障了新型电力系统的稳健运行。

中国台风巨灾模型支持本地部署及个性化定制，开发了针对电网输电线路的易损性模型与风险暴露模型、针对电网资产的金融模型，实现台风实时展示、输电塔易损性计算、电网资产损失实时预测、保险损失计算等功能，成功打造了集合灾害预警、查勘定价、数据分析的统一风险管理平台，在"狮子山""圆规"台风中发挥重要作用，累计提供5.2万次风险查询服务，发送预警19.6万人次。"风险云"系统通过强化数据展示和空间分析服务，对风险数据进行深入挖掘和集中管理，直观呈现电网资产及所面临的各类风险地理分布，有效推动了风险管控从事后向事前转移，描绘多维度全方位风险脸谱，为企业风险减量管理提供有效的数据参考。"风险云"投入至今，已为粤港澳大湾区地区电网资产防灾减损超过数千万元，为保险融入和服务大湾区建设、发挥保险"社会稳定器"和"经济助推器"作用提供了重要技术支持。

（三）巨灾风险管理服务平台

随着灾害风险预警与管理能力的不断提升，以及大数据、物联网、区块链、"3S"技术、人工智能、云计算等新科技的快速发展与应用，保险机构积极探索"保险+科技+服务"业务模式创新，业务与技术高度融合的平台生态逐步发展，形式多样的巨灾风险管理服务平台，为保险业风险管控提供重要支撑，推动行业进入智能风控阶段。

1．灾害风险管理数字化平台

灾害风险管理数字化平台是集合了"预警—减损—理赔"等业务场景服务为一体的智能风控管理平台，主要面向投保人服务，可为灾害风险识别、风险预警、风险处置、快速理赔等核心保险环节提供闭环数字化服务。依托科研团队和再保险机构的巨灾科技能力，主要保险机构纷纷研发自身的风险管理数字化平台。例如，人保财险建立了智慧气象灾害风控服务平台及理赔调度平台，支持以自动推送和人工调度相结合的方式，为重点保险客户及时发送防灾减损信息，向公司防灾减损专员分享应急处置调度任务，针对保险标的实施抢救减损行动。平安财险打造了鹰眼系统，基于物理空间的数字化风险分析和风控服务系统，基于自然灾害、承保理赔等数据，支撑承保客户快速筛选和精准预警，精准投放防灾减灾和救援力量；其3.0开放平台可为行业客户输出风险评级、灾害预警、客户地图和风控云平台等核心功能。太保财险利用高精监测装备研发了智能化风控平台"风险雷达"系统，围绕企业安全生产的风险防控问题，贯穿事前风险防范、事中监测预警、事后应急救援与保险赔付的全阶段，通过自有专业服务队伍，提供快速预警及精准防灾服务。国寿财险建立了基于空间化数字化的防灾防损云平台"安心防"平台（见图3），基于全国产化GIS可视化技术和时空大数据技术，实现了对承保标的风险精准预警，降低了出险频度和赔付率，为产品定价、承保决策提供了精细化风险评级支撑。阳光财险建立了天眼风险地图平台，实现了基于位置智能、大数据技术的风险管理系统建设，集合了9种自然灾害大数据的研究成果、14类气象预警信息和承保理赔风控等数据，实现了对标的地址的快速精准风险分析，支持承保企业风险监控和快速预警，及时有效提供防灾减灾服务。

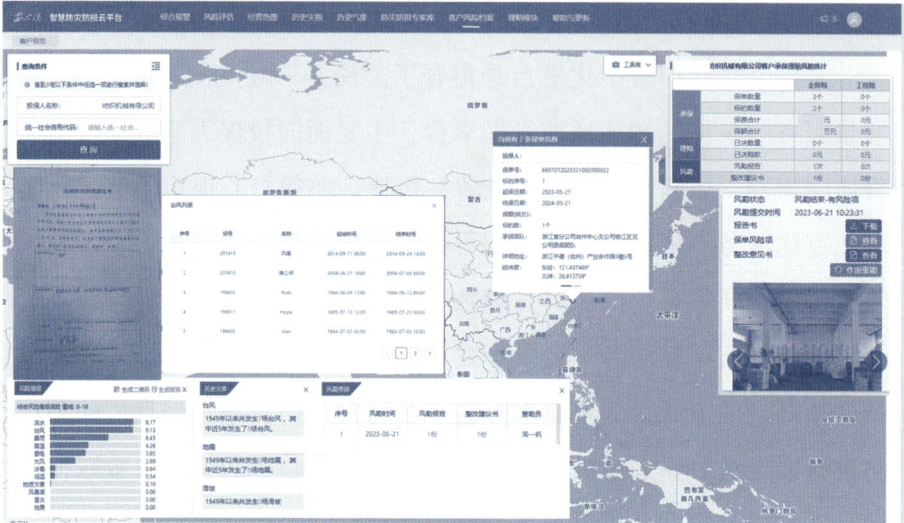

图3　安心防智慧防灾防损云平台示例

专栏：灾害风险管理便捷App工具

相较于大型灾害风险管理服务平台而言，新型App工具具有更加灵活便捷的特点，大幅提升了风险减量服务的可获得性和便利性。

中再基于中国巨灾模型创新研发了"风·眼""水·号"等应用App产品。"风·眼"以中国台风巨灾模型为核心引擎，实时对接最新台风预报数据，实现"1公里网格级"台风风场、洪涝淹没场及台风灾害损失快速计算（见图4）。"水·号"以中国洪涝巨灾模型为核心引擎，将抽象化预警信息转化为具象化风险可视信息，提供灾情预测、灾害仿真、损失评估等全流程数字化服务，进一步提升防灾减灾救灾能力。

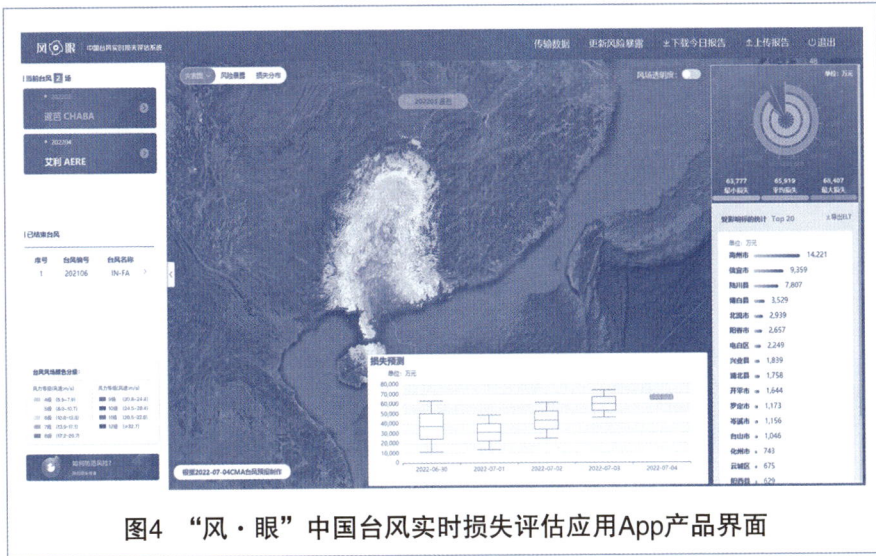

图4 "风·眼"中国台风实时损失评估应用App产品界面

2．灾害风险解决方案平台

巨灾风险解决方案平台是面向直保公司或客户公司提供巨灾产品自助服务或定制化解决方案服务的平台，是保险业再直融合及产业融合的新型服务模式。

2020年，中再依托自身农业风险管理优势和生态圈合作伙伴资源，研发了农业气象指数保险研发平台AWII（Agricultural Weather Index Insurance platform）（见图5），为行业提供特色林果、蔬菜园艺、水产养殖等特色指数创新保险产品方案，年均定制服务案例近20款。为加强农业风险减量服务，中再已启动建设集产品创新支持、风险识别评估、风险预警提示、灾情进展跟踪、风险减量管理应用场景于一体的"再耘"综合性农险科技平台。

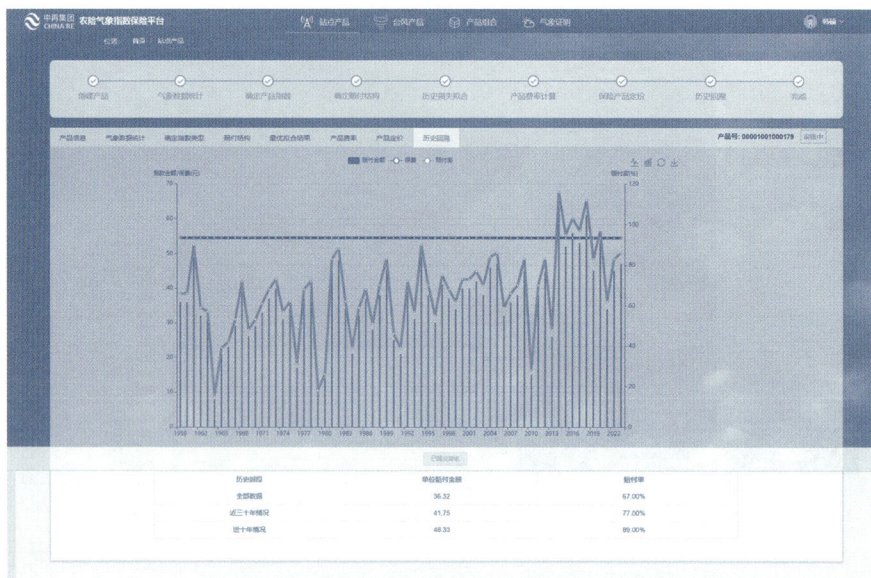

图5　AWII平台产品验证及回溯分析示例

瑞再自主研发了集定价和产品设计于一体的"禹志"巨灾保险定制平台，将自身累积的指数保险产品设计经验融入先进的算法模型，为保险机构提供定价指导及自动化的巨灾保险产品设计建议。2022年，瑞再发布"信瑞智农（SRAIRMP）2.0"，以农业灾害模型和大数据算法为核心，为客户公司提供线上化农险天气指数产品开发服务，并通过提供实时风险评估报告，为政府、保险机构及农户的防灾减损、灾后救援和风险管理提供量化参考。

（四）巨灾组合风险管理平台

保险再保险业务风险累积的量化评估及有效管理是保险机构关注的重要问题之一，直接关系整体业务风险限额管控。巨灾组合风险管理平台即是为保险机构风险累积提供量化管理的智能平台。中再面向业务发展及风控管理需要，搭建国际巨灾组合风险管理平台（CREST）

（见图6），实现了中国保险行业在统一定价和实时组合风险管理、统一巨灾和非巨灾风险管理、统一传统定价方法和边际定价法方面零的突破。该平台包括风险评估、组合管理、风险管理三大核心模块。

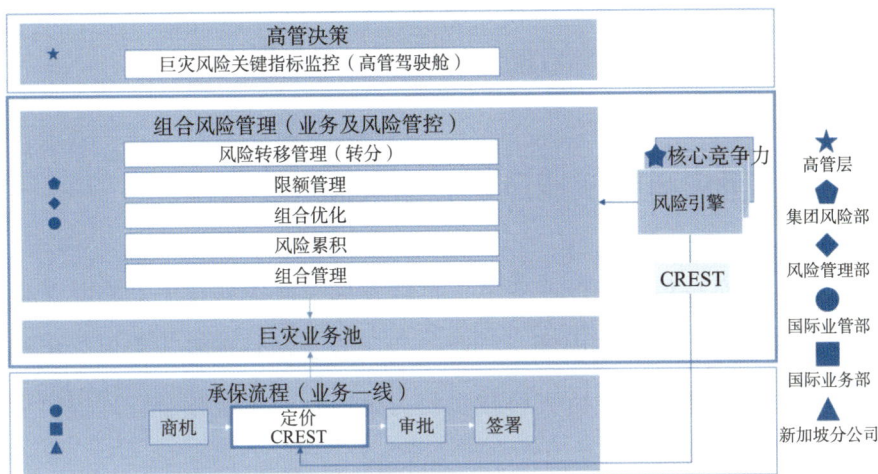

图6　国际巨灾组合风险管理平台（CREST）架构

风险评估模块对单笔再保险业务进行边际定价。围绕巨灾风险，通过与巨灾模型对接，实现风险事件的模拟计算、不确定性计算；围绕非巨灾风险，通过风险评估和经验费率两种方法实现最大损失和常规损失的模拟分析。平台同时考虑单笔业务在整个业务组合中的影响，以实现边际定价功能。该模块为业务部门判断业务质量、进行业务决策提供了量化依据。

组合管理模块包括三大主要功能：一是用于组合分析，根据业务实际需要支持将相同维度的业务组合进行风险累积、利润累积分析，实现对业务各板块、各条线、各区域、各灾因的累积状态进行管理；二是进行组合优化，不断调整业务组合结构，实现资本回报率最大化；三是实现特定风险事件的压力测试，在极端情况下了解公司业务组合表现，积极应对"黑天鹅"和"灰犀牛"事件。

风险管理模块主要实现公司关键风险指标同实际风险累积之间的对接。实时监测各维度风险累积状况，准确把握公司国际业务整体风险情况。该模块为公司提供业务组合数据，包括风险累积数据、利润累积数据和资本分配累积数据，为管理决策提供支撑。

三、巨灾科技赋能风险减量展望

新一轮科技革命和产业变革正迅猛发展，巨灾科技革新将赋予保险业风险减量管理新的内涵，行业长效风险减量管理将成为保险机构高质量发展的新动能，巨灾科技也将为赋能行业风险减量管理提供更大助力。

（一）强化巨灾技术支撑，全面量化灾害风险

有效的风险减量服务需建立在对风险的全面理解基础之上，即对各类风险因素、风险生成机制和风险传播链条等均有全面且深刻的认知。财产险承保标的种类多、风险差异大，需分层分类发展风险量化技术。一是保险机构应进一步加强人工智能等创新科技应用，加强数据积累，完善巨灾模型研发，筑牢行业基础设施，让灾害风险"看得清""算得明"；二是保险机构须面向市场应用场景，结合灾害风险智能研判、预测预警、信息共享及辅助决策等，拓展灾害管理数字化平台建设，为保险机构提供更准确、及时、便捷的量化服务，让灾害风险"管得住"。

（二）推进巨灾科技跨界融合，强化综合解决方案服务

保险机构正面临传统业务模式转型的挑战。巨灾科技与保险产业链深度融合，保险服务将在更广范围、更深程度上触及客户全业务流程。借鉴国际经验，科技与业务高度融合的风险减量管理与综合解决方案服务，对减少灾害损失具有明显成效。一是保险机构应加快推动内部业务数据治理与整合，加强外部产业数据引入与融合，利用联邦学习、隐私计算等数据脱敏技术，推进数据跨界融合；二是保险机构应延伸信息及服务链条，运用物联网、感知技术等，将更多上下游服务机构引入保险业数字化生态服务体系中，推动"产品+科技+服务"多维度全方位综合解决方案服务的升级。

（三）加强政策制度引领，完善风险减量长效机制

防灾减损常态化、标准化、制度化是保险风险减量不断发展的重要保障。风险管控前置所需的技术、人力及资金投入正面临成效难以量化的行业痛点问题，急需行业尽快研究制定效益评估技术标准体系。一是针对数据应用、监测预警、防灾处置、损失减少等建立风险减量成效评价标准，将技术指标转为价值指标；二是保险行业需逐步建立防灾减损成效评价长效机制，科学合理评估风险减灾成效，为科技赋能风险减量提供重要支撑。

专题八

（再）保险业损失评估技术与应用的
创新探索

保险作为一种市场化的、为应对各类灾害事故和突发事件而建立的风险转移机制，已成为现代社会风险管理的重要手段之一。如何衡量风险程度的大小，计算风险转移效率的高低，日益成为保险行业技术研究的焦点。最大可能损失评估是一套可以有效评估预期保险损失的方法体系，是全球保险业在非寿险保险领域衡量风险时通用的基础方法和标准动作。

随着中国保险业加快向专业化、精细化、集约化转型，再保险行业也不断发挥技术与数据优势，推进最大可能损失评估方法的研究和实践，不断提高风险分散效率、监控风险累积敞口，推进行业从风险等量管理向风险减量服务转型，为中国经济高质量发展贡献积极力量。

一、（再）保险业加强最大可能损失技术研发的意义

最大可能损失（Probable Maximum Loss，PML），通常指在给定的保险条件和风险因素的基础上，对单个损失事件在不同事故发生场景下对单个危险单位可能造成的最大损失金额。（再）保险行业加强最大可能损失评估技术的创新探索具有较大的现实意义。

1．有助于对承保风险进行精细化管理

借助PML评估，保单的保险金额与保单责任内的各种风险相关联，再被细分为风险单位，在不同事故发生概率的损失场景下，形成对不同场景的损失估计，并寻求其中最大值。该评估方法是对保险标的的风险度量，可以有效衡量各项概率场景下的预计损失，从而对承保风险进行有针对性的精细化管控。

2．有助于为风险量化评估提供依据

首先，借助PML评估，保险公司可以更好地决定是否承接某一业务，承接多少，自留多少。其次，PML评估还可以为同一类风险的选择和评估提供技术基准情景，有助于形成合理的价格机制。最后，PML评估基于有效衡量各项概率场景下的预计损失的特性，可以为同质风险的选择和评估提供基准情景，无疑是评判风险大小的最有效方法。

3．有助于形成合理的对价机制和顺畅的风险转移链条

PML评估为同质风险的选择和评估提供基准情景，能够建立起不同主体间风险交易的通路，使被保险人、经纪人、保险公司和再保险公司在风险转移的产业链条上实现定量化的沟通。

二、（再）保险业损失评估技术应用的最新探索实践

（一）国内外（再）保险业PML评估的应用情况

PML作为保险风险度量的一块基石，受到国际保险业的高度重视和广泛使用。各主要保险公司、再保险公司和经纪公司均制定了各自的PML标准，在风险检验、风险评估、风险控制和核保定价等诸多方面发挥着重要的作用。但是，PML在包括中国在内的各国市场之间、各公司之间的定义和评估标准并没有统一，形成了交流中的"术语壁

垒"，在参与国际市场时，必须特别注意核保资料的PML口径，否则有可能付出无谓而高昂的代价。

在总结长期保险经营实践、借鉴国际同行经验的基础上，人保再保险股份有限公司（以下简称人保再）系统研究形成了PML评估体系的总体方案和基本方法，并于2022年7月发布了最大可能损失（PML）评估及应用指引——《PML白皮书（2022）》。该成果着眼于PML评估的普适性原则，基于全球保险行业和工程技术的通行标准和方法，通过"场景+损失量化"的方法，全面展示了主要险种PML评估的基本规则和流程，是中国保险行业建立统一的PML评估标准方面一次重要的经验总结和保险专业技术创新。

（二）（再）保险行业PML评估技术探索

1．PML的分层评估方法

本着合理谨慎的原则，参考保险监管机构《财产保险危险单位划分方法指引》（保监发〔2006〕52号），人保再将最大可能损失定义为Possible Maximum Loss或Maximum Foreseeable Loss，将PML定义为在单次事件中，在所有保护系统失灵、相关应急处理人员以及公共救灾机构均无法提供任何有效救助的情况下，单一危险单位可能遭受的财产损失以及营业中断损失的合计最大金额。

根据上述PML定义，并基于对不同普通保险事故场景的考虑，开展PML评估需要设置一系列起始条件假设，包括单一地址且单一危险单位、导致最严重损失的灾因（通常为火灾或爆炸）、单一地址含多个危险单位、不考虑自然灾害场景假设、最不利损失场景假设。同时，为确保PML评估结果相对保守可靠，需要遵循最不利原则、审慎原则、重置价值原则、最大值原则[①]。

无论在何种损失事件下，PML评估应由五个主要部分组成：灾因（如火灾、爆炸等）、损失场景的时间线（如火灾的发展、蔓延和控制）、损失的范围、财产的损失和营业中断。

评估损失分层能否展示单一危险单位的风险全貌，是PML评估体系中的重要方法。不同程度损失按损失层进行量化是风险全面量化的基础，有助于保险人分析和管理单一危险单位的全面风险，优化承保能力在每个分层上的配置，有针对性地管控特定损失量级的风险。

简化的火灾损失场景下的保险对策如表1所示：

表1　　　　　　　　各损失分层的简化损失场景和保险对策

损失分层	简化的损失场景（火）	保险对策
Frequency 高频率损失	第一时间内，被保险人干预灭火	设置保单免赔额
NLE （Normal Loss Expectancy） 正常预期损失	喷淋器工作把火扑灭	保持保费充足度，足够的保费几年内即可以摊销损失
PML （Probable Maximum Loss） 最大预期损失	喷淋器工作但不能把火扑灭，应急措施有效，消防队到达灭火，结构分隔起作用	可自我摊销成本，或转嫁给再保险人，在一段时间内摊回成本
MFL （Maximum Foreseeable Loss） 最大可预见损失	喷淋器不工作，应急措施无效，消防队到达将火扑灭，结构分隔不起作用，间距起作用	将风险转嫁给再保险人；再保险人在较长的时间和空间内摊销成本
MAS （Maximum Amount Subject） 最大涉险标的价值	喷淋器不工作，消防队不能到达，结构分隔不起作用，完全焚毁，有延烧的可能	转嫁给再保险人，跨险种，在较长的时间和空间内摊销成本

[①] 最不利原则：在最大可能损失情境的推演和选择中，无论是损失波及的范围，还是损失的破坏性，均建议考虑最不利的可能性。尤其是在核保资料完备性不足的情况下，需始终考虑最坏的损失情况。审慎原则：开展PML评估时应采用审慎评估的方法，以避免因评估误差给公司造成意料之外的损失或准备金提取不足，确保PML评估的各项结果相对保守可靠。重置价值原则：所有PML评估都是以保险标的物的重置价值为测算基础。对风险敞口的评估必须基于实际重置价值而不是保险投保价值，因为后者会存在投保价值充分性的问题，而导致对实际在险价值的评估误差。最大值原则：PML或MFL不一定来自最大危险单位。若一张保单可划分多个危险单位，应逐一评估每个危险单位的最大可能损失，并从中选择PML和MFL中的最大值作为该保单的PML和MFL。

2．主要险种最大可能损失评估应用

（1）财产损失（Property Damage，PD）的MFL评估内容

MFL（Maximum Foreseeable Loss）评估的方法是在考虑保单条件和危险单位损失敞口风险因素的基础上，评估单个损失事件在最坏情况下对危险单位可能造成的损失金额。财产损失应考虑修理、更换损坏财产的总成本，包括清理、重建修复规划、聘请顾问、建筑师、工程师等；重建修复作业、设备安装和试车等各方面。财产损失一方面要考虑财产标的物的物质损坏或灭失，另一方面还要考虑标的物所承载的价值丧失。对于财产的损失金额应考虑事件的类型，以及给定的物理环境。

例如，有一个储存塑料制品的仓库，建筑材料为钢框架配合可燃塑料绝缘层，MFL事件就是失控的火灾。在这个场景下，建筑物、内部财产、仓储物均将会估计为100%损失。但是，对于钢筋混凝土建筑内的干式机械车间（不需要切削液的机械加工）的火灾，即使在MFL事件中，也可只考虑机械和建筑的有限损坏。

（2）营业中断（Business Interruption，BI）的MFL评估内容

在营业中断MFL评估中，应评估完全恢复现场营业所需的三个主要时间阶段中需要涉及的项目和所有费用。第一阶段包括权威机构调查、清理污染和生态环境影响、关于许可证等的讨论、清除残骸等；第二阶段包括施工，设计和许可证、对新建筑的法规相对原建筑的变更等；第三阶段包括装配，考虑设备的交付周期、设置、启动，和工艺或产品的质量保证，以及当局的批准（如需要）等。在评估中，同时还应考虑相互依赖性、缓解措施、额外收入损失、额外费用等因素的影响。

（3）投保价值和承保条件分析

保险人在进行PML评估时，应首先确定承保条件中对投保价值约定了何种评估基础。通常情况下，确定投保价值可以有三种方式。

重置成本（Replacement Cost）指保险人依据损失发生的时间和地点，承担被保险人对受损资产进行重置的成本。购置或修理后的财产，种类和品质与原先相同或接近。

实际现金价值（Actual Cash Value）相当于重置成本减去折旧值。折旧一般参考财产的实际剩余使用寿命，而非财务报表体现的残值。

销售价格（Sales Price）通常适用于财产保险中已经售出但尚未出库的库存，在销售价格基础上需要减去实际销售折扣和未发生费用。

承保条件对PML评估有三个方面的影响：一是扩大承保范围，二是扩展额外风险因素，三是扩展保险投保金额。这些方面都会不同程度地对PML评估产生影响。保险人对承保条件进行损失场景化分析后，需要把量化评估后的影响附加在PML评估结果之上。

（三）（再）保险行业PML评估的实践应用

1. 基于PML评估的承保能力投放

承保能力投放策略是保险公司的关键经营策略。目前，国内各主体普遍以承保保额为基础来确定承保能力投放，优点是保额直接来源于保单，数据直观、操作简单。但在市场竞争激烈化的驱动下，各主体对承保能力的需求越来越大，迫切需要更加科学和精细化的风险敞口测算和评估方法以制定更有效率的承保能力决策体系，既满足市场竞争的需要，又能守好风险敞口的底线。从以保额为基础逐步转向以PML为基础的承保能力决策体系，是发达保险市场走过的道路。

保险公司可以根据自己的风险容忍度选择使用最大可预见损失MFL或最大预期损失PML来测算所承担的最大风险敞口。在这种策略下，承保能力可能与以保额为基础投放的承保能力较大差异，市场竞争力也随之产生显著变化。

2．基于PML评估的再保险运用

（1）临时分保

PML方法可以帮助保险公司更科学地认识和评估风险，是提高保险公司风险分析和管理能力的重要方法。再保险是保险公司风险管理的主要手段之一，通过PML的合理评估与运用，可以达到优化再保险保障，提升再保险效用的作用。

图1显示在单个危险单位情况下PML各预期损失分层与几种再保险形式的结构对应关系。

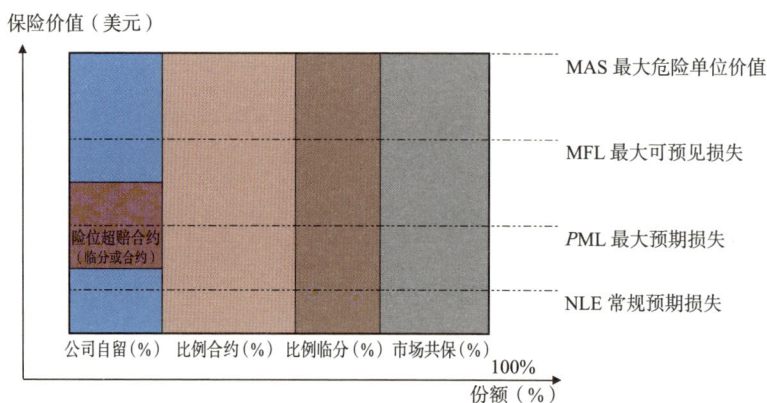

图1　最大可能损失评估中各预期损失分层与再保险结构的关系

无论是比例临分分出，还是超赔临分分出，PML均可发挥较大作用。

比例临分分出。PML的运用提供了一个更合理的分出依据。目前，国内分出公司在安排比例临分时，通常也是以保额为基础来确定分出比例。同理，由于标的保额越来越大，需要安排分出的比例相应越来越高，在现在的市场环境中，完成排分的难度自然很大。采用PML方法后，可以利用评估后的PML值来确定分出比例，相应地将降低分出压力。例如，如果公司以10%的份额承保了标的，在以保额为基础下，可能需临分分出5%（不考虑合约再保险）。但若以MFL为基础，则可能无须再安排临分分出。这一优势在地铁等线性工程险项目的使用中更为突出。一般而言，线性工程的MFL远小于保额，所以利用MFL为基础可以更合理地开展临分安排。

超赔临分分出。PML在超赔临分中运用的优势更加明显。相较于比例临分，超赔临分的难点在于选择合适的起赔点与保障限额。起赔点方面，一般可结合具体项目特点，与公司的承保风险偏好衔接。限额方面，实操中部分公司将超赔限额设置与保额一致，这样安排固然安全性很高，但负面影响是限额设置越高，需要的承保能力越大，成本支出也越高。采用PML的方法后，可在一定程度上优化超赔临分的方案。例如，超赔限额不用再与保额一致，可以使用评估后的MFL为限额，可以降低超赔购买的限额，节约再保险支出成本，但实质的保障程度基本相同。

精准化的临分分出方案。通常国内临分都是将保单的全部保险责任按照同一个比例分出，但有时分出可能仅是因为某类风险过高，比如自然灾害。如果可行，可仅对自然灾害风险部分进行分出，而无须对全部保单责任统一分出。在PML运用的场景下，既有意外事故MFL，也有按不同自然灾害评估的MFL，这就为临分分出提供了新的视角，可以单独分出某一类MFL较大的风险以实现承保风险的控制，从而减少不必要的分出。现实中，更多的是在超赔临分时，在PML分层的基础上设置超赔层，实现对不同风险的准确转移。

（2）合约分保

目前，国内的比例合约基本是以"保额"为基础来设置自留额与分出额。在实务中，还可以PML为基础来设计比例合约。PML为基础的再保险合约最大的好处在于进一步加大承保能力杠杆，更加符合通过再保险均衡公司业务组合的目标，提高资本经营效率。

当然，PML基础的再保险运用也是一把"双刃剑"，它对分出公司技术能力的要求是非常高的。分出公司必须具备扎实的PML评估能力，如果PML评估不足，导致再保险分出不足，一旦出现超出PML评估的损失，则意味着分出公司需要额外自行承担损失。此外，如果分出公司拟安排以PML为基础的比例合约，在PML定义、评估方法、评估信度等方面均需要获得合约再保险公司的认可，否则难以获得再保险公司的支持。要达成双方的默契在实务中是非常困难的，从全球范围来看使用是较为有限的，毕竟PML评估有主观成分。即使在运行的此类再保险合约中，再保险公司也往往会约束PML保额的最低比例，避免分出公司过于激进地评估PML，人为加大风险。

综上所述，虽然以PML为基础的再保险运用对分出公司承保技能、风险管理体系要求较高，但不失为一种很好的提高再保险效用的路径，在未来的运用可能会逐步扩大。

三、目前（再）保险业损失评估技术的局限性

（一）相对于实际发生的损失，风险评估可能并不准确

PML评估是保险行业在防灾减损领域的一项基础研究工作。相对于实际发生的损失，PML评估结果可能并不准确，它的意义在于为选择风险和评估风险提供一个技术基准。

（二）在具体风险和业务的评估中，可能因主客观因素导致偏差

在具体风险和业务的评估中，因有关风险资料不足、缺乏经验、环境变化，如新技术、敏感设备或储存环境等因素导致风险的增加或

减少，主观因素、通货膨胀或社会通胀等因素的影响，可能导致PML评估存在偏差。

（三）有待全行业共同努力，借助新技术提高数据收集和应用水平

PML评估技术的提升需要全行业共同努力，不断总结经验。未来应借助大数据和新技术提高数据收集和应用水平，为PML评估提供更加强大的数据支撑基础。同时，应强化精算方法在单个风险的风险量化过程的应用，提供信度和效度俱佳的PML定量标准。

四、（再）保险业损失评估技术的未来展望

PML的本质是一套风险量化方法，在互联网、大数据和万物互联的新时代它将更加具有现实指导意义。大数据和新技术使更加准确的PML风险敞口量化成为可能，并对保险的风险评估、损失预测和风控指导带来新的变化。

（一）新兴科技和风控技术使数据收集和更加精细的分析成为可能

互联网、大数据和万物互联使风险和损失数据的收集更加精细和准确的分析成为可能。在大量风险损失数据存在的情况下，PML将从比较粗犷的定量评估变成更加细致的以精算为基础的量化方法，从而更加有效地指导保险业务风险的评估和风险管理。PML评估本身是把风险评估进行定量化，对不同的损失场景进行判断和分析，从而更加准确地把握风险的损失强度的潜在变化，通过从损失频度和强度两个

维度所进行的损失量化预测，实现风险的精细化管理。

迄今为止，PML是由风险工程师或核保专业人员通过现场勘察和对单个风险的特征进行定性分析和估计而制定的，由于资源和数据的稀缺性和风险标的的可及性，PML的应用仍然局限在重大风险和一些特定风险领域，而且预测的不确定性极大地对冲了其对单个风险的科学指导意义。未来万物互联（IoT）所带来的监控和数据采集技术的广泛应用，可以做到动态监控风险标的的风险特征和状况，随时监测保险事故的前中后过程，并采集大量的三维即时损失信息的大数据。这些海量数据可以更加精确地按不同的行业类别、不同风险的大小，以及独特的风险局部特征进行分类，从而分析出风险现状和变化，更加精确地预测不同等级的损失的可能性（Likelihood）和出险强度（Loss severity），给更具科学统计意义的PML评估提供强大的数据支撑和基础。

（二）PML评估与大数据结合应用将使智能核保成为可能

大数据的存在使保险精算分析和损失分布模型搭建更加有效和更具现实指导意义。精算方法可以更加有效地使用在单个风险的风险量化过程中，提供信度和效度俱佳的PML定量标准，使保险原理最基础的大数法则发挥更大的作用。从核保和定价的具体实务中，具有更深更广的统计科学意义的PML方法不管是从组合的角度还是从单一风险角度，将会带来更强的现实指导意义。

PML方法和海量大数据相结合的应用将使商业保险领域的智能核保和更加准确的个性化费率厘定成为可能。在拥有极强的统计学意义的大数据下，PML的分层分析将变得更加有意义。在数据和信息有限的情况下，只有对最不利情况下损失（MFL）有相对确定性的量化预估，但对于变量更多的非"最不利情况"下的损失预估（FREQUENCY、NLE、PML）则存在极大的不确定性。然而，大数据和万物互联将改变这种状况，颗粒度非常细腻的海量数据和信息将会使不同损失层级的预测更加准确，其对应的概率和强度预期将给保险公司核保人提供最贴近真实情况的损失成本估计。基于PML方法的风险评估和不同层级风险敞口特征的风险专家系统可以完美结合，而这一切无疑会使商业保险领域的智能核保成为可能。

（三）人工智能将使PML获得更广泛的应用

过去几年，预测分析（Predictive Analytics）在财产和意外险业务中的应用大幅增长，许多保险公司已经开发了预测模型，用于承保定价和理赔管理。PML是传统预测模型中的典型代表，随着机器学习更广泛的应用，预测分析可以更加有效地识别数据中的模式，甚至超越模式直接形成预测结果，从而使PML各层级的损失敞口量级预测更加准确，尤其是对极低发生概率的损失事件的预测。传统分析在开发模型之前严重依赖于"干净"的数据集，而应用机器学习（Machine Learning）的预测模型（Predictive Modelling）能够从大量"不太干净"的数据中迅速并有效找出风险特征和损失特性，从而给风险评估、定价和承保提供更广泛和更深入的技术指导。以PML为风险损失量化方法论的预测模型在大数据和机器学习的加持下还可以向下游延伸，用来管理异常索赔。它能够对潜在的"异常值"提供模型预测模拟，并提供对极低概率的损失大案早期预警。

PML所代表的风险敞口量化的基本方法将展现前所未有的生命力和应用潜能。由于保险的基本原理是基于大数法则，数据是新时代的"石油"，是人类未来最重要的资源，基于互联网和万物互联（IoT）所产生的天量的大数据（Mega Data）将使保险计量技术发生革命性的跃进，PML将会是保险领域预测分析（Predictive Analytics）的最重要分析维度之一。未来，能够利用先进技术和经典损失敞口量化理论快速响应市场动态的保险公司将能够更好地竞争和发展。

CHINA RE

EMPOWER YOUR INSURANCE BY EXPERTISE

Report on the Development of Reinsurance Industry in China

(2023)

CHINA REINSURANCE (GROUP) CORPORATION

CHINA FINANCIAL PUBLISHING HOUSE

Preface.

The 20th CPC National Congress was successfully held in 2022, defining the historic mission of advancing the rejuvenation of Chinese nation on all fronts through Chinese path to modernization, drawing a grand blueprint for building China into a great modern socialist country in every respect and unifying the people across the country to strive for faster development.

At present, the changes unseen in a century accelerate, with the world entering a new period of turbulence and transformation amid sustained geopolitical tensions, global climate change and other prominent worldwide issues. China's economic development faces an even more grim and complex external circumstances, with higher risks and uncertainties. Insurance, as the main instrument to reduce risks and uncertainties, will play an even greater role in providing risk protection, serving the real economy and assuring a better life for the people.

Thanks to the strong guidance of the National Administration of Financial Regulation (NAFR), as well as sustained economic growth and industry collaboration, China has become the world's second largest insurance market and the most important emerging insurance market. As a growing economy, China is expected to become the world's largest insurance market by 2035. At a historic moment when the timeframes of the two centenary goals converge, China's insurance industry has consistently assumed its responsibility to serve the mission of Chinese path to modernization, proactively putting the principles of sustainable development as to ESG into practice. The industry has focused on key fields such as modernization of the national governance system and capacity, transition to green energy, high-level technological self-reliance, rural revitalization and agricultural modernization, elderly care system and reforms in the systems of medicine, medical insurance and medical management. The industry is boosting industrial integration, strengthening innovation-driven initiatives, and progressively achieving the transition from passive loss sharing to proactive risk reduction throughout the process, from a provider of simple risk protections to a provider of comprehensive risk solutions, fully integrating into the bigger ecosystem of social risk management, effectively functioning as a risk protection provider to serve the national strategies, participate in social governance and safeguard the people's lives and property in a vigorous fashion. Keeping in mind the bigger picture of the country and the people, China's insurance industry keeps pace with the times of national rejuvenation while resonating with the people's aspirations for a better life.

Digitalization has become a vital impetus for the transformation, upgrading and high-quality development of the insurance industry. Digital technologies such as Artificial Intelligence, Blockchain, Cloud

Computing, Big Data, the Internet of Things, Biometrics, 5G, Augmented Reality, Quantum Communication, etc., are accelerating innovation and are seamlessly integrating into the entire insurance business process, including product design, marketing innovation, underwriting and claims processing, operational management and reinsurance arrangements. This integration proves to be driving insurance institutions to deeply engage with various industries such as healthcare, new energy vehicles, and agricultural modernization, enhancing internal operational efficiency while simultaneously contributing to the development of external industry ecosystems. Digitalization is transforming the business chain and value chain of the insurance industry, reshaping the operational logic of insurance institutions, driving them to transition from fragmented and isolated technological applications to a systematic ecosystem, moving from technology-enabled incremental improvements to reform-oriented business model changes, and achieving transition from the technological applications (hard power) to the corporate organizational culture (soft power).

Taken the world over, the El Niño phenomenon is exacerbating the global climate crisis. In 2022, natural disasters such as Hurricane Ian are expected to cause economic losses up to $275 billion, with insurance losses reaching $125 billion, well above the previous five and ten-year averages. In addition, multiple factors such as the Russia-Ukraine conflict, energy crises, ongoing and recurrent pandemic situations, and major developed economies tightening their monetary policies have led to a significant reduction in both traditional and emerging capital in the global insurance market, resulting in a clear trend of rising insurance prices. China's insurance industry has seized the opportunities of financial sector's two-way opening, stepped up its development of internationalization, with a focus on responding to the Belt and Road initiative. Actively entering the competition in the international insurance market and proactively integrating into the global insurance value chain, the industry has greatly enhanced its own international influence.

It is evident from the global insurance history that every developed insurance market is backed by a strong and sound reinsurance system. As the "insurance for insurers", China's reinsurance industry has been a pioneer in opening up the financial industry on all fronts. It has become a level playing field for over 500 domestic and foreign, onshore and offshore entities. Reinsurance plays the role of risk diversification, technical guidance and financing mechanism, and served as a "stabilizer" and "governor" for China's insurance market. As the founder and main force of China's reinsurance industry, China Reinsurance (Group) Corporation ("China Re Group" or "China Re") has always been guided by the Xi Jinping Thought on Socialism with Chinese Characteristics for a New Era, resolutely implemented the guiding principles of the 20th CPC National Congress and put into action the decisions and plans of the CPC Central Committee and the State Council. Dedicated to reinsurance as its principal mission,

China Re has been working hard to build a reinsurance ecosphere, expedite digital transformation, help improving industry infrastructures, promote product and service innovation and cooperate with partners to provide one-stop, customized and comprehensive risk management solutions, with the aim of serving the national major strategies, spreading economic operation risks, assuring people a better life and participating in global risk governance.

In 2022, China Re organized the compilation of the industry's first annual report—*Report on the Development of Reinsurance Industry in China (2022)*, thanks to the guidance of the former China Banking and Insurance Regulatory Commission (CBIRC) and the Insurance Association of China as well as the strong support from insurance and reinsurance institutions in China. This year, China Re further compiled the *Report on the Development of Reinsurance Industry in China (2023)* in collaboration with industry forces. This new report sheds light on the new landscape, features and trends of the industry development, hoping to provide a useful viewpoint of reference for readers to gain a panorama of and insights into China's reinsurance industry, and play a positive role in promoting industry communications at home and abroad and enhancing the social influence of the reinsurance industry.

On the new journey of Chinese modernization ahead, China's reinsurance industry is still in an important period of strategic opportunities alongside many difficulties and challenges, which calls for pooled wisdom and shared insights. China Re will move proactively and conduct more research and collaborate with all industry players to promote the high-quality development of China's insurance and reinsurance industry. We hope to make yet greater contributions to serving the overarching causes of the Party and the country and realizing the "Chinese Dream" of rejuvenating the Chinese nation.

He Chunlei, Chairman of China Re

September 2023

Introduction.①

The year 2022 was an extremely important year in the history of the Party and the country. China successfully convened the 20th CPC National Congress. An ambitious blueprint has been drawn for building a modern socialist country in all respects. 2022 was also a year full of complex risks, enormous challenges and arduous tasks. Facing both global changes and a pandemic unseen in a century, the world economy is exposed to greater downside risks. The external environment for development showed notably higher complexity, severity and uncertainty. The CPC Central Committee with Comrade Xi Jinping at its core united and led the people of all ethnic groups across the country to rise to the challenges, better balance both domestic and international situations, coordinate epidemic response with economic and social development, and development with security. With intensified macro-control efforts, China managed to maintain steady economic performance, enhance the quality of development and keep the society stable across the board. In 2022, China's GDP exceeded RMB 121

---

① In this Report, "China's reinsurance industry" or "China's insurance industry" refers to the reinsurance or insurance industry and market in the Chinese mainland, excluding Hong Kong, Macao and Taiwan. Data in this Report come mainly from the *Yearbook of China's Insurance* for past years, the data disclosed by the National Administration of Financial Regulation (NAFR), the former China Banking and Insurance Regulatory Commission (CBIRC) and the annual reports of reinsurance companies as well as the research and survey data for the reinsurance industry available during the preparation of this Report.

trillion, up by 3.0% year-on-year, continuously ranking second in the world. The overall price level remained stable, imports and exports grew by 7.7% year-on-year, and the share of digital economy in GDP rose to 41.5%. The national economy has shown good momentum for sustained recovery, fostering a stable macro environment for steady development of the insurance and reinsurance industry.

In 2022, China's reinsurance industry remained guided by the Xi Jinping Thought on Socialism with Chinese Characteristics for a New Era, actively implemented the guiding principles of the 20th CPC National Congress, acted on the decisions and plans of the CPC Central Committee and the State Council and the regulatory requirements , and consistently upheld the political consciousness and people-centeredness of the finance sector. The reinsurance industry kept enhancing the innovation capability, further pursued digital transformation, constantly strengthened risk prevention and strove to serve the supply-side structural reform of the insurance industry, fully functioned as the safety valve and stabilizer for the insurance market. With an expanding overall capability, the reinsurance industry has been increasingly more capable of serving the real economy. In 2022, China's insurance market registered RMB 278.28 billion in ceded premiums, up by 13.3% year-on-year. The premium income of the reinsurance industry was RMB 225.02 billion, up by 7.7% year-on-year. The total assets of the reinsurance industry stood at RMB 671.95 billion, an increase of 10.9% over the beginning of the year. China took a share of about 9.0% in the global reinsurance market. The reinsurance industry shows a "3C" feature, namely, "Collaboration" between insurers and reinsurers is going deeper and deeper, "Creation" and alteration are speeding up and "Convergence" of domestic and foreign markets deepens.

In 2022, the reinsurance industry aligned its own development closely with the bigger picture of serving the Party's and the country's strategies. It heightened its stance and worked harder to shoulder the political, economic and social responsibilities of serving the national strategies and socioeconomic development. The new energy vehicle (NEV) chip quality and safety liability insurance was launched, the first of its kind across the industry and the country, to contribute to China's push for self-reliance and self-improvement in science and technology and for a manufacturing power. Taking rural revitalization and common prosperity as its mission, the reinsurance industry has provided more than RMB 2 trillion of risk protections in agricultural production for more than 300 million farmers. In helping local governments improve public safety management, the Inherent Defect Insurance (IDI) by the industry provided risk protection for more than 178 million square meters of building projects. In supporting the Healthy China initiative and addressing the population aging, the industry provided *Huiminbao* design and service solutions for 116 cities, benefiting more than 120 million people. The member companies of the China Belt and Road Reinsurance Pool provided nearly RMB 3.3 trillion insurance protections for Chinese businesses "going global" and overseas interests (property related), an increase of 19.0% year-on-year.

In the light of the new landscape, features and trends of China's reinsurance industry, the *Report on the Development of Reinsurance Industry in China 2023* (the "Report") expands the research perspective and enriches the research materials in the form of "main report + special report", throwing light on every respect of China's reinsurance market development. Based on analysis of international and domestic macro-economy, policy environment, market changes, catastrophe risks and other key factors affecting the industry development, the Report focuses on outlining the latest developments in the reinsurance industry, including market size, market landscape, business structure and innovation practices. After reviewing the past developments and practices of the reinsurance industry, the Report conducts an in-depth study on the new opportunities, new risks and future trends in the industry. The digital transformation of the industry is accelerating, thus we also invite the insurance technology collaborative innovation platform--Inslab to join us for the report.

We are so grateful to Li Youxiang, Head of the Property Insurance Regulation (Reinsurance Supervision) Department of the former China Banking and Insurance Regulatory Commission for valuable guidance throughout the preparation of this Report.

We acknowledge support from leaders and experts from the insurance industry in respect of the publication of this Report. We are in debt to Wang Jun, Jin Xuequn and Zheng Wandong from the Reinsurance Company Regulation Division, Property Insurance

Regulation (Reinsurance Supervision) Department of the former China Banking and Insurance Regulatory Commission for their meticulous guidance on the report's framework and regulatory contents. We extend our gratitude to the Insurance Association of China for coordinated efforts to conduct industrial surveys and solicit the whole industry for opinions. The compilation of the Report was led by China Re, and the following organizations also participated:

China Reinsurance (Group) Corporation

China Property and Casualty Reinsurance Company Limited

China Life Reinsurance Company Limited

China Agriculture Reinsurance Corporation

PICC Reinsurance Company Limited

Taiping Reinsurance (China) Company Limited

Swiss Reinsurance Company Ltd Beijing Branch

Inslab

Zhang Jian and Dou Xujie from China Re are responsible for final compilation and editing of the Report. The work on preparation of the Report is divided as follows: The main report section was prepared by China Re, with Chapter I prepared by Guan Bing, Chapter II by Sun Tao, Chapter III by Jin Xiaoquan and Li Fei, Chapter IV by Xue Yuan and Liu Shuang and Chapter V by Zheng Lina, Fan Lingjian and Zhang Kun. In the special report section, Chapter I was prepared by Jin Xiaoquan and Yu Yang (China Re), Chapter II by Wang Ke and Chen Cai Chunzi (China Agriculture Re), Chapter III by Lou Peng, Yuan Xinfang, Wang Guangzhi, Zhang Bingyu and Zou Yifei [Taiping Re (China), China Asia-

Pacific Reinsurance Research Centre], Chapter IV by Dai Xin, Chen Yaxin and Wang Xiaoyang (Swiss Re), Chapter V by Liu Yang (Inslab), Chapter VI by Ma Xiaojing (China Re), Chapter VII by Yue Xiliu, Feng Jian, Du Yue and Wang Mingchang (China Re) and Chapter VIII by Diao Ning and Li Zhongyi (PICC Re). The English version was proofread by Wang Shaokang (China Re).

The Report is published with the joint efforts of the reinsurance industry. It proves to be the fruit of industry's wisdom. We express our sincere gratitude to all the companies and colleagues participating in the compilation of the Report. We also extend our appreciation to our counterparts including Munich Re, Hannover Re, SCOR SE and General Re for providing information, materials and data, as well as professional comments, opinions and suggestions and other inputs for the Report.

In the end, we sincerely hope that the *Report on the Development of Reinsurance Industry in China* (2023) will, through the explorations in theory and practice, inspire readers' wisdom, promote communications among the industry and further contribute to the high-quality development of China's reinsurance industry.

China Reinsurance (Group) Corporation

September 2023

Contents

Chapter I

Overview of China's Reinsurance Market in 2022 and Development Outlook

Faced with the resurging COVID-19 pandemic and complex environment both at home and abroad, China's reinsurance industry remained in steady operation in 2022 with an expanding market size, improving momentum for innovation and effective risk prevention and control. Demonstrating growing international influence and new breakthroughs in high-quality development, the industry showed a "3C" feature in general: collaboration, creation and convergence. First, "Collaboration" between insurers and reinsurers. Reinsurance continued to enhance its support for the direct insurance market, warranting closer cooperation between the two sides and stronger ability to create value for direct insurers. Second, "Creation" is speeding up. The reinsurance industry attached greater importance to innovation in products, technology, services and models, with numerous achievements made in various fields of innovation. Third, "Convergence" of domestic and foreign markets. Global reinsurers remained optimistic about the prospects of China's reinsurance market, evidenced by their branching or offshore participation in China and their capital increase.

I. Reinsurance Market Environment

(I) Worldwide

2022 saw the world economy in a transformation and turbulence. The global economic growth decreased to 3.4% from 6.1% in the previous year due to the Russia-Ukraine conflicts, energy crisis, trade protectionism and protracted COVID-19 pandemic, coupled with drastic tightening of monetary policies in developed economies. With the economic development and trade growth losing dynamic, inflation rose from 4.6% in 2021 to 9.0%[1], the highest level in nearly four decades. Developed economies in the Europe and the United States were at a higher risk of recession, with the global debt levels elevated, financial markets volatile and commodity prices fluctuating wildly.

In 2022, the global insurance market faced such headwinds as economic slowdown, hot inflation and rapid rise in interest rates. The inflation-adjusted global premium income was about USD 6.8 trillion, and the real growth rate decreased to about –1.1%, versus a growth rate of 3.4% in 2021. Specifically, the non-life premium income was about USD 4.0 trillion, a real growth rate of about 0.5%. The life premium income stood at around USD 2.8 trillion, a real growth rate of approximately –3.1%[2].

Opportunities and challenges coexisted in the global reinsurance market in 2022. The impact of the COVID-19 pandemic has subsided, but the insured losses caused by natural disasters such as Hurricane Ian have exceeded the average level in recent years. The sharp interest rate hikes in major developed economies in a short period of time have triggered financial market turbulence and floating losses on bond investment, resulting in a substantial reduction in the supply of traditional reinsurance capital and third-party capital. Affected by various factors, global property reinsurance market was characterized by relatively notable hard trends in 2022. The global life reinsurance market remained stable in general due to controllable

---

① Source: World Economic Outlook published by the World Bank in April 2023.

② Source: Sigma 3/2023 - "World insurance: stirred, and not shaken", Swiss Re Institute.

mortality risks from the COVID-19 pandemic and relatively healthy risk-adjusted return on capital.

(II) China

China took effective steps to soften the economic shocks from multiple unexpected factors. To address the lack of effective demand, China stepped up macro-control efforts to stabilize the national economy. China's GDP exceeded RMB 121 trillion in the year, representing an annual growth rate of about 3.0%, ranking second in the world. Domestic supply and demand were generally balanced, with overall prices remaining stable. High-tech industries, new energy industries and new drivers of the digital economy continued to gain momentum. High-level opening-up expanded, and the quality of development steadily improved[1].

In 2022, China's insurance market recorded premium income of about RMB 4,695.8 billion, an increase of 4.6% year-on-year, consolidating its No. 2 position in the world. The insurance density was about RMB 3,369/person, with an insurance penetration of about 3.9%[2], still showing a gap from developed insurance markets and implying great potential for development in China's insurance market.

In 2022, China's property insurance companies registered RMB 1,486.7 billion in premium income, up around 8.7% year-on-year. The non-motor

---

[1] Source: Statistical Bulletin of National Economic and Social Development 2022, published by the National Bureau of Statistics of China on February 28, 2023.

[2] Based on the global statistics contained in the Sigma 3/2023 - "World insurance: stirred, and not shaken", Swiss Re Institute. The USD/RMB exchange rate of 6.89 as at December 31, 2022 in the inter-bank foreign exchange market was adopted.

line expanded by 12.5% year-on-year, representing a share of about 44.6% and becoming the growth engine for property insurance and reinsurance markets. The premium income of personal insurance companies was RMB 3,209.1 billion, an increase of about 2.8% year-on-year[1]. As the industry was still in a period of transition and adjustment, the new insurance premiums and the value of new business (VNB) remained negative growth, and personal insurance companies had stable cession demand in general. By the end of 2022, the balance of China's insurance funds utilized was about RMB 25.1 trillion, an increase of 7.9% year-on-year, and the median financial internal rate of return (FIRR) industrywide was between 3.25% and 3.5%, showing a relatively stable yield of insurance funds.[2]

II. Reinsurance Market Developments

(I) Market size

1. Ceded premiums from primary insurers

(1) Size of Ceded premiums from primary insurers

In 2022, China's insurance market recorded RMB 278.28 billion in ceded premiums, up by 13.3% year-on-year. Over the same period, the premium income of domestic primary insurers stood at RMB 4,695.8 billion, up by 4.6% year-on-year. In 2022, the growth rate of ceded premiums

---

[1] Source: Former CBIRC. The 2022 data do not include premium income data for insurers in the phase of risk disposal.

[2] Source: China Insurance Asset Management Industry Survey Report 2022-2023 published by the former CBIRC and the Insurance Asset Management Association of China.

was about 8.7 percentage points higher than that of primary premiums written, mainly due to the fact that some of the direct insurers saw their solvency adequacy ratios declining on account of the business cycle effects. Also, the former China Banking and Insurance Regulatory Commission (CBIRC) officially implemented the *Solvency Regulatory Rules for Insurance Companies* (II) ("C-ROSS Phase II") on January 1, 2022, with a sharper focus on risk-orientation and imposing more stringent requirements on capital determination and supervision, which drove up direct insurers' demand for cessions.

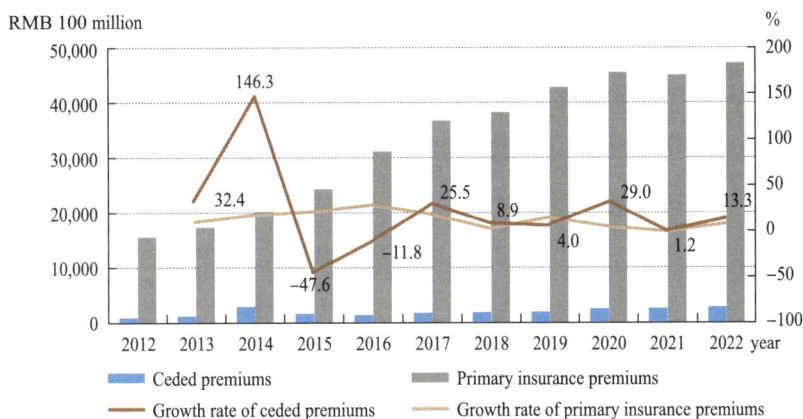

Figure 1   Primary Insurance Premiums, Ceded Premiums and Growth Rates (2012-2022)

(Source: Yearbook of China's Insurance and former CBIRC)

Table 1   Ceded Premiums, Primary Insurance Premiums and Cession Rates (2012-2022)

Unit: RMB 100 million, %

Year	Ceded premiums	Growth rate	Primary insurance premiums	Growth rate	Cession rate
2012	879.4		15,487.8		5.7
2013	1,164.0	32.4	17,222.1	11.2	6.8
2014	2,867.2	146.3	20,234.7	17.5	14.2
2015	1,501.6	−47.6	24,282.4	20.0	6.2

continued

Year	Ceded premiums	Growth rate	Primary insurance premiums	Growth rate	Cession rate
2016	1,323.8	−11.8	30,959.0	27.5	4.3
2017	1,661.2	25.5	36,580.9	18.2	4.5
2018	1,808.5	8.9	38,016.6	3.9	4.8
2019	1,881.6	4.0	42,644.8	12.2	4.4
2020	2,427.1	29.0	45,257.3	6.1	5.4
2021[1]	2,456.8	1.2	44,900.2	−0.8	5.5
2022[2]	2,782.8	13.3	46,958.0	4.6	5.9

Notes: The data on primary insurers' premium income in 2021 and 2022 do not include the data for insurers in the phase of risk disposal.

Source: Yearbook of China's Insurance and former CBIRC.

In 2022, the premiums ceded by property insurers in the Chinese market were RMB 162.95 billion, an increase of 11.6% year-on-year, accounting for 58.6% of the total ceded premiums. Personal insurance companies ceded RMB 115.33 billion of premiums to reinsurers, up by 15.8% year-on-year, accounting for 41.4% of total ceded premiums. In terms of the structure of ceded premiums in the past years, the ceded premiums showed a 60/40 split between property insurers and personal insurance companies.

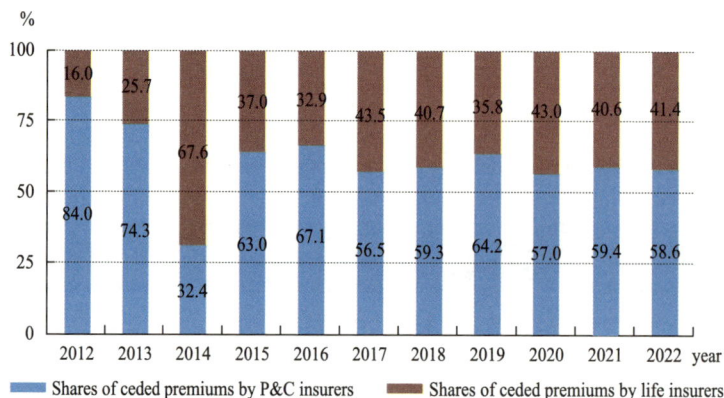

Figure 2   Premiums (%) Ceded by Property VS. Life Insurance Companies in 2012-2022

(Source: Yearbook of China's Insurance and former CBIRC)

From 2012 to 2022, reinsurance demand kept growing alongside China's insurance market expansion. Ceded premiums rose from RMB 87.94 billion to RMB 278.28 billion, representing an average annual growth rate of 12.2%. Over the same period, the premium income of primary insurers in China increased from RMB 1,548.78 billion to RMB 4,695.8 billion, an average annual growth rate of 11.7%.

In the past decade, ceded premiums and primary premiums have shown similar annual growth rates, yet with significant disparities in growth from year to year. The major fluctuations from 2014 to 2016 were mainly due to impact of C-ROSS Phase II. Having commenced in 2012, the C-ROSS Phase II project was officially launched in February 2015 and brought into a transitional phase before its full implementation from the first quarter of 2016. Compared with the size-oriented C-SI, C-ROSS Phase II is risk-oriented, which has a significant impact on insurers' cession demand and ceding strategy. Ceded premiums grew substantially from 2016 to 2017 and from 2019 to 2020, mainly driven by cessions from personal insurance companies.

(2) Cession rates of primary insurers

The cession rate in China's insurance market was around 5.9% in 2022. By segment, the cession rate was about 11.0% for property insurers and about 3.6% for personal insurance companies. Property insurers cover a broader range of risks，including catastrophe risks in particular when compared with life insurers. Thus property insurers have a greater demand for reinsurance and a higher cession rate.

The cession rate averaged about 6.1% in the domestic insurance market from 2012 to 2022. The years from 2014 to 2016 were the transitional period for C-ROSS Phase II regulatory policies, the cession rate experienced drastic fluctuations. The cession rate was as high as 14.1% in 2014 due to surge in demand and then gradually went down. Excluding impact of the fluctuations from 2014 to 2016, the average cession rate was 5.4%. The overall cession rate has gone up steadily since 2016, showing gradually increasing demand for spreading risks to reinsurers.

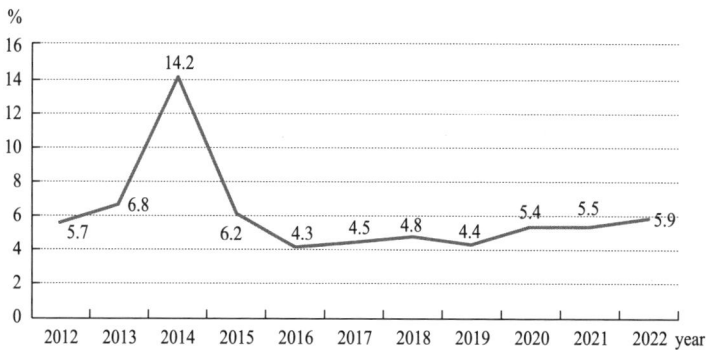

Figure 3   Cession Rates of the Primary Insurance Market (2012-2022)

(Source: Yearbook of China's Insurance and former CBIRC)

China's insurance market has a lower cession rate and a higher premium retention rate than the global market. According to estimates of the International Association of Insurance Supervisors (IAIS), the cession rate was about 8.5% for the global insurance market, 12.0% for North America and 8.5% for Europe[1].

2. Premium income in the reinsurance market

In 2022, the premium income of the domestic reinsurance market stood at RMB 225.02 billion, an increase of 7.7% year-on-year, higher

---

① Source: Global Insurance Market Report, published by the International Association of Insurance Supervisors (IAIS) in 2022.

than the growth rate of primary premiums, showing sound momentum for development of the industry. Specifically, the six Chinese reinsurers recorded RMB 162.55 billion in ceded premium income, up by 14.2% year-on-year, accounting for about 72.2%. The eight foreign reinsurers registered ceded premium income of RMB 62.47 billion, down by 6.4% year-on-year, accounting for around 27.8%.

From 2012 to 2022, the ceded premium income of reinsurers in China increased from RMB 69.12 billion to RMB 225.02 billion, an average annual growth rate of 12.5%. Overall, the ceded premium income of reinsurers showed similar average growth to primary premium income and premiums ceded by primary insurers, but the ceded premium income of reinsurers indicated significant differences and fluctuations in growth from year to year. In particular, the ceded premium income of reinsurers fluctuated significantly from 2014 to 2016 as the C-ROSS Phase II regulatory policies were in the transitional period. After C-ROSS Phase II was fully implemented in 2016, ceded premium income grew year by year.

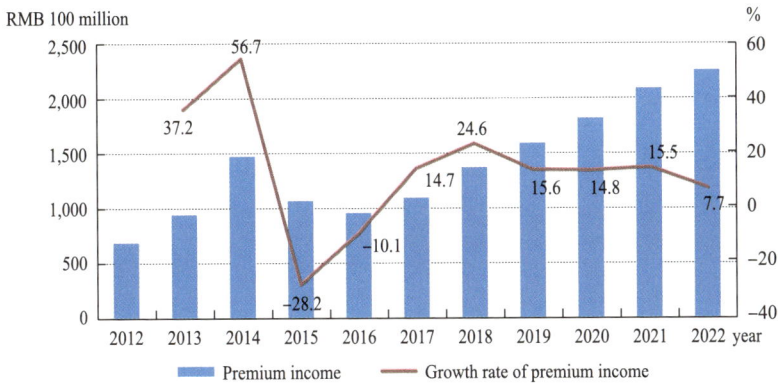

Figure 4   Premium Income of Reinsurers and Growth Rates (2012-2022)

(Source: Yearbook of China's Insurance and former CBIRC)

The premium income of Chinese reinsurers remained positive growth from 2012 to 2022. The premium income of foreign reinsurers operating in China was more volatile over the period with a growth rate of over 100% in 2014, down by nearly 47% in 2015 and down by about 6.4% in 2022, illustrating the different business strategies between Chinese and foreign reinsurers.

Table 2　Premium Income of Chinese VS. Foreign Reinsurers and Growth Rates (2012-2022)

Unit: RMB 100 million, %

Year	Premium income	Premium income of Chinese reinsurers	Growth rate	% of total	Premium income of foreign reinsurers	Growth rate	% of total
2012	691.2	400.3		57.9	290.9		42.1
2013	948.6	466.8	16.6	49.2	481.8	65.6	50.8
2014	1,486.0	502.5	7.6	33.8	983.5	104.1	66.2
2015	1,066.3	543.4	8.1	51.0	522.9	−46.8	49.0
2016	958.6	552.0	1.6	57.6	406.6	−22.2	42.4
2017	1,099.6	778.7	41.1	70.8	320.9	−21.1	29.2
2018	1,370.1	949.8	22.0	69.3	420.2	31.0	30.7
2019	1,576.1	1,044.9	10.0	66.2	533.0	26.8	33.8
2020	1,809.2	1,180.1	13.1	65.2	629.1	18.0	34.8
2021	2,090.2	1,422.9	20.6	68.1	667.3	6.1	31.9
2022	2,250.2	1,625.5	14.2	72.2	624.6	−6.4	27.8

Source: Yearbook of China's Insurance and former CBIRC.

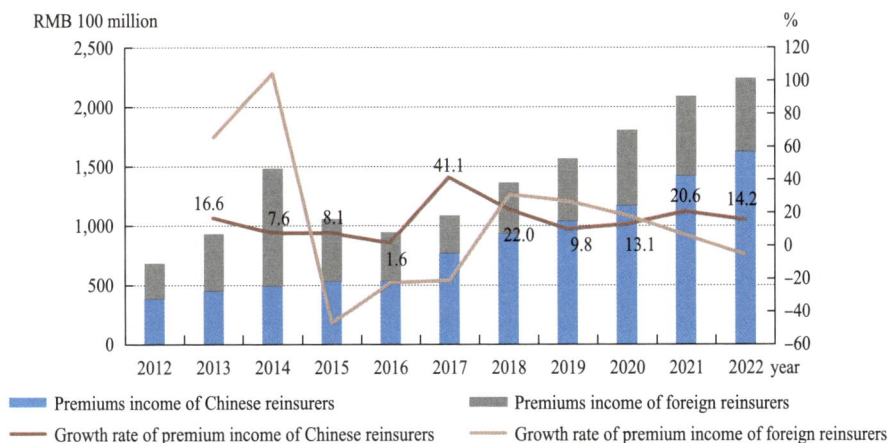

Figure 5   Premium Income of Chinese VS. Foreign Reinsurers and Growth Rates (2012-2022)

(Source: Yearbook of China's Insurance and former CBIRC)

3. Reinsurance claim payouts

The claim payouts of China's reinsurance industry totaled RMB 115.46 billion in 2022, up by 35.4% year-on-year, accounting for about 51.3% of the premium income for the year. Specifically, the six Chinese reinsurers recorded RMB 83.19 billion in claim payouts, up by 69.4% year-on-year, mainly due to a sharp rise in payouts from some reinsurers. The eight foreign reinsurers registered RMB 32.27 billion in claim payouts, down by 10.8% year-on-year.

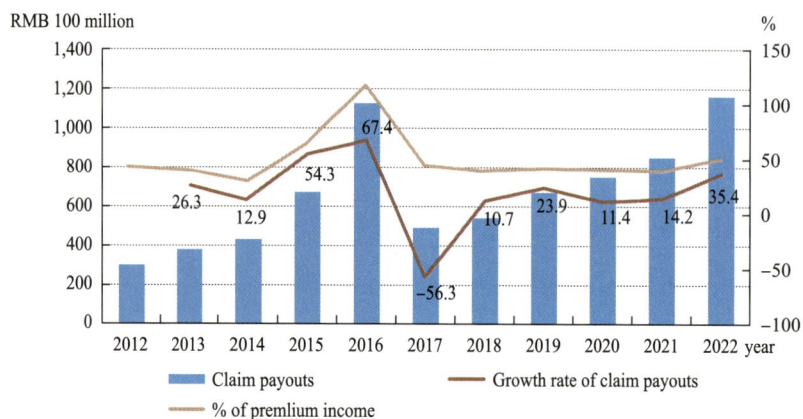

Figure 6   Reinsurance Claim Payouts (2012-2022)

(Source: Yearbook of China's Insurance and former CBIRC)

Table 3   Reinsurance Claim Payouts (2012-2022)

Unit: RMB 100 million, %

Year	Claim payouts	Chinese reinsurers' claim payouts	Growth rate	% of total	Foreign reinsurers' claim payouts	Growth rate	% of total
2012	303.8	151.8		50.0	151.9		50.0
2013	383.7	180.6	18.9	47.1	203.1	33.7	52.9
2014	433.2	210.5	16.6	48.6	222.6	9.6	51.4
2015	668.5	263.3	25.1	39.4	405.2	82.0	60.6
2016	1,119.4	301.2	14.4	26.9	818.1	101.9	73.1
2017	489.0	254.4	−15.6	52.0	234.6	−71.3	48.0
2018	541.2	278.3	9.4	51.4	262.9	12.1	48.6
2019	670.3	350.4	25.9	52.3	320.0	21.7	47.7
2020	746.5	432.7	23.5	58.0	313.8	−1.9	42.0
2021	852.6	491.0	13.5	57.6	361.6	15.2	42.4
2022	1,154.6	831.9	69.4	72.1	322.7	−10.8	27.9

Source: Yearbook of China's Insurance and former CBIRC.

RMB 100 million   %

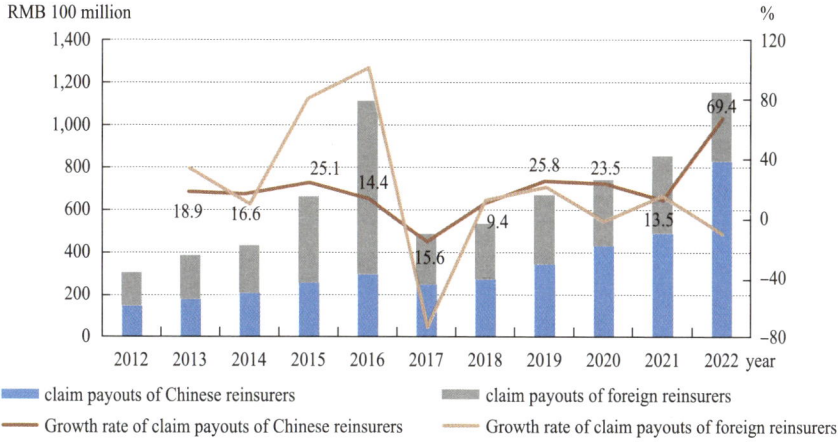

Figure 7   Claim Payouts of Chinese VS. Foreign Reinsurers and Growth Rates (2012-2022)

(Source: Yearbook of China's Insurance and former CBIRC)

From 2012 to 2022, the claim payouts of China's reinsurance industry rose from RMB 30.38 billion in 2012 to RMB 115.46 billion in 2022, representing an average annual growth rate of 14.3%. Overall, reinsurance payouts surged in 2016 when C-ROSS Phase II was initially implemented. Personal reinsurers' claim payouts grew substantially in 2016 before a marked decline in 2017, showing great fluctuations during the policy shift.

4. Total reinsurance assets

At the end of 2022, the total assets in China's reinsurance industry was RMB 671.95 billion, an increase of 10.9% from the beginning of the year, and 3.3 percentage points lower than the growth rate of premium income. From 2012 to 2022, the total assets in China's reinsurance industry increased from RMB 143.72 billion to RMB 671.95 billion, an average annual growth rate of 16.7%, outpacing the ceded premium income of reinsurers. Total assets were also volatile from 2014 to 2016 due to the impact of C-ROSS Phase II. Total reinsurance assets in China have kept expanding since 2016, in line with the trends in ceded premium income.

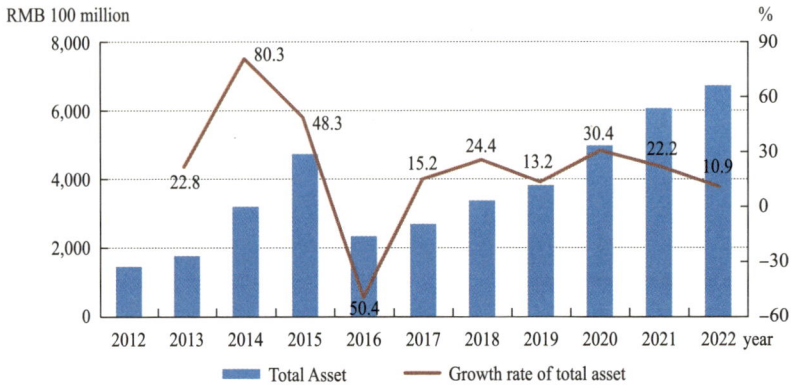

Figure 8 Total Assets of China's Reinsurance Industry and Growth Rates (2012-2022)

(Source: Yearbook of China's Insurance and former CBIRC)

From 2012 to 2022, total reinsurance assets represented a relatively stable share in total assets of the insurance industry, which stood at about 2.5% at the end of 2022. It shows that the reinsurance industry expanded gradually along with the insurance market, maintaining steady growth under the evolving regulatory policies and market environment. Meanwhile, the share of total insurance assets in total assets of the financial sector increased steadily from 5.6% in 2018 to 6.5% in 2022, indicating a growing role and heightening position of insurance in the financial sector.

Table 4 Total Assets and Proportions of Reinsurance, Insurance and Financial Sectors (2012-2022)

Unit: RMB 100 million, %

Year	Total reinsurance assets	Total insurance assets	Total reinsurance assets as % of total insurance assets	Total financial assets	Total insurance assets as % of total financial assets
2012	1,437.2	68,425.6	2.1		
2013	1,765.4	77,576.7	2.3		
2014	3,183.2	96,177.8	3.3		

continued

Year	Total reinsurance assets	Total insurance assets	Total reinsurance assets as % of total insurance assets	Total financial assets	Total insurance assets as % of total financial assets
2015	4,722.0	119,295.7	4.0		
2016	2,343.9	142,659.0	1.6		
2017	2,699.3	146,816.7	1.8		
2018	3,358.3	163,641.0	2.1	2,940,000	5.6
2019	4,261.3	187,495.6	2.3	3.186,900	5.9
2020	4,956.3	216,156.5	2.3	3,531,900	6.1
2021	6,057.5	248,874.0	2.4	3,819,500	6.5
2022	6,719.5	271,500.0	2.5	4,196,400	6.5

Source: Yearbook of China's Insurance, former CBIRC and the PBC website.

(II) Market Landscape

1. Higher diversity of market players

After years of development, China's reinsurance market has gradually formed a diversified landscape with domestic professional reinsurers as the mainstay and offshore reinsurers and direct insurers also playing in the market.

In terms of professional market players, by the end of 2022, there were 15 professional players in China's reinsurance market, including seven Chinese reinsurers (including 1 conglomerate, namely China Re Group) and 8 foreign reinsurers. Spanish reinsurer MAPFRE was approved to establish a branch in Beijing in August 2022 with working capital of RMB 500 million.

As for offshore market players, in recent years, offshore reinsurers have expanded their participation in the Chinese market by underwriting insurance ceded by domestic insurers through offshore transactions. In 2022, the domestic insurers conducted transactions with over 500 offshore reinsurers and ceded RMB 47.13 billion of premiums to overseas reinsurers, showing a basically stable size of cessions.

In addition, more than 100 domestic primary insurers in the property and Pesonal lines competed in the reinsurance market to various degrees. Some direct insurers conducted reinsurance transactions with overseas market players through business swap.

Table 5   Overview of Professional Reinsurance Companies in China[1]

Company name	Date of establishment	Place of registration	Nature of registration	Chinese/ foreign
China Reinsurance (Group) Corporation	1996	Beijing	Group	Chinese
China Property and Casualty Reinsurance Company Limited	2003	Beijing	Stand-alone Company	Chinese
China Life Reinsurance Company Limited	2003	Beijing	Stand-alone Company	Chinese
Munich Reinsurance Group Beijing Branch	2003	Beijing	Branch	Foreign
Swiss Reinsurance Company Limited Beijing Branch	2003	Beijing	Branch	Foreign
General Reinsurance Corporation Shanghai Branch	2004	Shanghai	Branch	Foreign
SCOR SE Beijing Branch	2008	Beijing	Branch	Foreign
Hannover Re Shanghai Branch	2008	Shanghai	Branch	Foreign
XL Reinsurance (China) Company Limited[2]	2011	Shanghai	Stand-alone Company	Foreign
Reinsurance Group of America, Incorporated Shanghai Branch	2014	Shanghai	Branch	Foreign
Taiping Reinsurance (China) Company Limited	2015	Beijing	Stand-alone Company	Chinese
Qianhai Reinsurance Company Limited	2016	Shenzhen	Stand-alone Company	Chinese
PICC Reinsurance Company Limited	2017	Beijing	Stand-alone Company	Chinese

continued

Company name	Date of establishment	Place of registration	Nature of registration	Chinese/ foreign
Korean Reinsurance Company Shanghai Branch	2020	Shanghai	Branch	Foreign
China Agriculture Reinsurance Corporation	2020	Beijing	Stand-alone Company	Chinese

Notes: 1. The name of each reinsurance entity is abbreviated as follows: China Re Group or China Re, China Re P&C or China Re, China Re Life or China Re, Munich Re or Munich Re Beijing Branch, Swiss Re or Swiss Re Beijing Branch, General Re or General Re Shanghai Branch, SCOR SE or SCOR SE Beijing Branch, Hannover Re or Hannover Re Shanghai Branch, XL Re, RGA or RGA Shanghai Branch, Taiping Re (China), Qianhai Re, PICC Re, Korean Re or Korean Re Shanghai Branch, and China Agriculture Re.

2. XL Insurance (China) Company Limited was established in 2011 and changed its name to XL Reinsurance (China) Company Limited in 2020.

Source: Yearbook of China's Insurance and annual reports of the reinsurance companies.

The number of players in the domestic reinsurance market kept growing from 9 in 2012 to fifteen in 2022, of which four players were Chinese reinsurers and eight were foreign reinsurers. One reinsurance company was established a year on average between 2014 and 2017, with another two reinsurers added in 2020 and one reinsurer approved in 2022.

2. A pattern of two-way opening-up began to take shape

In terms of "bringing in", the reinsurance market has become one of China's financial service sectors that have opened up earliest and most widely to the outside world since China's accession to the World Trade Organization (WTO) in 2001. All the world's major reinsurers have set up branch offices and carried out business in China, contributing talent, technology and capital to the onshore reinsurance market. In recent years, China's reinsurance industry has actively implemented the requirements of the CPC Central

Committee, further deepened its high-level opening-up, kept improving the national policies and standards in line with international standards and practices, further activated the internal impetus for industry development and continuously enhanced the capability of service innovation.

Since the 18th CPC National Congress, China has stepped up the development of Shanghai as an international reinsurance hub, which has yielded positive results. As at the end of 2022, Shanghai was home to more than 40 insurance corporations, 8 reinsurance institutions, 10 insurance asset management companies and 232 incorporated professional insurance intermediaries. The Shanghai International Reinsurance Center will focus on building an "international board" serving as the global trading venue for ceded reinsurance business. Its purpose is to pool global factors of production to gather in Shanghai, enhance the ability to allocate global resources and build a global reinsurance trading center with global influence and combining onshore and offshore operations, thereby creating a hub for the domestic reinsurance market while providing a strategic link between domestic and international markets.

Table 6   Distribution of Professional Reinsurance Companies in China

Company name	Distribution
China Reinsurance (Group) Corporation	Headquartered in Beijing
China Property and Casualty Reinsurance Company Limited	Headquartered in Beijing; branches in Shanghai and Shenzhen
China Life Reinsurance Company Limited	Headquartered in Beijing; branches in Shanghai and Shenzhen
Munich Reinsurance Group Beijing Branch	Branch in Beijing
Swiss Reinsurance Company Limited Beijing Branch	Branch in Beijing
General Reinsurance Corporation Shanghai Branch	Branch in Shanghai

continued

Company name	Distribution
SCOR SE Beijing Branch	Branch in Beijing
Hannover Re Shanghai Branch	Branch in Shanghai
XL Reinsurance (China) Company Limited	Incorporated in Shanghai
Reinsurance Group of America, Incorporated Shanghai Branch	Branch in Shanghai
Taiping Reinsurance (China) Company Limited	Headquartered in Beijing; branch in Shanghai
Qianhai Reinsurance Company Limited	Incorporated in Shenzhen
PICC Reinsurance Company Limited	Incorporated in Beijing
Korean Reinsurance Company Shanghai Branch	Branch in Shanghai
China Agriculture Reinsurance Corporation	Incorporated in Beijing

In terms of "going out", China's insurance market underwrites ceded reinsurance business from overseas primary insurers by means of offshore trading. The ceded premiums from overseas markets stood at about RMB 28.3 billion in 2022. Meanwhile, Chinese reinsurers are seeking distribution in overseas markets，which markedly broadens their horizons and strengthens their international competitiveness. China Re has become the eighth largest global reinsurer and one of the Chinese financial corporations and insurance companies with the broadest international distribution. China Re has extended its business to 11 countries and regions outside China with an overseas reinsurance team of over 500 professionals. China Re's overseas business accounts for 17.8%[1] of its reinsurance business, or 32.0% of its property lines.

---

[1] It is the ratio of China Re's total overseas income from insurance business to the Group's total premium income.

(III) Business structure

1. Premium income by type of business

In 2022, the premium income of China's reinsurance market stood at RMB 225.02 billion. Specifically, the premium income of treaty business was RMB 224.06 billion, up by 8.2% year-on-year, accounting for about 97.9% of the total premium income. The premium income of facultative business was RMB 4.8 billion, down by 3.1% year-on-year, accounting for about 2.1%[1] of the total. The treaty business maintained solid growth, versus a slowdown in facultative business.

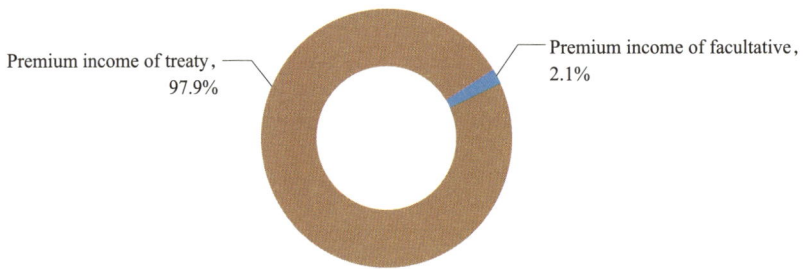

Premium income of treaty, 97.9%

Premium income of facultative, 2.1%

Figure 9   Proportions of Premium Income of Treaty VS. Facultative Business in 2022

(Source: Former CBIRC)

From 2012 to 2022, the premium income of treaty business increased from RMB 68.19 billion to RMB 224.06 billion, an average annual growth rate of about 12.6%. The premium income of facultative business increased from RMB 930 million to RMB 4.8 billion, an average annual growth rate of about 17.8%. In general, the treaty business is the dominant type of reinsurance business, accounting for more than 95% with a steady pace

---

[1] The impact of related party transactions between companies was considered in terms of premium income but not in terms of reinsurance premium income by treaty type.

of development. The facultative business represents a small share and grows fairly fast, though varying much over the years due to its nature of business.

Table 7 Premium Incomes, Growth Rates and Proportions of Treaty VS. Facultative Business (2012-2022)

Unit: RMB 100 million, %

Year	Treaty business premium income	Growth rate	% of total	Facultative business premium income	Growth rate	% of total
2012	681.9		98.7	9.3		1.3
2013	940.3	37.9	99.1	8.3	−10.7	0.9
2014	1,476.7	57.1	99.4	9.3	11.6	0.6
2015	1,055.2	−28.5	99.0	11.0	19.2	1.0
2016	917.9	−13.0	95.8	37.9	243.7	4.0
2017	1,080.2	17.7	98.2	19.4	−48.9	1.8
2018	1,339.4	24.0	97.8	30.7	58.5	2.2
2019	1,539.8	15.0	97.7	36.3	18.1	2.3
2020	1,774.3	15.2	97.5	45.8	26.2	2.5
2021	2,070.7	16.7	97.7	49.5	8.1	2.3
2022	2,240.6	8.2	97.9	48.0	−3.1	2.1

Source: Yearbook of China's Insurance and former CBIRC.

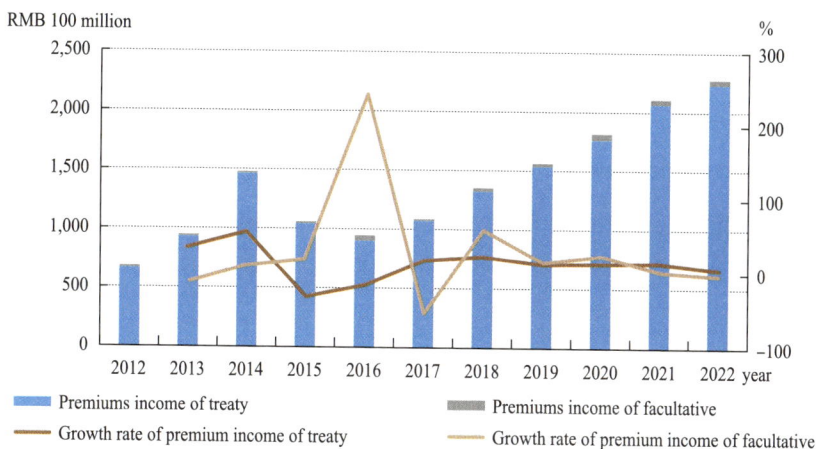

Figure 10 Premium Income of Treaty VS. Facultative Business and Growth Rates (2012-2022)

(Source: Yearbook of China's Insurance and former CBIRC)

2. Premium income by lines of business

In 2022, property reinsurance premium income of China's reinsurance market was RMB 122.05 billion, up by 13.5% year-on-year and accounting for about 54.2% of the total. Life reinsurance premium income was RMB 43.34 billion, down by 2.6% year-on-year and making up about 19.3% of the total. Health reinsurance premium income was RMB 53.22 billion, up by 7.2% year-on-year and accounting for about 23.7% of the total. Casualty reinsurance premium income was RMB 6.41 billion, down by 12.3% year-on-year and accounting for about 2.8% of the total.

Overall, firstly, the lines of business showed diverging growth rates of premium income. Property reinsurance grew rapidly, followed by health reinsurance, while the size of life reinsurance and casualty reinsurance remained basically the same as the last year's. Secondly, health reinsurance premium income was significantly slower than in previous years, consistent with the trends in health insurance in the insurance market, which recorded a significant decrease in demand for health reinsurance in 2022; Thirdly, compared with 2021, the share of property reinsurance premium income increased slightly, while that of life reinsurance, health reinsurance and casualty reinsurance saw a modest decline, indicating the impact of business structure adjustments in the insurance market on reinsurance.

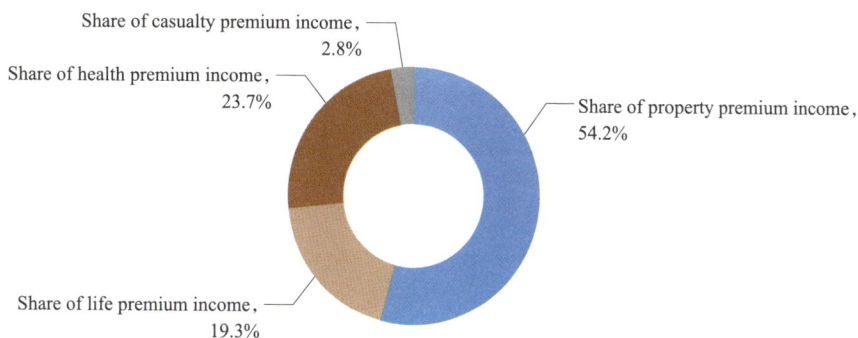

Figure 11   Proportions of Premium Income by Lines of Reinsurance in 2022

(Source: Former CBIRC)

From 2012 to 2022, the property reinsurance premium income in China's reinsurance market increased from RMB 46.26 billion to RMB 122.05 billion, an average annual growth rate of about 10.2%. Life reinsurance premium income grew from RMB 15.30 billion to RMB 43.34 billion, an average annual growth rate of about 11.0%. Health reinsurance premium income increased from RMB 5.06 billion to RMB 53.22 billion, an average annual growth rate of about 26.5%. Casualty reinsurance premium income expanded from RMB 2.5 billion to RMB 6.41 billion, an average annual growth rate of about 9.9%. Health reinsurance recorded the fastest growth with a growing share of premiums over the years, exceeding 20% for the first time in 2019, and its reinsurance premiums exceeded RMB 40 billion in 2020, which indicated its greatest growth potential. However, health reinsurance has slowed down in recent years. Given the rising share of health insurance among P&C insurers, the demand for health reinsurance is expanding. In particular, the increase in demand for short-term health insurance has generated higher premium income.

Table 8 Premium Income and Growth Rates by Lines (2012-2022)

Unit: RMB 100 million, %

Year	Property	Growth rate	Life	Growth rate	Health	Growth rate	Casualty	Growth rate
2012	462.6		153.0		50.6		25.0	
2013	562.8	21.7	297.3	94.3	63.5	25.6	24.8	–0.6
2014	588.0	4.5	799.6	168.9	65.7	3.4	32.7	31.7
2015	598.1	1.7	320.9	–59.9	112.1	70.7	35.1	7.4
2016	480.7	–19.6	285.9	–10.9	100.1	–10.8	43.5	23.9
2017	484.9	0.9	430.2	50.5	136.1	36.0	48.4	11.3
2018	600.4	23.8	484.4	12.6	218.2	60.4	67.1	38.5
2019	729.9	21.6	421.3	–13.0	353.1	61.8	73.6	9.7
2020	840.1	15.1	441.6	4.8	454.5	28.7	73.1	–0.7
2021	1,075.6	28.0	445.0	0.79	496.5	9.2	73.1	0.0
2022	1,220.5	13.5	433.4	–2.6	532.2	7.2	64.1	12.3

Source: Yearbook of China's Insurance and former CBIRC.

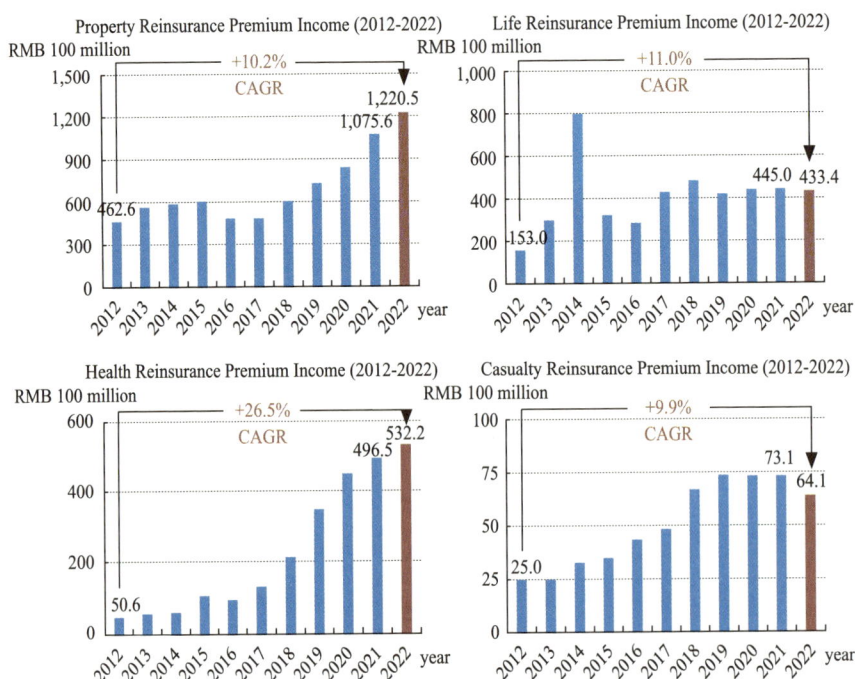

Figure 12 Property,Life,Health,Casualty Reinsurance Premium Income and Annual Growth Rate (2012-2022)

(Source: Yearbook of China's Insurance and former CBIRC)

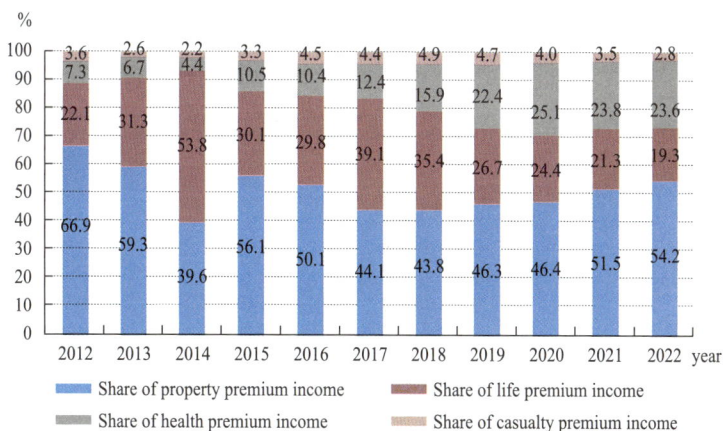

Figure 13   Proportions of Reinsurance Premium Income by Lines

(Source: Yearbook of China's Insurance and former CBIRC)

3. Innovation in reinsurance products and services

The traditional reinsurance services based on proportional insurance treaty have always been the basic way for reinsurers to provide stable underwriting capacity support, improve the solvency of primary insurers and maintain long-term partnership between direct insurers and reinsurers on a mutual benefit and win-win basis. Some reinsurers have explored how to strengthen the cycle management and portfolio management of traditional reinsurance business, in an effort to help the insurance industry optimize capital investment and stabilize the level of risks and returns.

In recent years, China's insurance industry has accelerated its push into ermerging risks, fields and markets. The reinsurance industry has gradually moved from behind the scenes to the front of stage leveraging on its strengths in data, product development and pricing. Reinsurers, in closer cooperation with direct insurers, provide comprehensive services ranging from product development to project design, data analysis, automated underwriting, intelligent claim settlement and risk control. Actively integrating themselves into the industry ecosphere, reinsurers provide one-stop customized solutions to meet the individualized needs of direct insurers and help clients enhance value.

(IV) Risk management

In recent years, the reinsurance industry has strengthened the risk management duties of relevant parties with growing awareness of risk management. A full-fledged risk management framework has been created, with a broad spectrum of risk management policies and procedures in place, the working mechanism for risk management more reasonable and the risk control toolkit diversified. In 2022, reinsurance companies generally demonstrated good solvency and overall risk evaluation, laying a solid and effective foundation for their business expansion, risk management and reputation maintenance.

1. Solvency capital requirement[1]

The core solvency ratio is the ratio of an insurance company's core capital to its minimum capital requirement (MCR). It measures the adequacy of an insurer's high-quality capital, subject to a minimum regulatory requirement of 50%. The comprehensive solvency ratio is the ratio of the available capital to MCR, which measures the overall adequacy of an insurer's capital, subject to a minimum regulatory requirement of 100%.

From the first quarter to the fourth quarter of 2022, the average core

---

[1] The solvency data below are all statistics under the C-ROSS Phase II rules.

solvency ratios of reinsurance companies were 267.5%, 281.2%, 278.5% and 268.5%, respectively, all exceeding the regulatory floor and the quarterly averages of P&C insurers and personal insurance companies in the quarters.

From the first quarter to the fourth quarter of 2022, the average comprehensive solvency ratios of reinsurance companies were 298.5%, 310.4%, 309.1% and 300.1% respectively, all exceeding the regulatory floor and the quarterly averages of P&C insurers and personal insurance companies in the quarters.

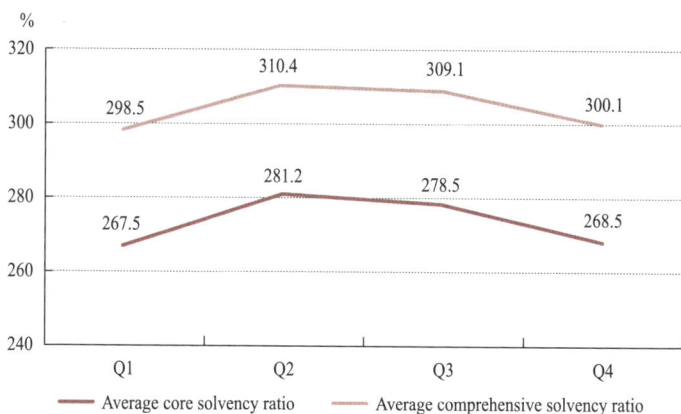

Figure 14   Solvency Ratios of Reinsurance Companies in 2022

(Source: Former CBIRC)

Compared with 2021, driven by shift to the new solvency standards and expansion of the reinsurance business, the minimum capital required for insurance risk in the reinsurance industry increased significantly in 2022. As the minimum capital requirement increased over the end of the previous year, both comprehensive solvency ratio and core solvency ratio declined in 2022.

2. Integrated risk rating (IRR)

IRR represents an evaluation of the integrated risk regarding an insurance company's solvency. It measures the overall solvency risk of an insurer with 4 classes: A, B, C and D, and the required regulatory rating is B.

In 2022, a total of 14 reinsurers received and disclosed their quarterly IRRs, all of which were rated Class B or higher.

3. Solvency-Aligned Risk Management Requirements and Assessment (SARMRA)

SARMRA is an important part of the functional supervision of the insurance industry. It reflects the risk management level of an insurance company by assessing the soundness of the system and the effectiveness of compliance. SARMRA is of great significance for improving the risk management level of insurers and enhancing the industry's ability to forestall and defuse risks. A SARMRA score of 80 or higher improves solvency adequacy.

In 2022, regulators conducted onsite SARMRA on eight reinsurers. The average score of reinsurers was 79.73, up by 1.11 from 2021, and six reinsurers scored more than 80.[1]

(V) Development of the reinsurance brokerage market

Reinsurance brokers are an important bridge and link for creating reinsurance relations between domestic reinsurers and direct insurers, and

---

[1] Source: The annual SARMRA results of insurance companies for 2022 published by the former CIBIRC on the website of the former CBIRC.

between domestic companies and overseas companies. They are also an important channel for Chinese insurers and reinsurers to access international professional services. With their thorough and timely knowledge of market information as well as their abundant expertise and experience, reinsurance brokers provide high-quality services for both sides of reinsurance, including designing reinsurance plans, implementing reinsurance arrangements and providing professional training.

China's reinsurance brokerage market is one of the most open financial sectors. Similar to domestic brokerage companies, foreign brokerage companies registered and approved in China Reinsurance Registration System can launch reinsurance business overseas. The China Reinsurance Registration System data show that there were 244 reinsurance brokers as at July 2023, of which 122 were overseas brokers and 122 were domestic brokers.

Players in China's reinsurance brokerage market are mainly composed of international reinsurance brokers, domestic reinsurance brokers and domestic direct insurance brokers who are concurrently engaged in reinsurance business. China's reinsurance broker market is mainly composed of three top-ranked foreign professional reinsurance brokers in the world, namely, Guy Carpenter, Aon and Willis. Their comprehensive services, professional teams and sufficient resources enable them to make complex reinsurance arrangements on a global scale. Chinese reinsurance brokers and direct insurance brokers have smaller market shares. Domestic professional reinsurance brokers including Zenith, Continental and Jiang

Tai are highly market-oriented and know customers' needs well, with professional teams for specific lines of business to provide a full range of services.

Treaty reinsurance is the principal business in China's reinsurance brokerage market, dominated by international reinsurance brokers. Chinese reinsurance brokers are more involved in the facultative business. They are engaged in facultative insurance of particular industries or enterprises according to their own resources or technical strengths.

(VI) Reinsurance Regulation

The regulatory authorities, with a focus on serving China's overall development, issued a series of rules, guidelines and directives with significant industry-wide influence in 2022, steering market players toward actively fulfilling the functions of insurance and bringing discipline to activities across the industry. C-ROSS Phase II has been officially implemented since 2022, enhancing overall risk control of the industry at the institutions level. Rules and regulations have been optimized with respect to the use of insurance funds, management of related party transactions, the corporate governance mechanism, the insurer supervision and assessment system, the insurer capital replenishment and measurement and the supervision of outbound data transfer, thereby giving a boost to high-quality development of the industry. Policy documents were promulgated in terms of the COVID-19 response, rural revitalization, boosting China's strength in transportation, micro, small and medium-sized enterprises, new urbanites, green development, inclusive insurance and digital transition. These documents guide the industry to better serve the national strategies and the real economy.

III. Reinsurance Services for Economical and Social Development

Reinsurance, as the "insurance for insurers", is an important means to support risk spreading, financial stability and innovative development of the insurance industry, and also a crucial safeguard for macroeconomic growth and insurance market stability. In 2022, China's reinsurance industry remained led by innovation, deepened reform and opening-up and accelerated high-quality development, continuing to contribute its professional value in serving economic growth, people's livelihood, social governance, and opening-up.

(I) Being a practitioner in risk reduction and serving the real economy for higher quality and efficiency

In serving China's push for a "world manufacturing power", China Re aimed at the key and core technologies and provided risk protections for the experiment and inaugural commercial flight of China's domestically built C919 airplane, solid backing for the aerospace industry. China Re developed the First (Set of) Major Technical Equipment insurance, covering risks in all high-end manufacturing segments including marine engineering, rail transit and environmental protection equipment.

In serving the "digital China" strategy, China Re strongly supported the digital economy's development and launched industry-finance cooperation with the Ministry of Industry and Information Technology, jointly promoting development of emerging industries such as information technology. China Re built a cybersecurity system jointly with the Chaoyang sub-park of the Zhongguancun Science Park, 360 Group and other parties to enhance the depth of industrial informatization.

In serving China's quest for technological self-reliance and self-sufficiency, China Re fully supported the first-reactor nuclear insurance for China's key technology project CAP1400, with a focus on such model projects as China's third-generation nuclear power plant Hualong One in which China has full intellectual property rights. China Re issued the first commercial quality and safety liability insurance policy for China-made chips for new energy vehicles (NEVs), the first of its kind in China and across the industry. This coverage provides risk protections for NEV manufacturers using China-made chips, enhancing the resilience of China's automobile industry chain and Chinese NEV makers' confidence in independent research and development.

In serving green development, the reinsurance industry continued to provide risk protections for renewable energy businesses such as offshore wind farms and NEVs. China Re released China's first NEV insurance pricing and risk control model "Re · Road", in an effort to promote the integrated innovation and collaborative development of the insurance and NEV industries. PICC Re served dozens of clean energy projects such as offshore wind farms, established an automated underwriting mechanism for offshore wind farms and provided a cumulative underwriting capacity of more than RMB 20 billion. Swiss Re assisted direct insurers in developing

China's first insurance plan for wetland carbon sequestration and ecological values and implemented the plan in Ningbo, providing risk protections for carbon sequestration and other ecological values of the Hangzhou Bay National Wetland Park.

Box: China Re Serves the "Strong Auto Chips & Stable Supply Chain" Initiative of China's Automobile Industry, Helping Build China into a World Manufacturing Power

In recent years, China has accelerated the localization of new energy vehicle (NEV) parts and components to achieve "strong auto chips and stable supply chain". It is imperative for the insurance industry to enhance its functions in disaster and loss prevention, risk transfer and financial compensation, thereby forming a virtuous cycle of "technology + industry + insurance". In recent years, bearing in mind the country's most fundamental interests, China Re has given full play to its strengths in product innovation and risk management in the fields of science and technology insurance and supply chain insurance. It released integrated risk solutions for the domestic NEV industry chain, including the product quality and safety liability insurance for China-made chips and the NEV pricing and risk control model, effectively facilitating the high-quality development of China's NEV industry chain.

First, the first ever NEV chip quality and safety liability insurance product was launched in China. In conjunction with insurance companies, China Re successfully launched and exclusively provided reinsurance support for China's first commercial quality and safety liability insurance for China-made NEV chips. The first product provided RMB 5 million of comprehensive risk protection for famous chip design, development and making company Unigroup Microelectronics. The product has effectively eliminated the worries of NEV manufacturers using China-made chips, enhanced the resilience of the automotive industry chain and the confidence in independent research and development, providing risk protections for accelerating the domestic chip replacement.

On this basis, under the guidance of the relevant departments of the

Ministry of Industry and Information Technology, China Re has broadened the coverage for chip localization and innovatively developed the first industry chain insurance product for the automakers, suppliers and chip designers. The product provides protections against risks in product quality, product liability, research costs and recall concerning automotive electronic components, providing crucial support for improving the risk protection system for localization of auto chips, breaking developed nations' clamp-down on China's chip sector that has bottlenecked the automotive industry chain, and achieving technological self-reliance and self-sufficiency by using China-made chips.

Second, China's first NEV pricing and risk control model "Re · Road" was developed. The model is divided between insurance pricing and risk control alarming. It adopts the world's cutting-edge actuarial technology and artificial neural network method. Featuring explainability, high precision and iteration, the model effectively meets the pricing and risk control needs regarding risks caused by thermal runaway of vehicle batteries, vehicle loss and dangerous driving behaviors. On the producer side, the model makes full use of the data analysis and risk control capabilities of the insurance industry to assist the NEV makers optimize the safety of various technologies and improve the fire control capabilities. On the consumer side, the model provides high-quality insurance and risk management services for NEV consumers through reasonable risk pricing, and gives a boost to the consumer demand for NEVs.

(II) Functioning as a builder of the new development pattern that serves rural revitalization and common prosperity

In serving rural revitalization and building up the national strength in agriculture, the reinsurance industry has achieved remarkable results ranging from the underwriting capacity support and product innovation and development behind the scenes to the use of technological power to help customers reduce risks in front of the scenes. China Agriculture Re has played a vital role in spreading agricultural disaster risks and promoting high-quality development of agricultural insurance. In the past two years, China Agriculture Re has provided nearly RMB 2 trillion of risk protections for agricultural production through treaty reinsurance, serving about 300 million rural households. China Re has actively expanded its underwriting capacity to help keep China's policy-oriented agricultural insurance market stable on track. Also, it has created new development models of commercial agricultural insurance, led the industry in developing an innovative insurance scheme for high-standard farmland development and implementing it in 12 provinces to improve farmland construction, management and maintenance. The weather index-based agricultural insurance product R&D platform went live, with more than 10 products bearing local characteristics launched and nearly RMB 90 billion worth of novel agricultural risk protections provided. In the past three years, PICC Re has provided a total of nearly RMB 20 billion of agricultural insurance-related risk protections, of which close to RMB 100 million covered rural housing projects in more than 20 provinces. Swiss Re rereleased Version 2.0 of its intelligent agricultural risk management platform SRAIRMP, providing insurance companies with multi-disaster, multi-scale, real-time and instant quantitative risk assessment, and helping the agricultural insurance industry improve risk management capabilities.

In terms of supporting common prosperity, China Re served small and micro businesses, exploring business interruption insurance for small and medium-sized enterprises (SMEs) and providing targeted coverage for 757,000 SMEs. It also provided innovative services to 230 million new urbanities including delivery riders. The "back-to-poverty insurance" provided RMB 23.708 billion of risk protections for 1,805,800 households lifted out of poverty in 20 provinces or regions including Gansu, Inner Mongolia and Heilongjiang.

(III) Functioning as a social co-governor that serves modernization of the national governance system

In terms of catastrophe risk management, China Re took in-depth part in designing China's earthquake catastrophe insurance system and piloting the comprehensive catastrophe insurance in various regions. Acting as the chief reinsurer in 80% of local catastrophe insurance pilot projects, China Re provided technical services such as disaster risk assessment, risk sharing mechanism research, insurance plan design and premium rate calculation, extending new protections to 40 million customers and accumulatively covering 130 million people, providing strong safeguards for disaster relief and post-disaster reconstruction. PICC Re took the initiative in joining the earthquake insurance pool for urban and rural residents and participated in the governmental catastrophe insurance programs in Guangdong, Guangxi, Hubei, Henan, Xiamen, Ningbo and Shenzhen, protecting the life and property security of more than 300 million urban and rural residents.

In terms of public safety management, China Re led the innovation of insurance products such as environmental pollution liability insurance, construction project workplace safety liability insurance, and inherent defect insurance (IDI). Specifically, IDI has covered a total floor area of 178 million square meters, effectively reducing social conflicts and disputes, promoting social management innovation and building a harmonious society. PICC Re actively participated in reinsurance business regarding vaccination, bail-out of service enterprises and business reopening in relation to the COVID-19 pandemic. Its service covered more than 700 million doses of COVID-19 vaccines given, and paid nearly RMB 7 million of indemnity support for 1,671 adverse reaction claims, helping building a national immunization shield and fulfilling its responsibility as a central state-owned enterprise.

(IV) Functioning as the guardian of the people throughout the lifecycle, and serving the Healthy China Initiative and the national strategy in response to population aging

In terms of protecting public health, China Re, as the chief reinsurer in China, actively participated in developing city-specific commercial medical insurance ("Huiminbao"), providing comprehensive support including product development, actuarial data, risk underwriting and system operation. The innovative solutions to inclusive insurance were promoted on a city-specific basis, benefiting 120 million people in 116 cities. In conjunction with the National Medical Alliance for Hypertension, China Re also established Qinghai Province's first Comprehensive Prevention and Control Demonstration Area for Co-management of Hyperlipidemia, Hypertension and Hyperglycemia in Xunhua County, Qinghai Province. It provided the first batch of 1,500 hypertension patients with the "chronic disease management + insurance" solution free of charge, protecting them from falling below the poverty line or returning to poverty due to illnesses. The project, as one of the first typical cases, has been extended nationwide by the National Rural Revitalization Administration.

In terms of the national strategy in response to population aging, China

Re has utilized its capabilities of insurance product design and strengths in professional investment of insurance funds, supporting endowment insurance startups on both ends of underwriting and investment and building the third pillar of the national pension scheme by joint efforts. China Re also cooperated with regulators in improving the long-term care insurance system and led the industry by launching 20 new products with a focus on old-age insurance, disability insurance and nursing insurance, providing one-stop care services for the elderly.

(V) Functioning as a participant in international cooperation that serves China's new development pattern of "dual circulation"

China Re chairs and manages the China Belt and Road Reinsurance Pool (CBRRP). In 2022, the member companies of the CBRRP provided nearly RMB 3.3 trillion worth of insurance for China's overseas interests (property category), an increase of 19.0% year-on-year. PICC Re has persistently strengthened its capability of serving customers along the Belt and Road and created an international intermediary service model. In the past two years, PICC Re has completed regulatory registration in Argentina and Chile, and accumulatively provided RMB 10.6 billion of risk protections for key customers such as Huawei, Goldwind and China Railway Construction and Sinovac's vaccine support for the COVID-19 fight in Latin American countries, earning RMB 17.5 million of premium income and delivering good social benefits. Taiping Re (China) has played an active part in building the Guangdong-Hong Kong-Macao Greater Bay Area, providing more than RMB 7.8 billion of risk protections for over 40 projects in the region, including the Shenzhen-Huizhou Intercity Railway and the Qianhai-Huanggang Port Section of Guangzhou-Dongguan-Shenzhen Intercity Railway, both being major projects in the Shenzhen Metropolitan Area.

(VI) Functioning as a stabilizer of the insurance market and a booster to the industry development, empowering high-quality development of the insurance industry

China Re established China Re Catastrophe Risk Management Co., Ltd. ("China Re CRM"), the first InsurTech firm specializing in catastrophe risk management in China's insurance industry. In 2022, China Re developed and launched the first Chinese flood catastrophe model with own intellectual property rights and iteratively developed Chinese typhoon and earthquake catastrophe models, shaping a China Re-branded spectrum of Chinese earthquake, typhoon and flood catastrophe models. These proprietary and controllable catastrophe models have made catastrophe risks "visible, calculable and manageable", effectively improving the ability to prevent and reduce disasters. To date, the Chinese typhoon and earthquake catastrophe models have been used by more than 30 insurance organizations and government agencies. China Re led development of the life insurance infrastructure, actively participated in compiling the fourth set of mortality tables and completed the data collection, cleaning and calculation for 904 million policies and 10.01 million claims across the industry, scientifically reflecting the death and longevity risks of life insurance and consolidating the data foundation of the industry. The trading information data exchange system developed by PICC Re won the "Global InsurTech Case Award", and

China Re CRM won the "Global InsurTech Enterprise Award". Swiss Re and Baidu jointly launched the industry's first customized insurance solution for the Baidu Apollo autonomous driving service, namely automatic parking product insurance, which won the "Annual Motor Insurance Innovation Award 2022" awarded by the *Insurance Asia*. In non-life lines, Munich Re established the Insurance Solutions Department in April 2022. Based on technical data analysis and oriented to product development and consulting services, this new function is committed to helping insurance companies efficiently improve the underwriting quality and strictly strengthen underwriting management. In the health insurance segment of the life lines, Munich Re launched iRISK, a tailor-made digital underwriting risk control solution for the Chinese market, helping insurers simplify the underwriting process, increase underwriting efficiency and reduce adverse selection risks.

IV. Outlook on China's Reinsurance Market

In 2023, China's reinsurance industry will continue to deepen reforms, keep to the right path while making innovations, stay true to the original mission of risk protections, accelerate the transformation of business models, effectively upgrade and appropriately expand the reinsurance business and march down the road to development with Chinese characteristics.

(I) Opportunities and Challenges

1. Opportunities

From the perspective of economic growth, major developed economies will slow down their pace of monetary tightening in 2023, softening the external pressure on China's stock, bond and foreign exchange markets. China has extricated itself from the aftermath of the COVID-19 pandemic, with gradual improvements in consumption environment and order as well as stable market expectations and confidence. The pro-growth policy will continue to work and steer the economy toward stabilization and recovery. With its annual economic growth projected to be about 5.0% for 2023, China will contribute one percentage point of the global economic growth and account for one third of the incremental global output. China's economy has great resilience and potential for growth. The fundamentals sustaining China's sound economic growth in the long run remain unchanged, laying a solid foundation for the high-quality development of the insurance market.

From the perspective of growth momentum, investment remains a major driver of a steady recovery of the economy. Both traditional and new infrastructures will continue to gain momentum, giving an impetus to engineering insurance, freight insurance, and new energy insurance. As consumption will play a bigger role in driving the economic growth going forward, motor insurance and home property insurance are expected to keep growing. Stabilizing foreign trade and playing the vital role of exports is China's long-term development strategy, implying huge insurance gaps in the development of Belt and Road Initiative and the protection of Chinese enterprises' overseas investment activities and overseas interests. With the "overall national security" strategy implemented, ensuring the security in food, energy, industrial chains and other sectors means huge potential demand for agricultural insurance, safety liability insurance and commercial property insurance, among others. China will value insurance more as a helper in social governance transition. The insurance industry will make up for the deficiencies in public services and social management in more sectors, including food and drugs, workplace safety, environmental protection and labor security. Annuity insurance and health insurance are expected to move onto the fast track as a series of favorable policies are promulgated, such as the personal pension system, data sharing between basic and commercial medical insurance programs, expansion of the tax-deductible health insurance and conversion between life insurance and long-term care insurance liabilities. Further, the demand for reinsurance will also be persistently released amid China's faster move to bridge the gap in risk protections and pursue higher-quality development.

2. Challenges

First, the macro environment is complex and volatile. China will face greater uncertainty in the external environment in 2023. The world will see the inflation still high, the economic and trade growth moderating and major central banks' policy tightening effects lingering, which will add to the pressure from the outside world. The International Monetary Fund (IMF) forecast a bleak outlook for the global economy in 2023, with growth rate decreasing to a historical low——2.8% while financial stability risks rising.

The foundation for the Chinese economy to stabilize and improve has yet to be laid. Insufficient aggregate demand remains a prominent problem in the economy at present, with economic transformation and upgrading facing new headwinds. The misalignment of macro cycles between China and the United States restricts the elbow room for China's macro policies to work. Climate change has led to frequent catastrophe events and increased complexity of economic and social risks, making risk management more difficult and increasing external risk factors for reinsurance companies.

Second, the policy impact will be further felt. The international accounting standard IFRS17 has been piloted among listed companies at home and abroad, expected to be extended industry-wide in 2026. China's motor insurance segment has embarked on another round of comprehensive reform, with the floating range of motor insurance's discretionary coefficient expanded nationwide before June 1, 2023, which will further widen the fluctuations in motor insurance premium rates. The C-ROSS II has been implemented for a full year, having a far-reaching impact on insurers' business behaviors. Policy changes have posed new challenges to the product forms, service models, service fields and technological capacity, with more constraints and rules requirements for reform and development.

Third, market competition is becoming increasingly fierce. In the property insurance lines, the competition in motor insurance has been intensifying to inflate the comprehensive cost rate. Growing revenue without growing profits is common in non-motor and non-agricultural lines of business. The engineering, marine and special insurance lines are struggling to recover pricing levels, coupled with grave accumulation of risk exposures in some commercial lines, which has been a tough test for reinsurers' business selection and risk management ability. In the personal insurance segment, the segment will remain in a transformation where the low-interest-rate environment has a great impact on conventional life insurance and annuity products as well as a long-term, sustained impact on business dealings and actuarial assumptions. The health insurance has entered a plateau period with deteriorating experience in critical illness insurance and increasing payout ratio of medical insurance, all affecting development of the personal reinsurance market. In the reinsurance lines, the underwriting capacity of traditional business is sufficient, aggravating the homogeneous competition. The needs of direct insurance customers are more diversified, putting higher requirements on reinsurers' pace of product innovation, efficiency of customer service and capability of platform operation.

(II) Trends

First, the reinsurance industry will sustain its momentum of sound growth. The macro economy will maintain a steady upward trend in the foreseeable future with interest rates stable and poised for a decline, and the investment and consumption gradually regaining momentum. The demand for insurance will pick up, and the external environment for the reinsurance market will continue to improve. The reinsurance industry will continue to promote customer-centered strategic transformation, further promote the use of cutting-edge technologies such as cloud computing, big data and artificial intelligence, accelerate the pace of digital, intelligent and ecosystem-based development, enhance professional, fine-grained and intensive management, create a distinctive reinsurance ecosystem and step up the development of industrial chain and cooperation networks. The reinsurance industry will show a more evident trend of stable and sound growth.

Second, the reinsurance industry development will be aligned more closely with national strategies. The reinsurance industry will focus on China's key sectors of development, such as economic growth, sci-tech innovation, digital economy, green development, people's livelihood, social governance and the Belt and Road Initiative. Reinsurers will leverage on their technological strengths in data accumulation, risk identification, risk pricing and product innovation to strengthen coordination of the liability and asset sides, bring services forward to earlier stages, carry out the "more protection, less risk" initiative and provide a broader range of insurance protections and services (e.g. risk prevention, risk management and loss financing) for property loss and personal health, especially a series of emerging risks, thereby expanding the breadth and depth of insurance protections and improving the efficiency and quality of services.

Third, the reinsurance market will keep moving towards higher levels of two-way opening-up and integrated development. In June 2023, the National Administration of Financial Regulation (NAFR) issued the implementation rules for building the Shanghai International Reinsurance Center jointly with the Shanghai Municipal People's Government, officially opening a global reinsurance trading market in Shanghai. The rules have clarified the path and support for building the Shanghai reinsurance center, which is expected to speed up. Further, China's reinsurance industry will seize the opportunity of a new round of financial sector opening-up, implement the international strategy in serving the new development paradigm with domestic circulation as the mainstay and domestic and international circulations reinforcing each other, accelerate the pace of international development, improve cross-border service capabilities and international operation, enhance international competitiveness and gain a greater say in the international market.

Fourth, the reinsurance industry will continue to optimize its policy framework. The policy framework for China's reinsurance industry will keep improving with the aim of continuously enhancing industry competitiveness, market attractiveness and national security. The business environment for reinsurance will continuously improve to make China's reinsurance market increasingly attractive worldwide. Efforts will be stepped up to enhance the reinsurance risk management capacity for special risks such as trade credit, maritime, aviation and war, address the shortage of reinsurance supply for major risks and emerging risks and expand the depth and breadth of reinsurance services for the national economy. The organizational system for reinsurance will be optimized to enhance the role of reinsurance as the "last resort" in terms of risk taking, and eventually improve the ability to serve the new development paradigm with domestic circulation as the mainstay and domestic and international circulations reinforcing each other.

Chapter II

Review and Outlook on China's P&C Reinsurance Market in 2022

I. Market Size

(I) Size of ceded premiums

In 2022, the total ceded premiums of China's P&C insurance companies stood at RMB 162.95 billion, up by 11.6% year-on-year. During the same period, the total primary insurance premiums of P&C insurers amounted to RMB 1.4867 trillion, up by 8.7% year-on-year, and the growth rate of ceded premiums was about 2.9 percentage points higher than that of primary insurance premiums over the same period.

Between 2012 and 2022, the ceded premiums of P&C insurance companies in China increased from RMB 73.9 billion to RMB 162.95 billion, with an average annual growth rate of about 8.2%. During the same period, the primary insurance premiums of P&C insurers increased from RMB 552.99 billion to RMB 1.4867 trillion, with an average annual growth rate of about 10.4%. The average annual growth rate of ceded premiums was about 2.2 percentage points lower than that of primary insurance premiums over the same period.

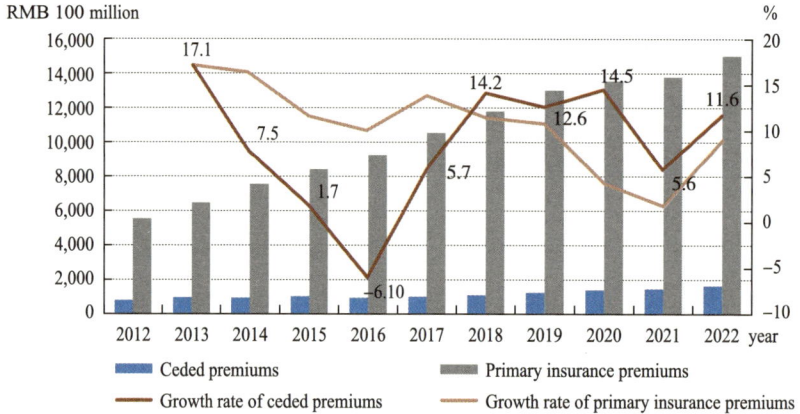

Figure 1   Primary Insurance Premiums, Ceded Premiums and Growth Rates of P&C Insurance Companies (2012-2022)

(Source: Yearbook of China's Insurance and former CBIRC)

Table 1   Ceded Premiums, Primary Insurance Premiums and Cession Rates of P&C Insurance Companies (2012-2022)

Unit: RMB 100 million, %

Years	Ceded premiums	Growth rates	Primary premiums	Growth rates	Cession rates
2012	739.0		5,529.9		13.4
2013	865.2	17.1	6,481.2	17.2	13.3
2014	929.8	7.5	7,544.4	16.4	12.3
2015	946.0	1.7	8,423.3	11.6	11.2
2016	887.9	−6.1	9,266.2	10.0	9.6
2017	938.8	5.7	10,541.4	13.8	8.9
2018	1,072.3	14.2	11,755.7	11.5	9.1
2019	1,207.7	12.6	13,016.3	10.7	9.3
2020	1,383.4	14.5	13,583.7	4.4	10.2
2021	1,460.5	5.6	13,676.5	0.7	10.7
2022	1,629.5	11.6	14,867.0	8.7	11.0

Source: Yearbook of China's Insurance and former CBIRC.

(II) Cession rates

In 2022, the cession rate of China's P&C insurance companies was about 11.0%, exceeding 10% for the third year in a row, up by 0.3 percentage point year-on-year.

The P&C cession rates saw a year-on-year decline from 2012 to 2015, yet remaining above 10%, and showed a falling trend followed by a rising one from 2016 to 2022. The P&C cession rate declined sharply to below 10% in 2016, mainly due to the implementation of C-ROSS II, and further dropped to less than 9% in 2017 amid the continued impact of C-ROSS II. Since 2018, the P&C cession rate have increased over time due to growing non-motor insurance business. The rate increased to over 10% in 2020, and further rose in 2021 and 2022, approximately 1.4 percentage points higher than in 2016.

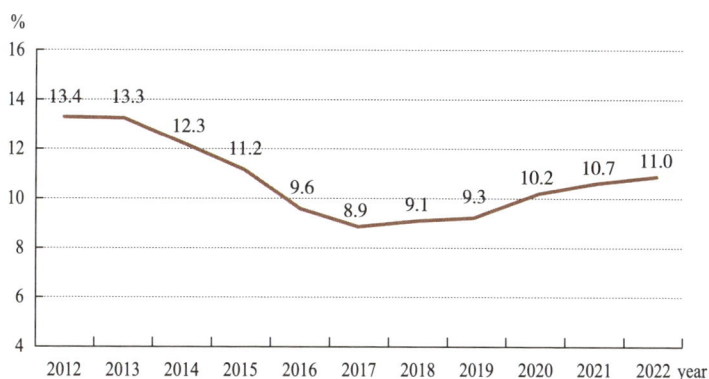

Figure 2   Cession Rates of P&C Insurance Companies (2012-2022)

(Source: Yearbook of China's Insurance and former CBIRC)

II. Demand-side Analysis

(I) Distribution of ceded premiums

In 2022, four P&C insurance companies had P&C ceded premiums over RMB 10 billion, totaling RMB 103.43 billion and accounting for 63.5% of the industry's total ceded premiums. A total of 15 P&C insurers had P&C ceded premiums ranging from RMB 1 billion to RMB 10 billion, totaling RMB 39.18 billion and accounting for 24% of industry-wide ceded premiums. A total of 50 P&C insurers had P&C ceded premiums ranging from RMB 0.1 billion to RMB 1 billion, totaling RMB 19.64 billion and accounting for 12.1%. A total of 18 P&C insurers had P&C ceded premiums of less than RMB 0.1 billion, totaling RMB 0.71 billion and accounting for 0.4%.

Table 2   Distribution of Ceded Premiums from P&C Insurance Companies in 2022

Unit: RMB 100 million, %

	Number	Total ceded premiums	% of total
Ceded premiums of more than RMB 10 billion	4	1,034.3	63.5
Ceded premiums of RMB 1 billion to RMB 10 billion	15	391.8	24.0
Ceded premiums of RMB 100 million to RMB 1 billion	50	196.4	12.1
Ceded premiums of less than RMB 100 million	18	7.1	0.4

Source: Former CBIRC.

(II) Changes in ceded premiums

In 2022, 65 P&C insurance companies saw a year-on-year increase in P&C ceded premiums, accounting for 74.7% of the total. More specifically, 16 P&C insurers had a year-on-year increase of less than 10%, accounting for 18.4% of the total; 18 had a year-on-year increase from 10% to 20%, accounting for 20.7% of the total; and 31 had a year-on-year increase of over 20%, accounting for 35.6% of the total.

Table 3   Distribution of Ceded Premiums Growth Rates of P&C Insurance Companies in 2022

Unit: company, %

	Number	% of total
P&C insurance companies with a YoY increase in ceded premiums	65	74.7
Of which: with a YoY increase less than 10%	16	18.4
with a YoY increase of 10% to 20%	18	20.7
with a YoY increase over 20%	31	35.6

Source: Former CBIRC.

(III) Distribution of cession rates

In 2022, 41 P&C insurance companies had a P&C cession rate of over 20%, accounting for 47.1% of the total, an increase of 2 companies year-on-year; 6 had a P&C cession rate from 15% to 20%, accounting for 6.9% of the total, and an increase of 1 company year-on-year; 10 had a P&C cession rate from 10% to 15%, accounting for 11.5% of the total, an increase of 2 companies year-on-year; 16 had a P&C cession rate from 5% to 10%, accounting for 18.4% of the total, a decrease of 2 companies year-on-year; 14 had a P&C cession rate of less than 5%, accounting for 16.1% of the total, a decrease of 4 companies year-on-year.

Table 4   Distribution of Reinsurance Cession Rates of P&C Insurance Companies (2016-2022)

Unit: company

Cession rates	2016	2017	2018	2019	2020	2021	2022
>20%	26	26	28	34	32	39	41
15% to 20%	4	5	8	2	10	5	6
10% to 15%	12	12	11	15	7	8	10
5% to 10%	14	17	15	11	12	18	16
<5%	24	24	25	25	27	18	14
Total	80	84	87	87	88	88	87

Source: Former CBIRC.

III. Supply-side Analysis

In 2022, there were 12 professional reinsurance companies registered and/or engaging in P&C reinsurance business in China. Specifically, one company had a market share of over 20%. China Re P&C gave full play to its role as the main channel of reinsurance in China, ranking first in terms of market share. One company had a share from 10% to 15%, three with a share from 5% to 10%, and seven with a share of less than 5%.

(I) Motor line of business

In 2021, the P&C reinsurance market recorded RMB 20.45 billion in professional reinsurers' premium income from the motor line of business, down by 10.3% year-on-year. From 2012 to 2021, the average annual growth rate was about −3.4%, showing an overall downtrend in business size. The annual premium income from the motor line showed the fastest growth in 2013, at around 27.7%, and the sharpest decline in 2016, at about 42.6%.

The business size shrank to around RMB 20 billion from more than RMB 30 billion in 2016.

Table 5   Premium Income of Professional Reinsurers from the Motor Line (2012-2021)

Unit: RMB 100 million

	2012	2013	2014	2015	2016	2017	2018	2019	2020	2021
China Re P&C	147.0	170.0	174.9	181.5	94.3	91.2	88.4	83.5	98.1	81.0
Munich Re Beijing Branch	39.3	65.6	46.6	45.5	43.3	30.3	41.6	28.3	28.7	25.7
Swiss Re Beijing Branch	78.2	103.1	106.3	83.1	38.3	38.5	33.8	42.9	44.7	42.9
SCOR SE Beijing Branch	3.7	9.1	14.1	16.4	14.6	12.5	12.1	10.6	4.5	4.3
General Re Shanghai Branch		0.1	0.1	0.2	0.2	0.2	0.2	0.2	0.2	0.2
Hannover Re Shanghai Branch	10.3	3.7	3.4	20.7	6.2	4.6	8.2	12.0	14.4	14.6
Taiping Re (China)		4.0	4.6	6.4	6.3	7.6	11.5	11.8	11.9	11.6
Qianhai Re						1.4	2.5	5.2	3.9	3.8
PICC Re						15.6	10.1	10.6	21.6	20.4
Korean Re										0.1
Total	278.4	355.5	350.0	353.8	203.2	201.8	208.4	205.1	228.1	204.5

Source: Yearbook of China's Insurance and former CBIRC.

Among market players, China Re P&C ranked first industry-wide by premium income from the motor line, which stood at RMB 8.1 billion in 2021 for China Re P&C, versus less than RMB 5 billion for all other players.

(II) Non-motor lines of business

In 2021, the P&C reinsurance market recorded RMB 82.31 billion in professional reinsurers' premium income from the non-motor lines of business, up by 48.6% year-on-year. From 2012 to 2021, the average annual growth rate was about 18.1%, showing rapid overall growth in business size. The annual premium income from non-motor lines remained the positive growth, except in 2015 and 2017. The non-motor lines showed strong growth, with the premium income passing the marks of RMB 40 billion, RMB 50 billion and RMB 80 billion in 2018, 2019 and 2021, respectively.

Table 6   Premium Income of Professional Reinsurers from Non-motor Lines (2012-2021)

Unit: RMB 100 million

	2012	2013	2014	2015	2016	2017	2018	2019	2020	2021
China Re P&C	93.5	114.2	118.1	114.8	123.6	128.9	162.9	203.7	235.4	269.3
Munich Re Beijing Branch	25.4	23.1	26.3	27.6	41.2	16.5	41.5	46.6	38.9	50.3
Swiss Re Beijing Branch	46.2	53.2	52.6	60.3	59.3	37.0	58.8	76.7	81.0	95.9
SCOR SE Beijing Branch	12.6	15.2	18.3	19.2	23.1	22.8	21.3	22.1	23.0	29.7
General Re Shanghai Branch	0.2	0.3	0.5	0.4	0.3	0.7	1.5	1.9	3.2	2.2
Hannover Re Shanghai Branch	6.3	5.5	30.7	10.5	16.2	20.7	33.4	54.5	81.4	68.4
XL Re										4.8
Taiping Re (China)		9.4	11.0	12.0	14.2	22.8	32.4	38.9	39.0	39.8
Qianhai Re						4.7	19.1	18.2	21.3	25.5
PICC Re						19.1	38.8	47.0	29.9	40.6
Korean Re									0.7	5.0
China Agriculture Re										191.7
Total	184.2	220.8	257.4	244.8	278.1	273.2	409.8	509.6	553.8	823.1

Source: Yearbook of China's Insurance and former CBIRC.

Among market players, China Re P&C ranked first industry-wide by premium income from the non-motor lines, which stood at RMB 26.93 billion in 2021 for China Re P&C, versus less than RMB 20 billion for all other players.

IV. Opportunities and Challenges in the P&C Reinsurance Market

(I) Opportunities for development of the P&C insurance market

The P&C insurance market is facing growth opportunities in the following four areas, driven by the macroeconomic recovery and policy tailwinds.

1. Insurance helps green transition

First, the "1+N" policy framework for "carbon peaking, carbon neutrality" has been gradually improved. Central and local governments issued action plans, including a roadmap for the insurance industry to create new products and foster new growth poles in line with relevant risk protection needs. Second, regulatory authorities have recently issued the *Green Finance Guidelines for Banking and Insurance Industries*, calling for more strategic support from green finance and requiring financial institutions for a green, low-carbon and circular economy. The guidelines also urge financial institutions to develop a green finance development strategy, set green finance targets, and report and disclose green finance information, which will further boost the "greenness" of insurance business development.

Insurance-driven green transition mainly involves the following segments. The first is new energy vehicle (NEV) insurance. In the first half of 2022, the number of Chinese-owned NEVs exceeded 10 million, with both production and sales reaching all-time highs. New car sales gave a boost to incremental premiums and improved underwriting performance. The second is green electricity insurance. After the installed capacity of wind energy and solar PV energy each exceeded 300 million kilowatts in 2021, there is still room for doubling compared with the goal of the state plan. Also, the large-scale pumped storage projects and the active, safe and orderly development of nuclear power projects have ushered in a historic period of development opportunities. The third is green building insurance. The lifecycle energy consumption of buildings in China accounts for 45% of the national energy consumption, equivalent to 50.6%[1] of the national carbon emissions. The green transition of the construction industry is vital to achieve the goal of "carbon peaking, carbon neutrality". At present, Beijing, Ningbo and Huzhou have implemented pilot operations. The fourth is forest and grassland carbon sequestration insurance. With the forest and grassland carbon sequestration insurance promoted as a hot area of innovation, a series of "first-of-its-kind" insurance policies were written to strengthen the role of ecosystems in carbon sequestration and enhance the carbon sequestration capacity. The next step of product innovation will focus on carbon asset insurance, losses on excess carbon emissions and other segments related to carbon trading.

---

[1] Data: Research Report on China Building Energy Compensation and Carbon Emissions 2022, published by China Association of Building Energy Efficiency.

2. Insurance supports technological innovation

Under a new system for mobilizing the resources nationwide to achieve breakthroughs in core technologies throughout key fields, insurance plays a role of risk protections and helps open up new space for sci-tech innovation. In addition, "serving strategic emerging industries" has been included in the evaluation metrics of the *Measures for Performance Evaluation of Commercial Insurance Companies* issued by the Ministry of Finance, fast tracking the insurance support for sci-tech innovation.

The insurance support for sci-tech innovation mainly involves the following segments. The first is the integrated circuit (IC) industry chain insurance. An IC insurance pool was established to jointly rise to the stranglehold problems existing in China's IC industry. The second is intellectual property insurance. At present, over RMB 20 billion of risk protections have been provided for 5,000 enterprises. The third is the equipment (first set)/new material insurance. The green and low-carbon innovation initiative for electrical equipment, which involves green development, is worth looking forward to. The next step of product innovation will focus on China-made auto chip insurance, intelligent robot insurance and other segments.

3. Insurance takes part in risk co-governance

First, the deep-going modernization of the national governance system and governance capacity will turn the huge potential demand for insurance into real needs at the institutions level. Second, the insurance industry promotes risk reduction management in an "Insurance Plus" way through third-party cooperation, which is conducive to realizing closed-loop operation and enhancing risk control.

Insurance takes part in risk co-governance mainly in the following segments. First, the IDI business for building quality management has provided coverage for 178 million square meters of floor space, with over RMB 8 billion of premiums written. Second, the cybersecurity insurance has formed the "pre-insurance security check + ongoing monitoring during insurance" risk control philosophy and model, with industry players participating in the preparation of the cybersecurity insurance and service standards. Third, the workplace safety liability insurance, mandated to provide accident prevention services, has officially become statutory coverage for just over one year and is expected to reach a market size of RMB 100 billion in the future. Fourth, the high-standard farmland insurance, which participates in the risk management of the construction, management and maintenance of high-standard farmland, has been piloted in many cities. In addition to the above segments, the insurance taking part in legal risk services will also become a new area of exploration.

4. Insurance serves the people's livelihood security

Serving the people's livelihood security directly reflects the essential attribute of "insurance for the benefit of people", and effectively aligns insurance with major strategies such as food and energy security and the Healthy China Initiative. "Serving the society and people's livelihood" has also been included in the evaluation metrics of the *Measures for Performance Evaluation of Commercial Insurance Companies* issued by the Ministry of

Finance. The regulatory authorities have also issued a series of guidelines requiring the banking and insurance industries to strengthen financial services for new urbanites and support the development of small and micro-sized businesses, steering the insurance industry toward strengthening the services for people's livelihood security.

Insurance serves the people's livelihood security mainly in the following segments. The first is Huiminbao. At present, the product has covered over 100 million people and written over RMB 10 billion of premiums. With information shared between basic and commercial medical insurance programs and the medical system reform being furthered, Huiminbao still has opportunity to further expand and deepen the coverage. The second is public health emergency-related insurance. The vaccine liability insurance continues to play a positive role. Some municipal governments have insured themselves against COVID-19 to ensure business reopening of service providers in the market. The third is the new urbanities insurance targeting 300 million people. Relevant data show that new urbanities have low social security participation and poor awareness of insurance, with 39% not covered by commercial insurance[1]. Relevant business opportunities remain to be tapped. The fourth is catastrophe insurance. The number of catastrophe pilot projects continues to increase, increasingly taking into account both disaster management and livelihood security. In addition, insurance is also vital to food security and energy security, which have close ties with people's livelihood.

---

[1] Source: White Paper on Financial Services for New urbanities 2022, published by Ping An Insurance in conjunction with third party survey agencies on July 8, 2022.

(II) Opportunities for development of the P&C reinsurance market

First, as high-quality development has become an industry-wide consensus, the role of reinsurance has been further highlighted. P&C insurers are generally heightening their underwriting standards. The underwriting profitability has become a core business indicator of most industry players. Safe and effective reinsurance arrangements have played a greater role in stabilizing underwriting results and supporting high-quality business development.

Second, with motor insurance into a new stage of development, reinsurance helps optimize operation and management of the motor lines. The pressure from comprehensive reform of motor insurance has been relieved, with the market competition landscape being improved. Market players are more responsive with significantly more accurate pricing of risks and well-controlled costs. NEV insurance has expanded rapidly into a strategic growth pole of the motor line of business, and an important growth engine for the motor insurance market going forward. However, the characteristic of "high growth, high payout" has exacerbated business challenges. Professional reinsurance companies will actively cooperate with primary insurance companies and third-party professional organizations to carry out data analysis and mining, optimize pricing models and improve underwriting performance.

Third, reinsurance takes part in collaborative innovation as product and service innovation has accelerated in non-motor lines. Focusing on facilitating green transition, supporting sci-tech innovation, participating in risk co-governance and serving the people's livelihood, P&C reinsurers will play a more professional function of risk management in serving the national strategies and integrating into the broader economy while pursuing their own business growth. The piloting of innovative products has gained pace amid persistently strong demand for reinsurance in emerging lines and innovative products.

(III) Risks and challenges facing the P&C insurance and reinsurance markets

First, China is sensitive to, and increasingly impacted by, global climate change. Climate change is a global topic. The latest report of the World Meteorological Organization shows that in the next five years, the world faces a 50% chance of warming of 1.5 degrees Celsius above pre-industrial levels[1], the limit on global warming set by the Paris Agreement. The *Blue Book on Climate Change of China 2022* once again confirmed that the warming rate in China is remarkably faster than the global average level in the same period, and the country is sensitive to climate change, showing higher frequency and intensity of extreme weather events such as heatwaves and heavy precipitation[2]. Also, the *National Climate Change Adaptation Strategy 2035* jointly issued by central government authorities believes that the climate change spillovers to the economic and social systems may lead to systemic

---

[1] Global Annual to Decadal Climate Update (Target Years: 2023-2027), published by the World Meteorological Organization in May 2023.

[2] Blue Book on Climate Change of China 2022, published by the National Climate Center of China Meteorological Administration on August 2022.

economic and financial risks associated with agricultural production, health, infrastructure and living environment, which are closely related to the insurance business scenarios.

Second, natural disasters remain severe in China, leading to rising losses. Natural disasters are the main factors affecting the underwriting performance of P&C insurers. Disastrous weather extremities hit China again in the first half of 2022. Guangdong Province experienced extreme "Dragon-boat Precipitation" and catastrophic floods, described as "once in more than a century" and "the heaviest in 60 years" respectively. A total of 17 cities in Guangdong Province triggered the conditions on catastrophe loss index (CLI)-based insurance claims, and some cities even triggered claims twice. In 2022, the typhoon disaster brought additional losses. Typhoon Chaba hit offshore wind farms hard. The offshore wind farm engineering vessel Fujing 001 got caught in typhoon in the Yangjiang sea area and sank after breaking anchor. In addition, the offshore wind turbines and submarine cables in the adjacent sea area were damaged due to collision and hauling, resulting in huge economic losses and insurance payouts.

Third, the risk exposure grows fast in green industries and green target assets. As offshore wind farms have been built and operated on a massive scale, the impact of typhoon has turned from threatening losses to cases of actual losses, but there is still a lack of quantitative risk analysis tools such as models. The new installed capacity of distributed solar photovoltaic (PV) projects, such as rooftop photovoltaic projects, has exceeded that of centralized projects, exposing more assets to the natural environment. Such risk exposure, coupled with risks in agriculture and rural housing, has added to the cumulative loss risks under disaster scenarios. The electrochemical energy storage projects aiming at stabilizing power grids will soon be carried out on a large scale, and their fire risks have attracted wide attention.

Fourth, the real estate risks and their impact on upstream and downstream operations in the industry chain deserve extra attention. In recent years, suspended construction and delayed delivery have become a prominent problem in China's real estate sector due to various factors. According to the monitoring data of All View Cloud (AVC) Real Estate Compass Big Data Platform, over 30% of the 3,162 projects scheduled for delivery in 2022 have been rescheduled for delivery, which means that nearly one-third of the projects will see delayed delivery in or after 2023. The situation will have a significant negative impact on the engineering performance bond and migrant workers' wage payment bond.

Fifth, more insurance types and products are affected by overseas risks. For example, the emerging comprehensive commercial liability insurance for Amazon sellers and overseas legal dispute insurance for intellectual property rights are both affected by overseas risks. Against the backdrop of ongoing product innovation, the overseas risks involved in the underwriting portfolio have begun to extend from asset risks represented by China's overseas interests to legal liability risks, posing greater challenges to risk control of the insurance industry.

Sixth, the risks of public security incidents and workplace accidents. Since 2022, public security incidents such as China Eastern Airlines plane crash and cyberattacks as well as workplace accidents such as fires and explosions at petrochemical plants have raised public awareness of risks and brought opportunities for innovation in insurance products.

Seventh, changes in the legal environment. The Chinese-style securities class action mechanism for investor protection has already been enforced in judicial practice. A number of listed companies have been investigated by the China Securities Regulatory Commission (CSRC) on suspicion of information disclosure in an illegal fashion. Many investors who suffered financial losses due to misrepresentations of listed companies have filed securities claims.

Eighth, impact of the COVID-19 pandemic. The pandemic has taken a heavier toll on micro, small and medium-sized businesses. Claim payouts have significantly increased for the financing guarantee insurance principally targeting the owners of micro and small businesses. In addition, COVID-19 insurance in Taiwan has encountered a peak of claims, and the COVID-19 outbreaks in Shanghai pushed up the claim payouts for COVID-19 lockdown risks. We should strengthen the control of major risk factors that may significantly affect business stability.

V. Outlook on the P&C Reinsurance Market

(I) Outlook on the changes in demand for ceding to reinsurance

In the conventional lines of insurance, P&C insurance companies maintain stable demand for reinsurance in general. Stabilizing operating results, spreading catastrophe risks and reducing capital pressure are the main objectives of reinsurance arrangements. First, as the cession rates of traditional insurance lines remain within a reasonable range as a whole, it is more urgent to further expand the reinsurance demand from high-quality business lines. Second, in a hard reinsurance market, most P&C insurers are tolerant of adjustments to the reinsurance contract terms and conditions. Third, in the excess-of-loss reinsurance arrangements, most P&C insurers can increase the cost budget to ensure full risk protections in a hard reinsurance market.

The emerging lines of insurance and innovative products see still-strong reinsurance demand from P&C insurers. First, green insurance has strong demand for product innovation and reinsurance. Regulatory authorities require financial institutions to strategically promote green finance and increase their support for a green, low-carbon and circular economy, which will further boost the "greenness" of insurance business development. Green electricity insurance, green building insurance, forest and grassland carbon sequestration insurance and carbon asset insurance show robust innovation in products and strong demand for reinsurance. Second, technology insurance has strong demand for reinsurance services. Regulatory authorities have issued multiple guidelines requiring the banking and insurance industries to support sci-tech self-reliance and self-sufficiency at higher levels and serve high-quality development of manufacturing. Insurance pools and ecosystems have been created as an innovative model of insurance services for high-tech industries, with a focus on integrated circuit (IC) industry chain insurance, intellectual property insurance, equipment (first set) and new material insurance, China-made auto chip insurance and intelligent robot insurance. Reinsurance is an essential part of the process. Third, integrated risk services such as "reinsurance + data" and "reinsurance + service" better cater to the business needs of P&C insurers. Professional reinsurance companies are more active in exporting data capabilities and experience, integrating service resources and networks, and working with primary insurers to develop innovative insurance products and risk solutions. In emerging lines of business such as catastrophe insurance and cybersecurity insurance, reinsurance companies continue to increase resource inputs and strengthen value outputs, fostering the transformation from business demand of the supply side to reinsurance cooperation.

(II) Outlook on changes in underwriting strategies of professional reinsurance companies

China's reinsurance market sees a tight supply of underwriting capacities, significantly adding to the difficulties in ceding risks. As P&C reinsurance will remain in a "hard market", offshore reinsurers will continue to transfer their underwriting capacity to countries and regions with greater price increases, resulting in an overall decrease in the supply of reinsurance underwriting capacity in the domestic market. P&C insurance companies will find it significantly more difficult to cede their risks, and the reinsurance gap already existing in some lines of business will be further widening.

The trend of price hikes in the international reinsurance market will be extended to China's local market. First, the natural catastrophe risks have shown "high incidence, high loss", coupled with Black Swan events such as the Russia-Ukraine conflict, eroding the underwriting profits in the international reinsurance market. Thus hiking reinsurance rates is a common demand among reinsurers. Second, professional reinsurance companies in the international market pay more attention to risk consideration, strictly control the cumulative liability for natural disasters and the exposure to certain areas of risks, and strictly control the further release of excess underwriting capacity. Finally, professional reinsurance companies in the domestic market have not seen their capital strength or underwriting capacity growing proportionately to the risks they underwrite. They still have to seek retrocession support from the international reinsurance market. However, the high cost of retrocession will inevitably increase their expected and quoted prices for the risks ceded to them.

3

Chapter III

Review and Outlook on China's Life Reinsurance Market in 2022

I. Market Size

(I) Overview

In 2022, China's life insurance market continued to move forward in rebalancing. The long-term savings lines grew fast while the protections lines showed a short-run decline. Life insurers is under pressure in operation and has increased demand for capital, which brought both opportunities and challenges to the life reinsurance market.

In terms of business size, the premium income of China's life insurance companies totaled RMB 3.2091 trillion in 2022, up by 2.8% year-on-year on a comparable basis.

In terms of business mix, in 2022, the life insurance premium income was RMB 2.4519 trillion, up by 4.0% year-on-year. The health insurance premium income was RMB 707.3 billion, up by 0.1% year-on-year, slowing down gradually over the years. The casualty insurance premium income was RMB 49.9 billion, down by 14.4% year-on-year, slowing down significantly.

(II) Size of ceded premiums

In 2022, the total ceded premiums of life insurance companies in China stood at RMB 115.33 billion, up by 15.8% year-on-year. During the same period, the total primary insurance premium income of life insurance companies was RMB 3.2091 trillion, up by 2.8% year-on-year on a comparable basis. Overall, the amount of life ceded premiums fluctuated from year to year. At present, against the backdrop of the fact that the Chinese economy faces triple pressures from shrinking demand, disrupted supply and weakening expectations at the macro level, the capital market is in a volatile decline and the primary insurance market is undergoing transition, posing certain shocks and challenges to growth of the life reinsurance market.

The ceded premiums of China's life insurance companies increased from RMB 14.04 billion in 2012 to RMB 115.33 billion in 2022, with an average annual growth rate of about 23.4%, securing a steady increase. The ceded premiums increased rapidly from 2012 to 2014, followed by a significant decline from 2015 to 2016 before a volatile pickup from 2017 to 2020, seeing a slight decline and a bounce-back from 2021 to 2022.

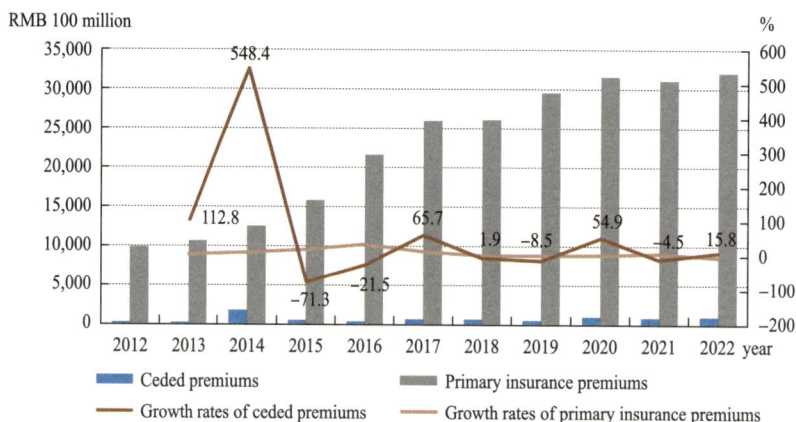

Figure 1   Primary Insurance Premiums, Ceded Premiums and Growth Rates of Life Insurance Companies (2012-2022)

(Source: Yearbook of China's Insurance and former CBIRC)

Table 1   Ceded Premiums, Primary Insurance Premiums and Cession Rates of Life Insurance Companies (2012-2022)

Unit: RMB 100 million, %

Year	Ceded premiums	Growth rates	Primary premiums	Growth rates	Cession rates
2012	140.4		9,957.9		1.4
2013	298.8	112.8	10,740.9	7.9	2.8
2014	1,937.4	548.4	12,690.3	18.1	15.3
2015	555.6	−71.3	15,859.1	25.0	3.5
2016	435.9	−21.5	21,692.8	36.8	2.0
2017	722.4	65.7	26,039.6	20.0	2.8
2018	736.2	1.9	26,260.9	0.8	2.8
2019	673.9	−8.5	29,628.4	12.8	2.3
2020	1,043.7	54.9	31,673.6	6.9	3.3
2021	996.3	−4.5	31,223.7	−1.4	3.2
2022	1,153.3	15.8	32,091.0	2.8	3.6

Source: Yearbook of China's Insurance and former CBIRC.

(III) Cession rates

In 2022, the cession rate of China's life insurance companies was around 3.6%, exceeding 3% for the third year in a row, up by 0.4 percentage points year-on-year. At present, China's life reinsurance cession rate is converging towards that of the world, which basically remains at around 3%, mainly due to the business mix and changes in the life insurance market. Traditional protection-oriented reinsurance business accounted for a relatively large cession share, while savings-oriented life insurance business has a lower share. Meanwhile, affected by such bulk transactions as international mergers and acquisitions, annuities, among others, the overseas existing market is stable with limited growth at present.

From 2012 to 2022, the cession rates of life insurance companies as a whole recorded a steady increase, with the exception of specific years. The cession rates saw a steady increase to a peak from 2012 to 2014, a significant decline in 2015 and a steady pick-up from 2016 to 2022. Overall, compared with 2012, the cession rate in 2022 was 2.6 times that of 2012, around 2.2 percentage points higher. This change was largely due to the rapid development of China's medical insurance market. Compared with the surplus reinsurance for critical illness, medical insurance has mostly adopted quota share reinsurance, which has led to a significant increase in the life insurance companies' demand for reinsurance.

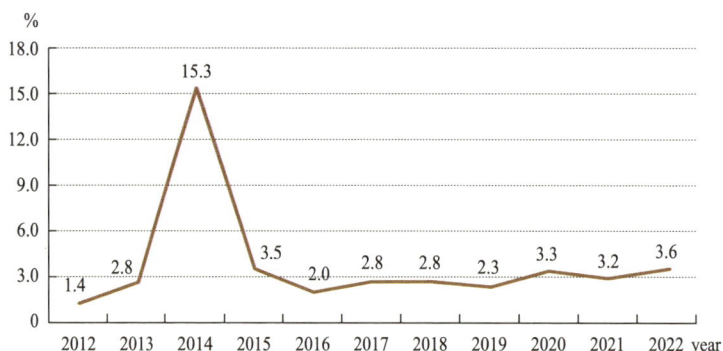

Figure 2   Cession Rates of Life Insurance Companies (2012-2022)

(Source: Yearbook of China's Insurance and former CBIRC)

II. Demand-side Analysis

(I) Distribution of ceded premiums[1]

In 2022, 10 life insurance companies had ceded premiums over RMB 5 billion, totaling RMB 69.18 billion, accounting for 60.0% of the industry's

---

[1] The values of ceded premiums by some life insurance companies in 2022 are negative.

total ceded premiums. 19 had ceded premiums between RMB 1 billion and RMB 5 billion, totaling RMB 40.9 billion, accounting for 35.5% of the total. 35 had ceded premiums between RMB 0.1 billion and RMB 1 billion, totaling RMB 13.61 billion, accounting for 11.8% of the total. 20 had ceded premiums of less than RMB 0.1 billion, totaling RMB 0.69 billion, accounting for 0.6% of the total.

Table 2   Distribution of Ceded Premiums from Life Insurance Companies in 2022

Unit: RMB 100 million, %

2022	Number	Total Ceded premiums	% of total
Ceded premiums of more than RMB 5 billion	10	691.8	60.0
Ceded premiums of RMB 1 billion to RMB 5 billion	19	409.0	35.5
Ceded premiums of RMB 100 million to RMB 1 billion	35	136.1	11.8
Ceded premiums of less than RMB 100 million	20	6.9	0.6

Source: Former CBIRC.

(II) Changes in ceded premiums

In 2022, 48 life insurance companies saw a year-on-year increase in life ceded premiums, accounting for 53.3% of the total. More specifically, 25 life insurers had a year-on-year increase of over 50%, accounting for 27.8% of the total; 6 had a year-on-year increase from 20% to 50%, accounting for 6.7% of the total; and 17 had a year-on-year increase of less than 20%, accounting for 18.9% of the total.

Table 3   Distribution of Ceded Premiums Growth Rates of Life Insurance Companies in 2022

Unit: company, %

	Number	% of total
Life insurance companies with a YoY increase in ceded premiums	48	53.3
Of which: with a YoY increase over 50%	25	27.8
with a YoY increase of 20% to 50%	6	6.7
with a YoY increase less than 20%	17	18.9

Source: Former CBIRC.

III. Supply-side Analysis

In 2022, there were 10 professional reinsurance companies registered / engaging in life reinsurance business in China. Specifically, one company had a market share of over 50%. One company had a share from 10% to 15%, three with a share from 5% to 10%, and five with a share of less than 5%. China Re Life gave full play to its role as the main channel of reinsurance in China, ranking first in terms of market share. Other major participants include the largest global reinsurers and Chinese reinsurers, such as Qianhai Re, Taiping Re (China) and PICC Re.

(I) Life line of business

In 2021, the life reinsurance market recorded RMB 58.71 billion in professional reinsurers' premium income from the life line of business, up by 4.4% year-on-year. From 2012 to 2021, the average annual growth rate was about 16.1%, showing a volatile uptrend. The annual premium income from the life line increased significantly from 2013 to 2014, decreased notably from 2015 to 2016 and began to pick up steadily in 2017. Except for 2019, the sector maintained positive growth from 2017 to 2021.

Table 4   Premium Income of Professional Reinsurers from the Life Line (2012-2021)

Unit: RMB 100 million

	2012	2013	2014	2015	2016	2017	2018	2019	2020	2021
China Re Life	125.7	142.2	166.0	178.1	252.9	368.5	404.6	390.0	464.8	443.7
Munich Re Beijing Branch	4.0	20.4	23.1	30.3	9.3	6.2	4.2	5.0	7.9	6.1
Swiss Re Beijing Branch	1.0	0.8	1.3	1.6	0.8	1.9	2.4	1.1	3.4	3.4
SCOR SE Beijing Branch	0.3	10.6	19.0	10.8	2.1	3.8	10.1	7.3	8.0	40.0
General Re Shanghai Branch	2.3	2.6	3.1	3.8	4.0	5.1	5.6	7.1	8.0	9.8
Hannover Re Shanghai Branch	19.7	120.7	586.9	96.3	16.7	9.3	12.5	17.6	18.8	16.4
RGA Shanghai Branch				0.1		2.1	2.9	2.0	2.4	2.5
Taiping Re (China)										0.1
Qianhai Re						33.3	42.2	29.0	49.1	62.5
PICC Re										2.4
Total	153.0	297.3	799.6	320.9	285.8	430.2	484.4	459.0	562.5	587.1

Source: Yearbook of China's Insurance and former CBIRC.

Among market players, China Re Life ranked first industry-wide by premium income from the life line of business, which stood at RMB 44.37 billion in 2021 with a market share of about 75.6%, followed by Qianhai Re and SCOR SE with the market shares of 10.6% and 6.8% in 2021, respectively. SCOR SE's premium income from the life line soared by 397.5% year-on-year. The remaining market players each recorded less than RMB 2 billion in premium income from the life line.

(II) Health line of business

In 2021, the life reinsurance market recorded RMB 48.05 billion in professional reinsurers' premium income from the health line of business, up by 12.3% year-on-year. From 2012 to 2021, the average annual growth rate was about 28.4%. The premium income from the health line has grown rapidly in recent years, with its value in 2021 being 9.5 times that of 2012. But its year-on-year growth decreased significantly in 2021, showing a moderation in growth.

Table 5　Premium Income of Professional Reinsurers from the Health Line (2012-2021)

Unit: RMB 100 million

	2012	2013	2014	2015	2016	2017	2018	2019	2020	2021
China Re Life	16.2	26.8	25.1	32.5	37.3	50.6	97.6	139.3	175.6	212.3
Munich Re Beijing Branch	10.6	10.8	10.8	17.3	24.5	28.5	26.3	36.4	44.3	37.5
Swiss Re Beijing Branch	18.9	18.7	21.1	20.3	21.5	20.1	17.3	38.1	46.6	48.6
SCOR SE Beijing Branch	1.5	2.0	2.5	1.4	1.2	5.0	13.7	21.8	30.7	26.3
General Re Shanghai Branch	0.5	0.4	1.2	2.1	2.9	7.8	23.4	37.0	40.9	41.7
Hannover Re Shanghai Branch	2.9	4.8	4.7	38.2	12.7	19.7	28.8	41.6	51.9	58.4
RGA Shanghai Branch				0.4		3.9	7.8	8.5	8.2	8.9

continued

	2012	2013	2014	2015	2016	2017	2018	2019	2020	2021
Taiping Re (China)								0.6	1.4	2.4
Qianhai Re						0.4	2.1	12.2	27.8	39.8
PICC Re									0.4	4.6
Total	50.6	63.5	65.4	112.2	100.0	135.9	216.9	335.6	427.8	480.5

Source: Yearbook of China's Insurance and former CBIRC.

Among market players, China Re Life ranked first industry-wide by premium income from the health line of business, which stood at RMB 21.23 billion in 2021 with a market share of about 44.2%. Hannover Re, Swiss Re, General Re, Qianhai Re, Munich Re and SCOR SE each recorded from RMB 2.5 billion to RMB 6 billion in premium income from the health line. Qianhai Re has grown fast since 2017, at an average annual rate of 211.8% between 2017 and 2021. Other companies each recorded less than RMB 1 billion in premium income from the health line.

(III) Casualty line of business

In 2021, the life reinsurance market recorded RMB 6.58 billion in professional reinsurers' ceded premium income from the casualty line of business, up by 4.5% year-on-year. From 2012 to 2021, the average annual growth rate was about 11.8%, showing a volatile uptrend.

Table 6   Premium Income of Professional Reinsurers from the Casualty Line (2012-2021)

Unit: RMB 100 million

	2012	2013	2014	2015	2016	2017	2018	2019	2020	2021
China Re Life	17.1	13.6	18.3	18.1	22.2	23.0	21.5	25.1	24.6	37.0
Munich Re Beijing Branch	2.8	1.3	6.2	3.8	5.5	8.3	11.5	12.6	13.0	11.6
Swiss Re Beijing Branch	1.9	0.9	0.6	1.1	–0.6	0.5	0.9	1.5	1.7	1.4
SCOR SE Beijing Branch	0.6	0.9	2.2	3.8	4.8	3.9	2.2	2.1	2.3	2.6
General Re Shanghai Branch	0.2	0.3	1.3	3.6	5.3	5.2	6.8	7.7	6.3	4.9
Hannover Re Shanghai Branch	1.4	7.0	3.1	4.1	5.5	6.0	12.3	13.1	14.1	6.8
Taiping Re (China)								0.3	0.5	1.0
Qianhai Re						0.1	0.6	0.5	0.6	0.4
PICC Re										0.1
Total	24.1	24.0	31.7	34.6	42.8	46.8	55.7	62.9	63.0	65.8

Source: Yearbook of China's Insurance and former CBIRC.

Among market players, China Re Life ranked first industry-wide by premium income from the casualty line of business, which stood at RMB 3.7 billion in 2021 with a market share of about 56.2%, followed by Munich Re and Hannover Re with the market shares of 17.6% and 10.3%, respectively. The remaining market players each recorded less than RMB 500 million in premium income from the casualty line.

(IV) Global market landscape for life reinsurance

In the global market, according to AM.Best data, life reinsurance generated at least 30% of the total premium income of global reinsurance groups, showing a fairly stable pattern of business. In the ranking of global life reinsurance companies for 2021, Canada Life Re surpassed Swiss Re to take the first place, and China Re Life overtook SCOR SE for fifth place.

Table 7 Top Ten Global Life Reinsurance Groups in 2021

Unit: USD 100 million

Rank	Company name	Gross reinsurance premiums
1	Canada Life Re	235.5
2	Swiss Re	160.7
3	Munich Re	142.3
4	RGA	133.5
5	China Re	108.5
6	SCOR SE	106.1
7	Hannover Re	96.7
8	Berkshire Hathaway	56.2
9	Transatlantic Re	40.9
10	Assicurazioni Generali SPA	24.3

Source: AM. Best.

IV. Opportunities and Challenges in the Life Reinsurance Market

The life insurance industry has ushered in a new stage of high-quality development as China's per-capita disposable income grows with the economy. At present, China's life insurance market has entered an in-depth transition period. Life insurers need to adjust their original business models to break the development bottlenecks and achieve long-term value growth.

(I) Opportunities for development of the life insurance market

From the macro-economic point of view, China adheres to the guiding principle of "giving top priority to stability and seeking progress while ensuring stability" amid the COVID-19 pandemic and complex international situation. The macroeconomy will sustain its recovery under the auspices of "macro-policy tailwinds", "expanding domestic demand", "reform and innovation" and "risk control and prevention". China continues to develop the three-pillar pension security system, bringing new opportunities for the insurance industry development and accelerating integrated development of the elderly care industry. The reform of "medical insurance system, health system and drug distribution system" has accelerated, and the separation of medical treatment and drug sales, the control of social security and medical expenses, and IT application in medical care have had a profound impact on the business environment of commercial insurance. The regional economic policies for the Greater Bay Area, Hainan, etc. have mentioned insurance, providing policy opportunities for innovation in insurance technology, integration of health care and elderly care and cross-border insurance.

In terms of regulatory policies, first, financial supervision is further enhanced to forestall and defuse major economic and financial risks. As for top-level design, the former China Banking and Insurance Regulatory Commission (CBIRC) was restructured into the National Administration of Financial Supervision to establish a unified supervision system for financial markets. The product supervision has been upgraded to driven down liability costs. The former CBIRC issued the *Information Disclosure Rules for Life insurance Products with a Term over One Year*, cancelling the "high, middle and low" tiers and requiring disclosure of participating insurance. A survey was conducted to solicit opinions and suggestions on measures taken by the regulatory authorities or industry associations to reduce the costs and improve the quality of liabilities. Second, the supply-side reform of products and services has been actively promoted. The General Office of the State Council issued the *Opinions on Promoting Development of Person Pensions*, clarifying the individual account system and tax exemption policy and accelerating the third pillar development. The former CBIRC issued the *Notice on Launching the Pilot Program on Conversion of Liabilities between Life Insurance and Long-term Care Insurance*, enriching the features of life insurance products and striving to improve the payment demand and supply capacity of long-term care insurance.

As for the life insurance market, in 2022, the premium income of the life insurance market increased by only 2.8% year-on-year, showing no signs of bottoming out. However, with the measures against COVID-19 optimized and the macro policies implemented effectively, the top insurance companies have transformed their business gradually, which will have a positive effect on the transition and recovery of the life insurance market. Meanwhile, the new development philosophy has given birth to new business models, substantially pushing up the demand for pharmaceuticals and medical value-added services, with the innovation in commercial payments continuing to heat up. New technologies have fostered new competition models. The Internet, blockchains, big data and artificial intelligence have been embedded into the industry at a faster pace, triggering an accelerated upgrade of insurance business from concept to model.

(II) Opportunities for innovation of life reinsurance products

The Healthy China Initiative has been furthered in recent years. The Report to the 20th CPC National Congress called for "vigorously developing commercial medical insurance". The regulatory authorities have also issued numerous policy documents to promote health insurance development, bringing huge opportunities for growth of the commercial health insurance. The life reinsurance industry will contribute professional value in terms of the innovation of health insurance products.

1. Critical illness insurance

In recent years, the innovation of critical illness insurance products has been reflected more in the product structure changes. In cooperation with primary insurance companies, life reinsurers continue to develop critical illness products with such features as medical expense reimbursement and disability compensation. The innovation of product structure mainly includes modular design for critical illness and "lifetime critical illness + time-bound critical illness" design. The modular product design is flexible and diversified. The modules may be in units of individual insurance types or individual liabilities for critical illness. The clients may flexibly combine them according to their own needs. With the shrinking size of new lines of critical illness insurance, the care or disability lines of critical illness have become a new hot topic. In addition, the critical illness insurance for substandard risks has also become one of the directions of the critical illness insurance innovation.

2. Medical insurance

Advanced medical care has always been a major direction of medical insurance upgrade. With the help of intensive exploration and innovation in the medical industry, life reinsurance can improve the availability and affordability of advanced treatment solutions for patients, and also help advanced medical technologies give play to their market efficiency and raise customers' awareness and recognition of insurance. In addition, the zero-deductible million-*yuan* medical insurance and the tax-exempt medical insurance have also become an important direction of medical insurance innovation. The new regulation on tax-exempt health insurance will take effect on August 1, 2023. In addition to medical insurance, long-term care insurance, disease insurance and other products are also included in the tax-exempt scope. The design of tax-exempt health insurance products attach greater importance to public wellbeing and alignment with basic medical insurance. Against this background, life reinsurance can support the design of tax-exempt exclusive products that are zero-deductible and available to people with prior illness by virtue of in-house product R&D and data strengths, and promote the sustainable development of tax-exempt health insurance through a reasonable product-specific actuarial mechanism.

3. Silver insurance

In response to population aging, life reinsurance seeks to develop a system of elderly insurance products. By identifying the needs of elderly customers with different health conditions and income levels, such products as million-*yuan* medical insurance for the elderly, care insurance for the elderly, cancer insurance for the elderly and casualty insurance for the elderly have been promoted across the industry to meet the differentiated protection needs of the elderly. These products provide risk protections for the elderly who previously had little access to commercial insurance, also offering insurance solutions for the aging society.

4. Reimbursement-type medical insurance

Life reinsurers design products in conjunction with scarce medical resources under such scenarios as early cancer screening and vaccine services. For example, the "Intestinal Security" medical insurance for colorectal cancer and cervical cancer products for specific female diseases have been developed. For example, the "Intestinal Security" medical insurance not only provides private clinic colonoscopy and polypectomy for customers, but also covers the future special drug costs incurred by the colorectal cancer. Cervical cancer products targeted at specific female diseases not only provide customers with scheduled HPV vaccination service, but also cover future medical expenses for cervical cancer. These products meet customers' current medical needs while providing long-term risk protections to customers and raising their awareness of insurance protection.

Table 8   Innovation Trends of Life Reinsurance Products

Type	Direction of development	Life reinsurance support
Critical illness insurance	Product liability innovation	Based on needs of primary reinsurers, developing critical illness products combing the features of medical expense reimbursement and disability compensation
	Product structure innovation	Modular design for critical illness and "lifetime critical illness + time-bound critical illness" design: modules are in units of either individual types of insurance or individual liabilities for critical illness
Medical insurance	Advanced medical treatment	With the help of the intensive exploration and innovation of the medical industry in different fields, enhancing the accessibility and affordability of advanced treatment solutions to patients and raising customers' awareness and recognition of insurance
	Zero-deductible million-*yuan* medical insurance	Leveraging on in-house product R&D and data strengths to support the design of tax-exempt exclusive products that are zero-deductible and available to people with prior illness, and promoting the sustainable development of tax-exempt health insurance
	Tax-deductible medical insurance	
Silver insurance	Providing insurability support to the elderly who previously had little access to commercial insurance	By identifying the needs of elderly customers with different health conditions and income levels, promoting such products as million-*yuan* medical insurance for the elderly, care insurance for the elderly, cancer insurance for the elderly and casualty insurance for the elderly
Reimbursement-type medical insurance	Meeting the current medical needs of customers while providing protections against future risks in the long run	Designing insurance products based on scenarios such as early cancer screening and vaccine services in collaboration with scarce medical resources

(III) Risks and challenges facing life insurance and reinsurance markets

First, under the triple pressures of shrinking demand, disrupted supply and weakening expectations amid the COVID-19 pandemic and geopolitical conflictions, China's macro-economy is still on a fragile footing of recovery that has yet to be strengthened. In financial markets, the risk of global stagflation has increased, and continued interest rate hikes have triggered fluctuations in global capital markets. Second, the domestic life insurance market is under multiple pressures from the demand side, the seller side and the asset side, resulting in a short-term decrease in the demand for insurance, an increase in the demand for long-term savings and a significant drop in the sales manpower. The agent channel has to explore new sales orders and value of new business in depth, and the overall market morale has yet to be boosted. Third, China's life insurance market is in transition amid deteriorating morbidity experience in critical illness, increasing medical expenses and underdeveloped management mechanism for long-term medical insurance. Health insurance development is facing such challenges as growing risk exposures and mounting management difficulties.

V. Outlook on the Life Reinsurance Market

China's economy is expected to stop its downward trend and recover in 2023. The life insurance market will continue to benefit from the macro-economic recovery and policy tailwinds. From the perspective of channel side, despite the great challenges facing market development, the agent channel is expected to basically bottom out after three years of transition, securing some achievements in pursuing higher quality and efficiency. Driven by long-term savings insurance and tax-deferred pension finance, the bancassurance channel will be further developed. Against the background of pursuing common prosperity and inclusive finance, the new model of group or quasi-group business featuring high efficiency and low marketing cost will create growth opportunities for business transformation and upgrading of the group insurance channels, and bring new opportunities for the development of job-based marketing. From the perspective of products and services side, with market interest rates steadily declining, life insurance products have formed its competitive edge with steady and good yields. Inclusive insurance such as Huiminbao is expected to become an innovative integration platform to drive the integration of social security and commercial insurance and the combination of "medical insurance system, health system and drug distribution system". Critical illness insurance is likely to get integrated with emerging health insurance products such as long-term care and disability. Long-term savings and annuity products remain the mainstream of the market. From the perspective of assets side, the weakening capital market is expected to stage a transitional recovery, fueling a pickup in the overall return on investment.

It is expected that the life insurance industry will continue to deepen the cooperation between primary insurers and reinsurers, thereby giving full play to the strengths in data accumulation, product design and platform-based ecosystem and accelerating the transformation and upgrading of the life insurance industry. First, responsiveness to market conditions will be boosted. The price war is fierce among life insurers and traditional casualty insurers, leading to a narrow profit margin. The reinsurance demand is relatively strong for health insurance and novel lines of casualty insurance. Product development and service innovation with data and technology as the core have become important ways to access new protection business opportunities. Affected by the population aging and the tax-deferred pension policy, the longevity risk-related demand has gradually emerged. The implementation of C-ROSS II and IFRS 17 will complicate and diversify non-traditional risk transfer methods, such as financial reinsurance, testing reinsurers' ability to adapt and innovate. Second, innovation and iteration will be accelerated. Health insurance is currently the main field where life insurers compete with one another. Primary insurance companies are increasingly demanding the responsiveness of reinsurers in terms of product iteration and pricing support. While expanding the coverage of health insurance products to include more people and liabilities, reinsurers will pay due attention to and study the innovation opportunities regarding specific medical care and diseases, such as in-vitro fertilization (IVF), and explore the protection products for the sick and sub-healthy population. Third, ecosystem-based collaboration will be emphasized. Reinsurers will expand the business scenarios and extend the industrial ecosphere to strengthen cooperation with hospitals, medical service institutions and health service organizations, thereby building a "insurance + medical service/health management" service system, realizing the in-depth combination of products and services and helping primary insurers tap into the health market. Fourth, technological empowerment will be enhanced. Reinsurers will use the big data technology to integrate reinsurance business data, primary insurers' data, third-party organizations' data and other data resources to establish a health insurance data pool, strengthen data integration and analysis and assist primary insurers in reducing costs, selecting customers, optimizing decisions and strengthening risk management.

Chapter IV

Review and Outlook on Two-way Opening-up of China's Reinsurance Industry in 2022

I.   Development of Foreign Reinsurance Companies in China

II. International Development of Chinese Reinsurance Companies

III. Outlook on International Development of China's Reinsurance Industry

Over the past 45 years since China began its reform and opening-up, the Chinese insurance industry has remained steadfast in implementing the basic state policy of opening up to the outside world, adhered to the combination of "bringing in" and "going out" and unceasingly attained a series of remarkable new developmental success along the road. Benefiting from the high-level opening-up of the insurance industry, the Chinese market has seen improved local presence and distribution of foreign insurance and reinsurance companies. Against the backdrop of accelerating efforts to foster a new pattern of development that is focused on the domestic economy and features positive interplay between domestic and international economic cycles, China's reinsurance companies have also continued to pursue coordinated development of domestic and overseas markets.

I. Development of Foreign Reinsurance Companies in China

(I) Overview of the international reinsurance market

The premium income of the world's top 50 reinsurers in 2022 is USD 363.6 billion, or about RMB 2,505.4 billion[1], up by around 3% year-on-year. In 2022, China's reinsurance market recorded RMB 225.02 billion in premium income, accounting for about 9.0% of the global total.

---

[1] Source: AM.Best, Global Reinsurance-Segment Review 2022. The USD/RMB exchange rate of 6.89 as at December 31, 2022 in the inter-bank foreign exchange market was adopted.

Premium income in other global reinsurance markets, 91.0%

Premium income in China's reinsurance market, 9.0%

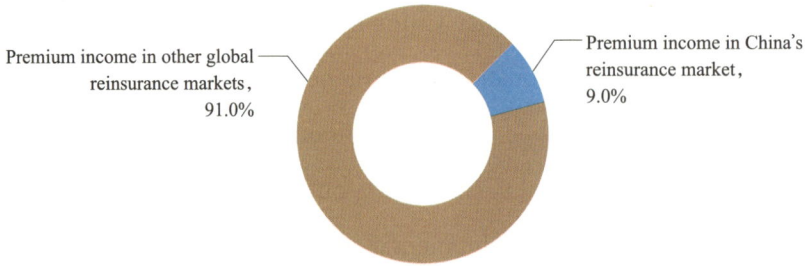

Figure 1   China's Share of Premium Income in Global Reinsurance Market in 2022

(Source: Former CBIRC and AM.Best)

By category, non-life reinsurance premium income in 2022 accounted for about 68% of the global gross reinsurance premium income, while life reinsurance premium income accounted for about 32%.

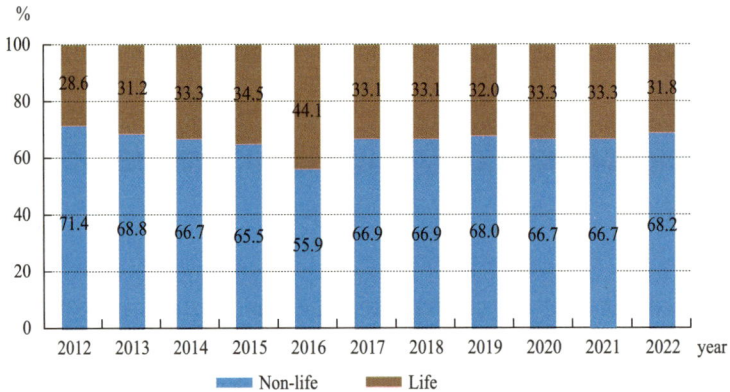

Figure 2   Business Mix of the World's Top 50 Reinsurers

(Source: AM.Best, Global Reinsurance-Segment Review (2012-2022))

By competitive landscape, according to AM.Best's annual ranking of global reinsurers in 2022, Munich Re Group ranked first with reinsurance premiums of USD 51.3 billion, an increase of 9.6% year-on-year driven mainly by its property and casualty segments. Swiss Re Group ranked second with reinsurance premiums of USD 39.7 billion, an increase of 1.2% year-on-year. Hannover Re ranked third with reinsurance premiums of USD 35.5 billion, an increase of 13.1% year-on-year driven mainly by its property and casualty segments. Canadian Life Re, which specializes in life reinsurance, continues to be ranked fourth. Berkshire Hathaway ranked up to fifth place. The world's top 50 reinsurance groups had about USD 363.6 billion in reinsurance in 2022, up by 2.8% year-on-year.

Table 1   Ranking of International Reinsurance Groups by Premiums in 2022

Unit: USD 100 million

Rank	Reinsurance group	Reinsurance premiums in 2022
1	Munich Re	513
2	Swiss Re	397
3	Hannover Re	355
4	Canada Life Re	234
5	Berkshire Hathaway	221
6	Scor SE	211
7	Lloyd's	185
8	China Re	169
9	RGA	138
10	Everest Re (Bermuda)	93

Source: AM.Best, Global Reinsurance-Segment Review, 2022.

(II) Development of foreign reinsurers in China

Since the State Council promulgated the *Regulations on the Administration of Foreign-Funded Financial Institutions* in 1994, foreign financial institutions have begun to do business in China. Swiss Re and Munich Re set up representative offices in Shanghai in 1996 and 1997, respectively, before other top reinsurers of the world entered the China market. After its accession to WTO in 2001, China made institutional arrangements for opening up its financial industry to the outside world. Since then, China's reinsurance market has grown bigger and bigger at an accelerating pace, now standing firm as one of the world's most open and fastest-growing reinsurance markets.

By the end of 2022, there were 15 professional players in China's reinsurance market, including 7 Chinese reinsurers (including 1 conglomerate, namely China Re Group) and 8 foreign reinsurers. Top international reinsurers enter the Chinese market through their branches. For example, the gross premium income of Swiss Re and Munich Re in China has accounted for around 10% of their global reinsurance premiums in recent years, highlighting China as an important market.

Table 2　Ranking of Foreign Reinsurers by Premium Incomes in China in 2022

Unit: RMB 100 million

Rank	Foreign reinsurers in China	Premium income in 2022
1	Swiss Re Beijing Branch	185.2
2	Hannover Re Shanghai Branch	158.4
3	Munich Re Beijing Branch	123.4
4	Scor SE Beijing Branch	87.9
5	General Re Shanghai Branch	46.4
6	RGA Shanghai Branch	14.1
7	KRC Shanghai Branch	6.1
8	XL Insurance	3.1

Source: Annual disclosure reports of the above companies for 2022.

Foreign reinsurers adopted differentiated development strategies according to their own operating characteristics. For example, some foreign reinsurers focused their China business on the governmental and sci-tech sectors. On the one hand, they cooperate with the Chinese government by extending covers to health, agricultural and liability risks in priority areas identified by the government, including healthcare, agriculture, rural areas and farmers, environmental pollution and food safety. On the other hand, they have expanded sci-tech innovation to cooperate with direct insurers in Internet of Vehicles, Internet of Things, data mining and other technology-intensive areas. For another example, some foreign insurers pay more attention to quality of business and emphasize sustainable and profitable growth in business, thus placing a particular emphasis on technology upgrading, market research and early investment. Some other foreign reinsurers emphasize business performance. They attach more importance to business profits and are good at reducing costs through delicacy management to remain more profitable than competitors.

(III) Operations of foreign reinsurers in China in 2022

In 2022, foreign reinsurers maintained steady business development in China with growing profitability and competitiveness, becoming an integral part of China's reinsurance market.

1. Business size

From 2017 to 2022, foreign reinsurers kept their business scale stable in China. In 2022, the premium income of foreign reinsurers decreased slightly from 2021. Swiss Re Beijing Branch still ranked first among foreign reinsurers in terms of business scale, with premium income of RMB 18.52 billion in 2022, followed by Hannover Re Shanghai Branch, Munich Re Beijing Branch and Scor SE Beijing Branch in descending order.

RMB 100 mn

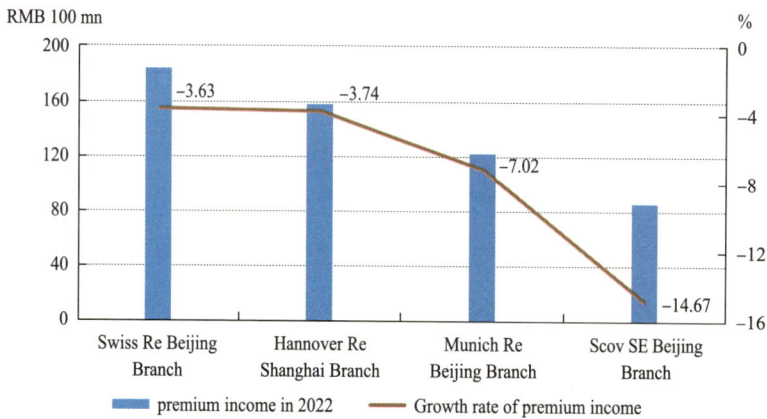

Figure 3   Foreign Reinsurers' Premium Income and Growth Rates in 2022

(Source: Annual disclosure reports of the above companies for 2022)

(1) Swiss Re Beijing Branch

By premium income, Swiss Re Beijing Branch, as the top foreign reinsurer, had a premium income of RMB 18.52 billion in 2022, down by 3.6% year-on-year. Swiss Re has achieved notable growth in the property segment in recent years, with Swiss Re Beijing Branch generating more than 70% of its total premium income from the property business, far more than that from life and health segments.

By business mix, the property segment contributed 70.6% of the premium income of Swiss Re Beijing Branch in 2022, with property and liability insurance (43.8%) and motor insurance (17.7%) taking bigger shares. premium income from personal insurance accounted for 29.4%. In the past two years, premium income from the personal line of business kept growing as China's life and health insurance markets enjoyed bright prospects and were less affected by the COVID-19 pandemic.

Table 3   Business Mix of Swiss Re Beijing Branch

Unit: RMB 100 million, %

Business line	Premium income in 2022	% of total
Personal insurance	54.5	29.4
Life insurance	6.0	3.2
Health insurance	48.5	26.2
Property insurance	130.7	70.6
Motor insurance	32.8	17.7
Property and liability insurance	81.2	43.8
Marine insurance	12.4	6.7
Others	4.4	2.4
Total	185.2	100

Source: Annual disclosure report of Swiss Re Beijing Branch for 2022.

(2) Hannover Re Shanghai Branch

Hannover Re Shanghai Branch recorded RMB 15.84 billion in ceded premium income, down by 3.7% year-on-year. By ceded premium income, Hannover Re Shanghai is second only to Swiss Re Beijing Branch at present, ranking second among foreign reinsurers.

By business mix, Hannover Re Shanghai Branch showed a 60/40 split between life and non-life segments. Of the life segment, health insurance took the largest share of 29.7%. Of the non-life segment, liability insurance accounted for 13.2%, property insurance 11.3%, credit insurance 11.2% and motor insurance 8.6%.

Table 4   Business Mix of Hannover Re Shanghai Branch

Unit: RMB 100 million, %

Business line	Premium income in 2022	% of total
Life	65.5	41.4
Health insurance	47.0	29.7
Life insurance	10.2	6.5

continued

Business line	Premium income in 2022	% of total
Casualty insurance	8.3	5.2
Non-life	92.9	58.6
Liability insurance	20.8	13.2
Property insurance	17.9	11.3
Credit insurance	17.7	11.2
Motor vehicle and third-party liability insurance	13.5	8.6
Agricultural insurance	8.1	5.1
Engineering insurance	6.8	4.3
Cargo transportation insurance	3.5	2.2
Health insurance	1.6	1.0
Hull insurance	1.6	1.0
Casualty insurance	0.6	0.4
Others	0.6	0.4
Total	158.4	100

Source: Annual disclosure report of Hannover Re Shanghai Branch for 2022.

(3) Munich Re Beijing Branch

The ceded premium income of Munich Re Beijing Branch was RMB 12.34 billion in 2022, down by 7.0% year-on-year. Specifically, the non-life segment recorded RMB 8.16 billion in ceded premium income, up by 5.3% year-on-year, while the life segment registered ceded premium income of RMB 4.18 billion, down by 24.3% year-on-year.

By business mix, Munich Re Beijing Branch showed a 33.9/66.1 split between life and non-life segments. Life premium income, in a downward trend, represented a shrinking share in ceded premium income, while non-life insurance became the principal business.

Table 5   Business Mix of Munich Re Beijing Branch

Unit: RMB 100 million, %

Business line	Premium income in 2022	% of total
Non-life insurance	81.6	66.1
Life insurance	41.8	33.9
Total	123.4	100

Source: Annual disclosure report of Munich Re Beijing Branch for 2022.

(4) Scor SE Beijing Branch

The premium income of Scor SE Beijing Branch was RMB 8.79 billion in 2022, down by 14.7% year-on-year. Specifically, the life segment recorded RMB 5.31 billion in ceded premium income, down by 20.0% year-on-year, while the non-life segment registered ceded premium income of RMB 3.48 billion, down by 5.1% year-on-year.

By business mix, Scor SE Beijing Branch has seen the percentage share of its life segment expanding in recent years, surpassing the non-life segment and become its largest line of business. In 2022, Scor SE Beijing Branch showed a 60.4/39.6 split in ceded premium income between life and non-life segments.

Table 6   Business Mix of Scor SE Beijing Branch

Unit: RMB 100 million, %

Business line	Ceded premium income in 2022	% of total
Life insurance	53.1	60.4
Non-life insurance	34.8	39.6
Total	87.9	100

Source: Annual disclosure report of Scor SE Beijing Branch for 2022.

2. Profitability

In 2022, foreign reinsurers operating in China showed good profitability in general. Some foreign reinsurers have diversified lines of business, with early distribution in Internet and mid-range medical insurance, a smaller share of critical illness insurance, showing good profitability. It should be noted that given the high retrocession rate of foreign reinsurers, their profitability will be impacted by retrocession arrangements, so the net profit indicators do not necessarily provide an accurate and full picture of their operations.

Table 7　Net Profits of Foreign Reinsurers in China

Unit: RMB 10,000, %

Company	Net profit in 2021	Net profit in 2022	Growth rate
Swiss Re Beijing Branch	8,069	27,617	242
Hannover Re Shanghai Branch	−2,940	−84,973	−2,790
Munich Re Beijing Branch	37,700	39,374	4
Scor SE Beijing Branch	18,113	24,129	33

Source: Annual disclosure reports of the above companies for 2022.

3. Solvency

The four foreign reinsurers mentioned above had high solvency ratios in 2022, of which Swiss Re Beijing Branch boasted the highest solvency ratio of 315%. In 2022, Swiss Re Beijing Branch increased its capital by RMB 3 billion and Hannover Re Shanghai Branch increased its capital by RMB 1.525 billion. Foreign reinsurance companies generally maintain strong capitals to underwrite high-quality business, laying a solid foundation for their further push into China's reinsurance market.

Table 8   Solvency Ratios of Foreign Reinsurers in China

Unit: RMB 100 million, %

Company	End-2022 comprehensive solvency ratio	End-2022 working capital	End-2022 net assets
Swiss Re Beijing Branch	315	43.6	85.3
Hannover Re Shanghai Branch	233	72.5	70.3
Munich Re Beijing Branch	254	16.5	47.0
Scor SE Beijing Branch	225	20.6	27.4

Source: Annual disclosure reports of the above companies for 2022.

II. International Development of Chinese Reinsurance Companies

In the two-way opening-up of China's financial sector, Chinese reinsurers including China Re and Taiping Re are "going global" to provide risk protection for Chinese enterprises operating overseas. They compete in the global reinsurance market, fitting in with the global insurance value chain at a faster pace and enhancing the international image and influence of Chinese reinsurance companies.

(I) International development of China Re

As the forerunner and vanguard of Chinese reinsurers going global, China Re Group has been implementing its international strategy over the years and has made major breakthroughs. China Re set up a representative office in London in 1999 and another two in Hong Kong and New York in 2008 and 2013, respectively, which served as a bridgehead for overseas information collection and market connection. China Re went public on Hong Kong Stock Exchange in 2015 and established a subsidiary of China

Re AMC in Hong Kong, creating an integrated platform for overseas asset management. During the 13th Five-Year Plan period, China Re set up a Singapore branch in 2016 by riding on the national strategy of "going global", seeking to gain a firm footing in Singapore as a hub of the "Maritime Silk Road" and strive to expand greater Asian-Pacific reinsurance market and business. In 2018, China Re seized the then market opportunity to acquire the century-old British insurer Chaucer, one of the largest members of Lloyd's, to substantially boost its international business capacity. In 2019, China Re Life set up a subsidiary in Hong Kong to conduct international personal reinsurance business in Hong Kong, Macao and Southeast Asia. In 2020, China Re P&C established a branch in Malaysia to conduct property reinsurance business in the local market.

After years of hard work, China Re has expanded its overseas distribution to more than 10 countries and regions including Hong Kong, Singapore, the United Kingdom, Ireland, Malaysia and Bermuda, covering three business segments: property reinsurance, personal reinsurance and asset management. In 2022, China Re's premium income from international business stood at RMB 30.21 billion, accounting for 17.8% of the group's consolidated premium income. The overseas premium income from property reinsurance was RMB 19.62 billion, accounting for 32% of the total property reinsurance premium income.

(II) International development of Taiping Re

Taiping Reinsurance Co., Ltd. ("Taiping Re"), the parent of Taiping Re (China), was incorporated in Hong Kong in September 1980. As a specialized reinsurance subsidiary of China Taiping Insurance Group, Taiping Re underwrites property and life reinsurance worldwide. Headquartered in Hong Kong, Taiping Re operates wholly-owned subsidiaries in Beijing and London, a branch office in Labuan, Malaysia and representative offices in Tokyo and Macao.

Relying on the strong support of its listed parent company, China Taiping Insurance Holdings Co., Ltd., and its strategic shareholder, Belgium-based Ageas Insurance International N.V., Taiping Re maintains prudent, efficient and flexible underwriting policies and management methods. In recognition of its sound financial strength and good performance, Taiping Re has received Financial Strength Rating of A from international rating agencies like Standard & Poor's, AM. Best and Fitch for consecutive years.

Taiping Re is a well-known professional reinsurer in Asia and the No. 1 player in Hong Kong's property reinsurance market, with its own scope of business covering more than 100 countries and regions across five continents and serving more than 1,000 customers. In 2022, Taiping Re's gross premium income reached USD 2.59 billion (HKD 20.2 billion), with its total assets standing at USD 7.93 billion (HKD 61.9 billion) and overseas business accounting for about 60%.

(III) Chinese reinsurers' service for the Belt and Road Initiative

China Re chairs and manages the China Belt and Road Reinsurance Pool ("CBRRP") which was jointly initiated and established by China Re and other institutions in Beijing in 2020. At present, the CBRRP provides about RMB 19 billion worth of risk protections for over 30 overseas projects. China

Re has also led the establishment of Belt and Road insurance and reinsurance trade organizations in Singapore and the United Kingdom. Leveraging on the three platforms, China Re operates a global network of high-quality risk protection services in support of the Belt and Road cooperation. By filling in the domestic gaps in political violence insurance and terrorism insurance and creating a terrorism risk assessment system of foreign countries from the perspective of China, China Re provides exclusive reinsurance support for the first ever "overseas surety bond" of Chinese insurers, and helps domestic enterprises address special risks in "going global". In the past three years, China Re P&C has provided about RMB 400 billion worth of stable and reliable comprehensive risk protections for more than 1,000 projects of Chinese companies across 40 countries and regions along the "Belt and Road".

PICC Re has persistently strengthened its capability of serving customers along the "Belt and Road" and created an international intermediary service model. In the past two years, PICC Re has completed the registration of offshore cedant qualifications in Argentina and Chile, and accumulatively provided RMB 10.6 billion of risk protections for key customers such as Huawei, Goldwind and China Railway Construction and Sinovac's vaccine support for the COVID-19 fight in Latin American countries, earning RMB 17.5 million of premium income and obtaining good social benefits.

Taiping Re (China) has played an active part in building the Guangdong-Hong Kong-Macao Greater Bay Area, providing more than RMB 7.8 billion of risk protections for over 40 projects in the region, including the Shenzhen–Huizhou Intercity Railway and the Qianhai-Huanggang Port

Section of Guangzhou-Dongguan-Shenzhen Intercity Railway, both being major projects in the Shenzhen Metropolitan Area.

III. Outlook on International Development of China's Reinsurance Industry

(I) Foreign reinsurers' outlook on the Chinese market

In terms of market potential, China's reinsurance market is huge in size with the potential for sustained development. According to Swiss Re Institute's estimates, China will continue to expand it share in the global insurance market and remain a major growth engine for the global insurance industry. In the next decade, China's insurance market is expected to grow at a compound annual growth rate (CAGR) of 8%. By 2031, the total premiums in the Chinese market will double from 2022.

In terms of regulatory policies, the Chinese market remains open to the outside world with a favorable and predictable regulatory environment. In recent years, the former CBIRC has introduced more than ten measures for opening-up of the insurance industry. Foreign reinsurers are rushing to expand their strategic distribution in China. Swiss Re, for example, initially positioned China as an emerging market but now has repositioned China as a high-growth market.

(II) Outlook on International Development of Chinese reinsurers

Thanks to the post-pandemic economic recovery, the sharp increase in commercial insurance rates and the growth of emerging markets, the global insurance market will likely regain growth momentum. Chinese reinsurers will seize the opportunity to further chart the course as to the strategy for international development, continue to enhance international management and global competitiveness, improve coordination of domestic and overseas operations, and strengthen the innovative cooperation with national authorities and industry players. Focusing on serving the "Belt and Road", Chinese reinsurers will help Chinese enterprises go global with high-quality and professional expertise. They will better participate in international competition and make positive contributions to the new development pattern that features positive interplay between domestic and international economic cycles.

The global reinsurance market still faces many challenges from the COVID-19 impact, geopolitical tensions, climate change and other factors. For example, climate change has aggravated the frequency, scope, intensity and concurrence of extreme weather events, posing great challenges to reinsurance activities. Other challenges facing reinsurers include the continued geopolitical tensions spurred by Russia-Ukraine conflicts, frustrated confidence in global economic stability, more volatile currency rates and elevated inflation in major economies. In the course of international development, Chinese reinsurers will further strengthen risk analysis and effectively balance development and security.

Recently, China has made another move to deepen its reinsurance industry opening-up. In June 2023, the National Administration of Financial Regulation (NAFR) and Shanghai jointly announced an "international board" for reinsurance. The move is to, relying on the digital and technology-driven international reinsurance platform, build a transparent, convenient and efficient international market for reinsurance trading, upgrade China's reinsurance market from "one-way opening-up" to "two-way opening-up", take an in-depth part in the global cooperation in reinsurance, provide Chinese solutions to the global risk protections and financial governance system and help maintain a diversified and stable international landscape for risk protections and financial cooperation for partnership. China's reinsurance industry will also take this turning point to grasp new opportunities, keep improving cross-border service capabilities and international operations and better serve the new development pattern that features positive interplay between domestic and international economic cycles.

Chapter V

Review and Outlook on China's Reinsurance Regulation in 2022

I. Overall Regulatory Framework of the Reinsurance Industry

II. Important Reinsurance Regulatory Policies Issued in 2022

III. Trends in Reinsurance Regulation

In 2022, China's reinsurance regulation upheld the political stance of serving the people and supported the task of pursuing high-quality development under the overarching requirement of "containing the pandemic, stabilizing the economy and ensuring safe development". A number of regulatory policies that have a substantial effect on the reinsurance industry were issued to effectively prevent and control reinsurance risks, help ensure overall economic stability and guide market players to improve their risk protection capability. The regulatory work delivered positive results.

I. Overall Regulatory Framework of the Reinsurance Industry

(I) A three-pillar reinsurance regulatory framework

After decades of development, China's insurance and reinsurance industry has formed a three-pillar regulatory framework, with solvency regulation as the core, corporate governance regulation as the foundation and market practice regulation as the emphasis.

Specifically, solvency regulation lies at the core of regulating the modern insurance industry. It is intended to ensure that insurers are solvent enough to meet underwriting requirements and keep the insurance market stable through comprehensive evaluation, supervision, and inspection of insurance companies' solvency adequacy ratios, comprehensive risk profile and risk management ability. In 2021, the former CBIRC successfully completed the C-ROSS Phase II and issued the *Regulations on the Administration of Solvency of Insurance Companies* (CBIRC Order No. 1 of 2021) and the

Rules on the Regulation of the Solvency of Insurance Companies (II) (Y.B.J.F. [2021] No. 51). These regulatory policies have clearly established a three-pillar framework for solvency regulation, consisting of quantitative capital requirements (Pillar I), qualitative regulatory requirements (Pillar II) and market discipline mechanism (Pillar III) and introduced three closely connected indicators of solvency regulation, namely, core solvency adequacy ratio, comprehensive solvency adequacy ratio and integrated risk rating. These policies have further tightened and refined the solvency regulatory requirements for insurers and reinsurers, making the insurer solvency supervision more scientific, effective and comprehensive, and guiding China's insurance market down the road for robust and healthy development.

Corporate governance is the cornerstone of the modern enterprise system. Its purpose is to improve the governance of an enterprise and maintain healthy and stable operations of an insurance institution through the establishment of a corporate governance framework that includes governing bodies like the (general) meeting of shareholders, board of directors, board of supervisors and senior management, defining the scope of roles and requirements of performing duties for these bodies, and improving mechanisms like risk control, checks and balances, and incentives and restraints. In January 2006, the former China Insurance Regulatory Commission ("CIRC") issued the *Guiding Opinions on Regulating the Governance Structure of Insurance Companies (Trial)* (B.J.F. [2006] No. 2), formally introducing corporate governance supervision into the regulatory system of China's insurance industry. Since then, China has gradually enriched and improved corporate governance regulation in both practical and theoretical terms. Regulatory authorities have issued a series of regulatory policies on corporate governance, including the *Code of Corporate Governance of Banking and Insurance Institutions* (Y.B.J.F. [2021] No. 14) and the *Measures for Regulating the Conduct of Majority Shareholders of Banking and Insurance Institutions (Trial)* (Y.B.J.F. [2021] No. 43), detailing and clarifying the composition, division of duties and working mechanisms of insurers' governing bodies, namely, the general meeting of shareholders, the board of directors, the board of supervisors and the management. As a Chinese characteristic, the Party leadership has been integrated into every respect of the corporate governance of insurance institutions. The corporate governance requirements for insurance institutions have been comprehensively and systematically standardized to keep refining the regulatory system for corporate governance in the insurance industry. In 2022, the former CBIRC revised and issued the *Measures for Regulatory Assessment of Corporate Governance of Banking and Insurance Institutions* (Y.B.J.G. [2022] No. 19), incorporating good practices in regulatory assessment and regulatory policy developments in recent years, further improving the regulatory assessment mechanism for corporate governance of insurance institutions and facilitating insurers to enhance their own corporate governance.

Regulation of market practices, as an important guarantee to ensure orderliness of the insurance market, covers the formulation of insurance terms and premium rates, and the regulation of insurance practices concerning sales, intermediaries, services and anti-frauds. Putting protecting the rights and interests of insurance consumers at the core, it aims to maintain the insurance market in normal order by bringing discipline to market practices of insurance institutions. The regulatory policies and measures are specific to the particular market practices of regulated entities. Considering the differences between P&C insurance, personal insurance and reinsurance in terms of trading entities, management model, business nature, and risk characteristics, regulators usually adopt a category-specific approach to regulating various insurance institutions and business. As for reinsurance, the former CBIRC revised and issued the *Provisions on the Administration of Reinsurance Business* in July 2021 (CBIRC Order No. 8 of 2021), strengthening the supervision of insurance institutions in respect of top-level reinsurance strategy formulation, reinsurance security management and reinsurance management standards. It emphasized that insurance companies should use reinsurance tools properly and stay committed to the core role of reinsurance as "insurance for insurers".

(II) Regulatory policy system for the reinsurance industry

At the legislative level, both insurance and reinsurance in China are governed by the *Insurance Law of the People's Republic of China*.

At the regulatory policy level, the National Administration of Financial Regulation ("NAFR") has introduced the following two categories of regulatory policies on reinsurance. (1) Regulatory policies applicable to the insurance industry as a whole, such as regulatory policies on solvency, corporate governance and the use of insurance funds. Such regulatory policies are based on the common characteristics of reinsurance and direct insurance, usually applicable to both reinsurers and direct insurers, or applicable to direct insurers and applicable *mutatis mutandis* to reinsurers. (2) Special regulatory policies applicable to the reinsurance industry, which cover the regulation of reinsurance market practices and the special regulation targeting the international nature of reinsurance. These special regulatory policies include standardizing the establishment of reinsurance companies, clarifying the norms for reinsurance business management and strengthening the safeguards for reinsurance by establishing an information disclosure mechanism for connected reinsurance transactions, creating a reinsurance registration mechanism and requiring offshore reinsurers to provide qualifying guarantees. To ensure effective implementation of the above regulatory policies, the National Administration of Financial Regulation will combine on-site supervision with off-site supervision and adopt such regulatory methods as formulating management standards, carrying out capacity assessment and imposing administrative penalties on illegalities or irregularities of insurance institutions, thereby causing insurers to maintain reasonable solvency, improve corporate governance and bring discipline to market activities.

In light of policies issued by other relevant regulatory authorities, in addition to the three-pillar regulatory framework of the National Administration of Financial Regulation, China's insurance and reinsurance industry are also subject to supervision by the People's Bank of China, the Ministry of Finance and the Cyberspace Administration of China in terms of anti-money laundering, counter-terrorist financing, finance and accounting, state-owned assets management as well as cybersecurity and personal information protection. In addition, the guidelines and plans issued by the CPC Central Committee, the State Council and relevant regulatory agencies with respect to the national economic and financial work will also have a far-reaching effect on the regulatory policies for China's insurance and reinsurance industry.

II. Important Reinsurance Regulatory Policies Issued in 2022

In 2022, the important regulatory policies on China's reinsurance industry mainly involved regulating the use of insurance funds, strengthening the administration of connected transactions, refining the regulatory assessment system, clarifying the capital replenishment and measurement mechanism, improving the cybersecurity review mechanism and improving the regulatory system for outbound data transfer.

(I) Further regulating the use of insurance funds

1. Refining the regulatory requirements for investing insurance funds in financial products

Investing in financial products is one of the important ways to use insurance funds. In December 2012, the former CIRC issued the *Circular on Investment of Insurance Funds in Financial Products* (B.J.F. [2012] No. 91) to regulate the insurance fund investment in financial products. However, some provisions of this regulatory document are out of date as the practices and regulatory rules for insurance fund utilization keep evolving. Therefore, the former CBIRC revised and issued the *Circular on Investment of Insurance Funds in Financial Products* (Y.B.J.G. [2022] No. 7) in April 2022 to refine the regulatory requirements for investing insurance funds in financial products issued by non-insurer financial institutions.

The new rules, aligned with the *Circular on Refining the Supervision over Investment Management Capabilities of Insurance Institutions* (Y.B.J.F. [2020] No. 45), set forth the following requirements: (1) Insurance institutions shall possess appropriate investment management capabilities to invest in financial products. The insurance group (holding) companies and insurance companies shall meet requirements regarding the investment in financial products and single asset management plans. Investing insurance funds in wealth management products and other financial products also shall meet relevant requirements. (2) Insurance group (holding) companies and insurance companies may invest in financial products directly or through insurance asset management companies, but shall not entrust insurance asset management companies to invest in single asset management plans or private wealth management products offered to single investors. (3) An insurance institution shall, when investing in financial products on its own account or on behalf of its clients, properly carry out such work as risk assessment, post-investing management, connected transaction management and regular reporting. The insurance asset management company investing in financial products on behalf of its clients shall assume the responsibility of active management.

The new rules mainly include the following changes: (1) Deleting provisions on investing insurance funds in the infrastructure investment plans, real estate investment plans and asset-backed plans issued by insurance asset management companies. These three types of investment are governed by the *Interim Measures for the Administration Management of Insurance Asset Management Products* (CBIRC Order No. 5 of 2020) and other relevant policies. (2) Expanding the scope of investable financial products to include wealth management products issued by wealth management companies, single asset management plans and debt-for-equity swap plans. (3) Removing external credit rating requirements for investing insurance funds in credit asset-backed securities, among others. (4) Strengthening insurance institutions' look-through risk supervision over financial products invested in.

2. Improving the regulatory mechanism for entrusted investment of insurance funds

In May 2022, the former CBIRC revised and issued the *Administrative Measures for Entrusted investment of insurance funds* (Y.B.J.G. [2022] No. 9) to further improve the provisions on the eligibility requirements, investment norms, risk management and regulatory requirements for entrusted investment of insurance funds. The new rules have incorporated the latest industry practices and regulatory policy developments: (1) The entrusted investment of insurance funds is defined as an activity whereby an insurance company (or insurance group (holding) company) entrusts its insurance funds to an insurance asset management organization, which acts as an trustee and carries out active investment management in the name of the insurance company. (2) The trustees of insurance fund investment are limited to insurance asset management organizations, deleting former provisions allowing non-insurance asset management organizations, e.g. securities companies, securities asset management companies, securities investment fund management companies and their subsidiaries, to qualify as trustees under the old rules. The investments conducted by non-insurance asset management organizations, such as securities companies, as entrusted by insurers, are included in the scope of single asset management plans, which are governed by the *Circular on Investment of Insurance Funds in Financial Products* mentioned above. (3) The new rules set forth the eligibility requirements for insurance companies to conduct entrusted investments, and for insurance asset management organizations to act as trustees, and stipulate that the entrusted investment assets of insurance funds are limited to those falling within the scope of insurance fund utilization approved by the National Administration of Financial Regulation, excluding direct equity investment and investment property held in the form of real rights and equity.

(II) Strengthening the administration of connected transactions of banking and insurance institutions

China's banking and insurance industries have developed rapidly in recent years. However, it is a common problem that banking and insurance institutions circumvent supervision and take illegitimate profits through hidden or complex connected transactions. Therefore, connected transactions of banking and insurance institutions have always been a key area of financial supervision. Previously, the supervision of connected transactions of banking institutions and insurance institutions were mainly governed by the *Administrative Measures for Connected Transactions* between *Commercial Banks and Insiders and Shareholders* (CBRC Order [2004] No. 3) and the *Administrative Measures for Connected Transactions of Insurance Companies* (Y.B.J.F. [2019] No. 35). Since the former China Banking Regulatory Commission ("CBRC") and the former China Insurance Regulatory Commission ("CIRC") were merged into the former China Banking and Insurance Regulatory Commission ("CBIRC") in 2018, the regulatory documents and standards for banking and insurance have been sorted out to gradually form a unified regulatory framework for banking and insurance.

In this context, to further regulate connected transactions of banking and insurance institutions, the former CBIRC revised and issued the *Administrative Measures for Connected Transactions of Banking and Insurance Institutions* (CBIRC Order No. 1 of 2022), setting forth centralized regulatory requirements for banking and insurance institutions in respect of related parties, connected transactions, internal management of connected transactions as well as their reporting, disclosure and supervision. (1) In terms of the identification of related parties, the scopes of related parties of banking and insurance institutions were unified. The identification approach continues to combine direct identification with the "substance over form" doctrine. The revised policy lists five types of related natural persons and five types of related legal persons and unincorporated organizations. (2) In terms of the identification and criteria for connected transactions, the revised policy has clarified the types of connected transactions, how to calculate the values of connected transactions, criteria for major connected transactions, proportion of connected transactions falling in the category of funds utilization and prohibitive provisions for different types of institutions, such as banks, insurers, trust companies and other non-bank financial institutions. The connected transactions of insurance institutions are recategorized into funds utilization, services, interests transfer, insurance business and others, with tighter requirements on the allowed proportion of connected transactions in the category of funds utilization. (3) In terms of the management of connected transactions, requirements have been laid out for the internal management mechanisms, look-through identification, sources and flows of funds, dynamic assessment, information system development and internal accountability for the connected transactions of banks and insurers. The exemption provision "except and unless the controlled subsidiaries are listed companies or financial institutions subject to industry supervision" has been cancelled. Aligned with the *Administrative Measures for the Supervision and Administration of Insurance Group Companies* (CBIRC Order No. 13 of 2021), the revised policy has made it clear that "where CBIRC imposes any other rules on the establishment of special committees of the board of directors, such rules shall apply".

(III) Improving the regulatory assessment system for insurance institutions

1. Refining the regulatory assessment mechanism for corporate governance of banking and insurance institutions

Regulatory assessment of corporate governance is one of the main regulatory measures adopted by the National Administration of Financial

Regulation in recent years. In November 2019, the former CBIRC issued the *Measures for Regulatory Assessment of Corporate Governance of Banking and Insurance Institutions* (trial) (Y.B.J.F. [2019] No. 43), setting three steps of assessment, namely compliance evaluation, effectiveness evaluation and rating downgrade for significant events. The regulatory assessment focused on banking and insurance institutions' Party leadership, shareholder governance, connected transaction governance, board of directors governance, board of supervisors and senior management governance, internal risk control, market discipline and stakeholder governance. After release of these measures, the former CBIRC further issued a series of important regulatory rules for corporate governance, including the *Code of Corporate Governance of Banking and Insurance Institutions* (Y.B.J.F. (2021) No. 14), and some of the original assessment indicators need to be updated urgently.

In November 2022, therefore, the former CBIRC revised and issued the *Measures for Regulatory Assessment of Corporate Governance of Banking and Insurance Institutions* (Y.B.J.G. [2022] No. 19) to refine the regulatory assessment mechanism for corporate governance. (1) Refining the assessment mechanism. The new rules allocate assessment resources according to the specific corporate governance standard of banking and insurance institutions. In principle, regulatory assessment should be conducted at least once a year for banks and insurers. For institutions with assessment results of grade B or above, the assessment frequency can be lowered to once every two years. A combination of off-site assessment and on-site assessment is adopted. For on-site assessment, the requirement of "achieving full coverage every three years" is added. The working methods and requirements are further refined for on-site assessment and off-site assessments, urging institutions to carry out the basic work on corporate governance in a more rigorous and effective manner. (2) Updating assessment indicators. The new rules focus on major shareholders' illegal intervention and insider control, adding "shareholders and banking and insurance institutions conducting illegal connected transactions that seriously affect the authenticity of the capital adequacy ratio or solvency adequacy ratio of such institutions" to the circumstances that result in a direct rating as Grade E institutions, further enriching the key indicators regarding Party leadership, shareholders and shareholdings, connected transactions as well as the nomination and performance of directors, supervisors and senior managers, adjusting the weights of indicators and reducing the number of indicators. (3) Strengthening the application of assessment results. The new rules impose extra regulatory concern on banking and insurance institutions assessed to be Grade D or below, with additional regulatory actions including early intervention and timely correction of major corporate governance risks to guard against "unhealthy operation". For Grade E institutions, additional regulatory actions are imposed, including restricting their connected transactions and conducting on-site inspection.

2. Establishing and improving an off-site regulatory system for insurance companies

Off-site regulation is an important means of insurance regulation, by which the institutional regulators comprehensively track and assess the operations and risk profile of insurance companies. To establish and improve an off-site regulatory system for insurance companies, the former CBIRC issued the *Interim Measures for Off-site Regulation of Insurance Companies* in January 2022 (CBIRC Order No. 3 of 2022) based on the historical experience in off-site regulation and the current division of regulatory duties. The interim measures provide standardized procedures and mechanisms for off-site regulation of insurance companies, including the division of duties and work requirements, information collection and sorting, day-to-day monitoring and regulatory assessment, application of assessment results and information archiving. (1) Emphasizing the leading role of institutional regulators. The institution regulator, as the lead body for off-site regulation, is responsible for studying and formulating the policies, rules, workflows and working standards for off-site regulation. (2) Clarifying the principle of category-specific regulation. After the *Interim Measures for Off-site Regulation of Insurance Companies* set forth the workflows and mechanisms for off-site regulation, the relevant institutional regulators also formulated and issued guidelines for risk monitoring and off-site regulatory assessment of P&C insurers, personal insurers and reinsurers separately, taking into account the differences in business operations and risk characteristics of different types of insurance companies. (3) Highlighting the principle of coordinated regulation. Off-site regulation should be effectively linked with administrative approval, on-site inspection and other regulatory means to form a synergy in key regulatory areas such as corporate governance.

(IV) Clarifying the capital replenishment and measurement rules for insurance companies

1. Permitting insurers to replenish capital by issuing perpetual capital bonds

To further broaden the capital replenishment channels of insurance companies, enhance insurers' ability to forestall and defuse risks and serve the real economy, the People's Bank of China and the former CBIRC jointly issued the *Circular on Matters Concerning Issuance of Perpetual capital bonds by Insurance Companies* (Y.F. [2022] No. 175) in August 2022, permitting insurance companies other than insurance group (holding) companies to issue perpetual capital bonds. The circular defines the issuance of perpetual capital bonds by insurance companies, setting forth the requirements regarding application for issuance, write-down or conversion clauses, redemption, information disclosure, credit rating and capital replenishment. (1) Perpetual capital bonds should be attached with write-down or conversion clauses, with a list of events that will trigger the write-down or conversion. (2) When the redemption of a perpetual capital bonds or the payment of interest on the perpetual capital bonds will bring the insurer's solvency adequacy ratio below the required level, the insurer shall not redeem the bonds or pay interest, and the investors of the perpetual capital bonds shall not apply for bankruptcy of the insurer due to its failure to pay interest as agreed. (3) Insurers are allowed to replenish core Tier 2 capital by issuing perpetual capital bonds, provided that the balance of perpetual capital bonds does not exceed 30% of the core capital.

2. Improving the regulatory system for non-life insurance reserves

For the regulation of reserves for non-life insurance business ("Reserves"), the former CBIRC revised and issued the *Administrative Measures for Reserves for Non-life Insurance Business of Insurance Companies* (CBIRC Order [2021] No. 11) in alignment with the accounting standards and solvency regulatory rules. In March 2022, the former CBIRC issued the *Rules for Implementing the Administrative Measures for Reserves for Non-life Insurance Business of Insurance Companies* (No. 1-7) (Y.B.J.G. [2022] No. 6), covering unearned premium reserves, claim reserves, risk margin and discount, branch reserves, retrospective analysis of reserves, reserve assessment report and working paper for reserves, and other provisions under Rule No. 7. (1) Explanations, interpretations and additions are provided for matters not yet specified in the *Administrative Measures for Reserves for Non-life Insurance Business of Insurance Companies*. (2) In view of the existing problems of insurance companies manually adjusting branch reserves and adjusting profits through reserves, the outdated provisions in the earlier regulatory documents for reserves have been revised. (3) Regulatory gaps are filled with respect to the risk margin and discounting of reserves, favorable reserve development and the reserves of branches.

(V) Improving the mechanisms for cybersecurity regulation and data protection

1. Improving the cybersecurity review mechanism

Cybersecurity review is an important measure to ensure the supply chain security for China's critical information infrastructure, ensure cybersecurity and data security and safeguard national security. In late 2021, the revised *Cybersecurity Review Measures*[1] were promulgated by 13 agencies, including the Cyberspace Administration of China, effective on February 15, 2022. Compared with the old measures, the revised version has extended the cybersecurity review requirement from "critical information infrastructure operators procuring network products and services that influence or may influence national security" to "online platform operators conducting data processing activities that influence or may influence national security". In addition, "online platform operators holding the personal information of more than 1 million users" must apply to the Cybersecurity Review Office for cybersecurity review prior to "listing abroad". Cybersecurity review is focused on assessing the national security factors of the relevant objects or scenarios, including the influence on critical information infrastructure (such as the risk of illegal control, disturbance or destruction and the harm to business continuity) and the influence on core data, important data or massive personal information (e.g. being stolen, leaked, damaged, or illegally used or illegally transmitted abroad).

If an insurer or reinsurer has any information system identified as

---

[1] Decree No. 8 of the Cyberspace Administration of China, the National Development and Reform Commission of the People's Republic of China, the Ministry of Industry and Information Technology of the People's Republic of China, the Ministry of Public Security of the People's Republic of China, the Ministry of State Security of the People's Republic of China, the Ministry of Finance of the People's Republic of China, the Ministry of Commerce of the People's Bank of China, the People's Bank of China, the State Administration for Market Regulation, the National Radio and Television Administration, the China Securities Regulatory Commission, the National Administration of State Secrets Protection and the State Cryptography Administration.

"critical information infrastructure" or is identified as an "online platform operator", it should attach great importance to its network and data compliance management, especially the security management of personal information, important data and core data it holds, and shall conduct network security reviews as required.

2. Improving the regulatory system for outbound data transfer

In 2022, with the introduction of the *Measures for Security Assessment for Outbound Data Transfer.* (Order No. 11 of the Cyberspace Administration of China), the *Announcement on the Implementation of Personal Information Protection Certification* (Announcement No. 37 of the State Administration for Market Regulation and the Cyberspace Administration of China in 2022) and the *Provisions on the Standard Contract for Outbound Transfer of Personal Information (Exposure Draft)*[①], China has initially established a regulatory mechanism for outbound data transfer that consists of "outbound transfer assessment + standard contract + certification", which is substantially consistent with those in other countries or regions.

(1) Assessment of outbound data transfer. The data subject to outbound transfer restrictions in China include important data and personal information. Outbound transfer of important data is subject to mandatory assessment. Outbound transfer of personal information that meets the following criteria must be assessed: First, the nature of the relevant entities should be assessed, including operators of critical information infrastructure

---

[①] In February 2023, the Cyberspace Administration of China formally issued the *Measures for the Standard Contract for Outbound Transfer of Personal Information* (Order No. 13 of the Cyberspace Administration of China).

and data processors that process the personal information of more than 1 million people. Such entities shall conduct assessment of outbound data transfer regardless of the amount of personal information transferred abroad. Second, assessment is required if the personal information transfer reaches a certain amount, that is, providing personal information of 100,000 people or sensitive personal information of 10,000 people across borders since January 1 of the previous year. The assessment of outbound data transfer includes the self-assessment of the data processor and the regulatory assessment by the provincial cybersecurity administration. Such data shall not be transferred abroad unless the assessment is passed. (2) Entry into a standard contract on outbound data transfer. In addition to the above circumstances, the data processor may lawfully transfer personal information abroad by signing a standard contract for outbound data transfer with the overseas recipient. However, the signing of such contract does not mean "once signed, once and for all". The data processor is also obliged, at least, to conduct an assessment of impact on personal information protection; file the standard contract and the impact assessment report for personal information protection with the local provincial cybersecurity administration; and ensure the contract is duly performed. (3) Certification for cross-border processing. According to the *Personal Information Protection Law*, "the certification by a professional agency for personal information protection in accordance with the rules of the national cybersecurity administration" is also a legitimate way to provide personal information abroad. According to relevant certification standards, the certification of cross-border personal information processing activities is mainly applicable to cross-border personal information processing activities within a multinational company, or among subsidiaries or affiliates of the same economic or public entity.

In the case of insurance and reinsurance companies, either international business operations or overseas institution management may involve outbound data transfer. Insurers and reinsurers shall sort out their outbound data transfer scenarios in the business and management activities, identify the types and entity nature of outgoing data, and select appropriate ways of outbound data transfer to ensure compliance.

III. Trends in Reinsurance Regulation

In 2023, China's reinsurance industry is stable and improving with growing market demand. At the same time, it also faces such challenges as global geopolitical tensions, frequent natural disasters, weak macroeconomic growth, aggravated financial market volatility and rising information technology risks. While strictly forestalling systemic risks, the reinsurance regulation will seek to keep improving the policy environment in light of the latest industry developments, so as to facilitate high-quality development of the reinsurance industry and better serve the economic and social development.

First, reinsurers will be further encouraged to serve economic and social development. As an important part of the financial sector, insurance and reinsurance play a crucial role in mobilizing social resources, enhancing economic resilience, supporting social development and improving people's living standards. In 2022, the former CBIRC issued a series of policies to strategically promote green finance across the insurance industry, pursue green transition of economic and social development and support urban development and governance, affordable rental housing development and high-quality development of road transportation. In the future, regulatory policies will further guide insurance institutions to focus on the needs of economic and social development and major national strategies, play a better role as "shock absorber" and "stabilizer" by working hard on product supply, service support, risk prevention and financing and provide a broader range of higher-quality risk protections and insurance services.

Second, reinsurers will be further encouraged to pursue innovative development. Reinsurers will enhance their pricing, underwriting, claim settlement and management capabilities for risks in high-tech fields such as electronic information, advanced manufacturing, biomedicine, modern agriculture, smart transportation, new energy and aerospace as well as other medium- and large-scale risks and special risks, so as to provide innovation momentum for China's insurance and insurance industry to further enhance their core competences and build world-class reinsurers.

Third, a further regulatory emphasis will be placed on the development of technological capabilities and prevention of relevant risks in the insurance and reinsurance industry. In 2022, the former CBIRC issued the *Guidelines for Digital Transformation of the Banking and Insurance Industries* (Y.B.J.B.F. [2022] No. 2), requiring banking and insurance institutions to strengthen the top-level design, overall planning and day-to-day management of digital transformation. In the future, the industry regulation will continue to promote the digitalization of insurance institutions and improve their ability to identify and tackle the information technology risks. In response to the rapid development of information technology across the insurance industry and the increasingly complex financial risks, the industry regulation will continue to make regulatory tools more scientific, standardized and procedure-based and enhance the efficiency of regulatory resource allocation and the level of regulatory technology (RegTech), eventually enabling more efficient development of the reinsurance industry while ensuring the compliance of business and safeguarding the market order.